BASIC PHILOSOPHICAL WRITINGS

Studies in Continental Thought
John Sallis, general editor

Consulting Editors

Robert Bernasconi
Rudolf Bernet
John D. Caputo
David Carr
Edward S. Casey
Hubert L. Dreyfus
Don Ihde
David Farrell Krell
Lenore Langsdorf
Alphonso Lingis

William L. McBride
J. N. Mohanty
Mary Rawlinson
Tom Rockmore
Calvin O. Schrag
†Reiner Schürmann
Charles E. Scott
Thomas Sheehan
Robert Sokolowski
Bruce W. Wilshire

David Wood

Emmanuel Levinas

Basic Philosophical Writings

EDITED BY

ADRIAAN T. PEPERZAK,

SIMON CRITCHLEY, AND

ROBERT BERNASCONI

Indiana University Press

BLOOMINGTON AND INDIANAPOLIS

The paper used in this publication meets the minimum requirements of American National Standard for Information Sciences—Permanence of Paper for Printed Library Materials, ANSI Z39.48-1984.

Manufactured in the United States of America

Library of Congress Cataloging-in-Publication Data

Levinas, Emmanuel.
  [Essays. English. Selections]
  Emmanuel Levinas : basic philosophical writings / edited by Adriaan T. Peperzak, Simon Critchley, and Robert Bernasconi.
    p. cm. — (Studies in Continental thought)
  Includes bibliographical references and index.
  Contents: Is ontology fundamental? — Transcendence and height — Meaning and sense — Enigma and phenomenon — Substitution — Truth of disclosure and truth of testimony — Essence and disinterestedness — God and philosophy — Transcendence and intelligibility — Peace and proximity.
    ISBN 0-253-33078-5 (cl : alk. paper). — ISBN 0-253-21079-8 (pb : alk. paper)
    1. Philosophy.   I. Peperzak, Adriaan Theodoor, date.
  II. Critchley, Simon, date.   III. Bernasconi, Robert.
  IV. Title.   V. Series.
  B2430.L482E6   1996
  194—dc20
                                                                95–49540

1 2 3 4 5 01 00 99 98 97 96

CONTENTS

PREFACE

Although interest in Emmanuel Levinas's thought has been growing steadily in the English-speaking world, teachers wishing to introduce their students to his work have been hampered by the absence of a volume that makes a representative selection of his philosophical writings readily accessible. The present book is intended to remedy this lack. Some of the essays, such as "Transcendence and Height" and "Transcendence and Intelligibility," have been selected because in the view of the editors they offer the best introduction to Levinas's philosophy. Other essays, such as "Meaning and Sense" and "Substitution," are among Levinas's most groundbreaking texts. With the addition of editorial notes and introductions to each essay, the editors hope that students encountering Levinas for the first time as well as scholars of contemporary European philosophy will benefit from this presentation of his writings and better understand why Levinas is now ranked among the most important philosophers of the twentieth century.

Emmanuel Levinas was born in Kovno (Kaunas), Lithuania, on January 12, 1906 (or, according to the Julian calendar which was used in the Russian Empire at the time, on December 30, 1905). The Levinas family belonged to Kovno's large and important Jewish community. As a child, Levinas learned to read the Bible in Hebrew; however, Russian was the language of his formal education and the language that was spoken at home. As a youth Levinas read the great Russian writers Pushkin, Gogol, Dostoyevsky and Tolstoy; together with Shakespeare, they would remain important influences on his thinking. In 1916, during World War I, the family moved to Kharkov in Ukraine where Emmanuel attended a Russian high school and experienced the upheaval of the revolutions of February and October 1917.

In 1920 the family returned to Lithuania. In 1923 Emmanuel traveled to Strasbourg, where, having studied Latin for a year, he matriculated at the university. In his autobiographic essay "Signature" (1963 and 1966), as well as in an interview published as *Ethique et Infini* in 1982, he mentions Charles Blondel, Henri Carteron, Maurice Halbwachs, and Maurice Pradines as the four professors who in his view embodied the virtues of the French university. These years also mark the beginning of his lifelong friendship with Maurice Blanchot.

After obtaining his *license* in philosophy, Levinas began a close study of Husserl's *Logical Investigations*. Phenomenology, especially the analysis of intentionality and its horizons, revealed entirely new ways of thinking, different from induction, deduction, and dialectics. Levinas chose Husserl's theory of intuition as the topic of his dissertation. He spent the academic year of 1928-29 in Freiburg-in-Breisgau, where he gave a presentation in one of Husserl's last seminars. He also published a long review article on Husserl's *Ideen I* in the *Revue Philosophique de la France et de l'Etranger* (1929).

At Freiburg it was Heidegger, however, who, through his teaching and his major work *Sein und Zeit*, impressed Levinas as a highly original innovator and a great thinker on the level of Plato and Kant. Levinas was present at the famous encounter between Cassirer and Heidegger in Davos in 1929.

Returning to Strasbourg, Levinas defended his dissertation, "Théorie de l'intuition dans la phénoménologie de Husserl," which received a prize from the Institut. The dissertation was published in 1930. This and Levinas's later publications on Husserl and Heidegger introduced phenomenology to Sartre and other key figures of postwar French philosophy.

In 1930 Levinas became a French citizen, married, and performed his military service in Paris. In the same year he obtained a teaching position at the Alliance Israélite Universelle in Paris. The Alliance was an important philanthropic and educational institution whose mission was to promote the "emancipation" of Jews living in Mediterranean lands such as Morocco, Tunisia, Algeria, Turkey, and Syria. At the Sorbonne Levinas attended the courses of Léon Brunschvicg and - although irregularly - the famous lectures of Alexandre Kojève on Hegel's *Phenomenology of Spirit* at the Ecole des Hautes Etudes. There he also met Sartre, Hyppolite, and other intellectuals who would later find prominence, and participated in the monthly soirees of Gabriel Marcel.

In his early Parisian years, Levinas, together with Gabrielle Peiffer, translated Husserl's *Cartesian Meditations* (1931). He began work on a book on Heidegger but abandoned it when Heidegger became involved with the Nazis. A fragment of the projected book entitled "Martin Heidegger et l'ontologie" was published in 1932. His next published essay on Heidegger, a Spanish translation of a paper which Levinas had read in 1940 to the students of Jean Wahl at the Sorbonne, did not appear until 1948. The French text was published in 1949 in a collection of Levinas's articles on phenomenology, *En découvrant l'existence avec Husserl et Heidegger* (1949; augmented edition 1967).

Levinas's first thematic essay, "De l'évasion," was published in 1935. In it one can recognize the central question of his later work: is it possible to transcend, in thinking, the horizon of Being? Although the question was not expressed in a polemical way, this essay was a first attempt by Levinas to wrestle free from Heidegger's "ontology" (as Levinas consistently calls Heidegger's "thought of Being").

In 1939 Levinas was drafted into the French army, and served as an interpreter of Russian and German. In 1940 he became a prisoner of war. Because he was a French officer, he was not sent to a concentration camp but rather to a military prisoners' camp, where he did forced labor in the forest. Most members of his family in Lithuania were murdered by the Nazis. Levinas maintained that the forebodings, the reality, and the memory of the Holocaust always dominated his thinking.

His first original book, *De l'existence à l'existant* (*Existence and Existents*), most of which had been written during his captivity, appeared in 1947, two years after the end of the war. Its title, which translates literally as "*From existence to existents*" proclaims the need for a thinking beyond ontology; it reverses the orientation of Heidegger's thought, which aims to transcend the "metaphysics" of beings (*Seiendes, l'étant, l'existant*) to Being (*Sein, être, existence*). Levinas points to another transcendence: the Good commands an exodus beyond the limits of Being. In 1946 Levinas had published a fragment of this book under the title *Il y a*. The expression *il y a* translates the German *es gibt* (there is), but it receives a very different interpretation from Heidegger's: rather than the generosity of a radical Giving, *il y a* is the name of a dark and chaotic indeterminacy that precedes all creativity and goodness. It was not until 1951, in his article "L'ontologie est-elle fondamentale?" that Levinas presented an explicit critique of Heidegger's enterprise.

In the context of postwar existentialism, with Marcel, Sartre, and Camus dominating the philosophical scene, Levinas's first thematic publications went almost unnoticed, perhaps because of their originality and extreme difficulty. Another publication of 1947 drew more attention, however. At the invitation of Jean Wahl, professor of philosophy at the Sorbonne and director of the *Collège Philosophique*, Levinas gave a series of four lectures on Time and the Other ("Le temps et l'autre") during the academic year of 1946–47. The text of these lectures was published as part of a collective book entitled *Choice-World-Existence*. Despite its still partially experimental character, "Le temps et l'autre" already expressed the core ideas of Levinas's later work: the Other is the center, and time, as the ultimate horizon, determines the relations between the Other and me.

Before 1961, Levinas was known as a specialist of Husserlian and Heideggerian phenomenology. His modest publications up to that time did not suggest the impressive body of work that would make him one of the most important thinkers of the century. His contributions to philosophy were overshadowed by his writings on questions related to Jewish spirituality. Because of his affiliation with the Alliance school, of which he had become the director in 1947, and because he did not hold an academic position at a French university, his influence in philosophy was limited in comparison to his growing impact in the field of Jewish thought. After the war, Levinas studied the Talmud with some of the finest scholars, and in 1957 he began giving Talmudic readings with contemporary interpretation at the annual Colloquium of Jewish Intellectuals of French Expression. Then, in 1961, he gained philosophical renown with the publication of *Totalité et Infini* (later published in English as *Totality and Infinity*). He presented this book as the main thesis for his *doctorat d'état*, while a collection of his previously published philosophical works was accepted as a complementary thesis. As his international stature grew, he received many invitations to lecture, prompting the production of a vast number of philo- sophical papers. In 1961 Levinas became professor of philosophy at the University of Poitiers, and in 1967 he was appointed to the University of Paris- Nanterre. He moved to the Sorbonne (Paris IV) in 1973 and became an honorary professor there in 1976.

Totality and Infinity, Levinas's first major work, proposes a revolution not only in phenomenology but also with regard to the entire history of European philosophy, from Parmenides to Heidegger. Levinas presents a critique of the whole of Western civilization, which he sees as dominated by the spirit of Greek philosophy. Western thought and practice in his view are marked by a striving for totalization, in which the universe is reduced to an originary and ultimate unity by way of panoramic overviews and dialectical syntheses. This kind of monism, according to Levinas, must be criticized from the point of view of a thinking which starts from phenomena as they present themselves. Such a critique is consonant with ancient traditions of thought that reach back to Biblical and Talmudic sources, but it also occurs in Plato and Descartes.

Against Western totalitarianism Levinas maintains that the human and the divine Other cannot be reduced to a totality of which they would only be elements. A truthful thought respects the nonsynthesizable "separation" that characterizes the relations between the Other and me, or - to borrow the terminology of Plato's *Sophist* - it respects the irreducible nonidentity of the Same (*tauton*) and the Other (*to heteron*). The Same is clearly connected to the traditional subject, the Ego or the Consciousness of modern philosophy, a subject for whom the totality of beings is spread out as a panoramic universe, but the Other is associated with the Infinite. Whereas the category of *totality* summarizes the way in which the Ego inhabits the world - its worldly economy - *the infinite* names the Other's ungraspable or incomprehensible character. "The Other" is in the first place the other human being I encounter; in a later development it also stands for God.

Levinas refers to Descartes's third *Metaphysical Meditation* for a formal analysis of the relation that simultaneously links and separates the infinite and the Ego, whose consciousness originarily contains "the idea of the infinite" and thus thinks more than it can fathom. Levinas's own, more concrete approach is given through a phenomenology (or "trans-phenomenology") of the modes in which the human other is revealed to me. The other's face or speech (or any other typically human aspect that reveals the other) is revealed as a refutation of any totalitarian or absolutist form of economy. Thus the Other presents him- or herself neither as a phenomenon in the normal sense of phenomenology, for which all phenomena belong to wider horizons, nor as a being within the totality of beings. "The Face" transcends all phenomenality and beingness and is, in this sense, "invisible," other than being, "ab-solved" and "absolute." The Ego's contact with the other's face or speech is incomprehensible but not unreal. It cannot be expressed in an ontological framework; the description must also use ethical terminology. To encounter another is to discover that I am under a basic obligation: the human other's infinity reveals itself as a command; the fact of the Other's "epiphany" reveals that I am his or her servant.

The intentional (or, rather, quasi-intentional) analysis of the relation between the other and me reveals an asymmetrical relationship which precedes every possibility of choice or decision. The tension between this asymmetry and the economy of ego's enjoyment of the world is unfolded in analyses of all the topics of twentieth-century philosophy, such as freedom, language, corporeality, sensibility, affectivity, work, history, love, and death, and many consequences for a radical transformation of phenomenology are made explicit. In constant discussion with Heidegger, Levinas struggles to develop a non-ontological language in order to express the beyond of being, but in doing so he uses that very same language to overcome it. This struggle continues to lead in a direction that can be perceived in those parts of the book that were written last, for example its preface.

After 1961 Levinas produced a considerable number of texts that prepared the way for his second magnum opus, *Autrement qu'être ou au-delà de l'essence* (1974), translated as *Otherwise than Being or Beyond Essence* (1981). The title, more explicit than *Existence and Existents* or *Totality and Infinity*, is a double translation of Plato's characterization of the Good as "beyond the *ousia*"; it declares Levinas's intention to overcome ontology. New descriptions of being, interest, sensibility, language, ethics, and the like are given. The asymmetrical relation between the Other and me is further analyzed as contact, being touched, proximity, vulnerability, responsibility, substitution, being a hostage, obsession, and persecution. Time is analyzed as radical diachrony. The unchosen character of responsibility is unfolded as a passivity more passive than the passivity that is opposed to activity. *Me voici* (see me here; here I am) is shown to precede any self-consciousness, and God is referred to as having passed into an immemorial past, a passing that has left a trace from which the human Other rises up as primary command.

The difficulty of any attempt to think beyond Being lies in the philosophical unavoidability of a thematizing language. In thematizing the asymmetry of substitution, Levinas's text betrays the nonobjective, nonthematic, and nonontological nature of that asymmetry. The resulting incongruency is made explicit in the distinction between the Saying (*le Dire*) and the Said (*le Dit*). Philosophy produces instances of the Said, but every Said is preceded and transcended by a Saying, to which the Said must be brought back. This reduction refers all philosophical texts to the proximity of "the-one-for-the-other." If philosophy is love of wisdom, it is also, and primarily, the wisdom of love.

Levinas's extensive writings on Judgaic topics and the prominence of God and religion in his philosophical work have sometimes led to characterizations of Levinas's thought as a masked theology rather than as phenomenologically rooted philosophy. *Difficile liberté* (1963, 1976), translated as *Difficult Freedom* (1990); *Quatre lectures talmudiques* (1968) and *Du sacré au saint* (1977), combined in the English edition *Nine Talmudic Readings* (1990); and *L'au-delà du verset* (1982), translated as *Beyond the Verse* (1994), show his attachment to the Talmudic tradition and *De Dieu qui vient à l'idée* (1982) is an example of his philosophical concern about the question of God. Levinas, however, without ever denying his roots, always insists on the philosophical character of his work. In his philosophical studies his approach is similar to the approaches of Descartes, Hegel, and Heidegger; even when he quotes from the Bible, his argumentation does not appeal to extraphilosophical authorities. He invites all readers of his texts to validate the truth of his arguments on the basis of their own experiences and thought. But philosophy, as a language that strives for universality, does not exclude the explicit and implicit thoughts of particular traditions and spiritualities.

The relevance of Levinas's philosophical work for our time can be shown by highlighting various facets of his originality. The most obvious aspect of his work is its ethical character, but it must not be misunderstood as an attempt to elaborate a treatise of moral philosophy. In Levinas's writings "ethics" is as basic as any attempt at "first philosophy"; in *Totality and Infinity* it is even identified with "metaphysics." Levinas's "ethics as first philosophy" pursues a purpose similar to the purposes of Plato's *Republic*, Spinoza's *Ethics*, and the ensemble of Kant's three *Critiques*. Of the modern philosophers Kant is certainly the one with whom Levinas's thinking shows the most affinity, but far from being neo-Kantian, his style is postmodern, postphenomenological, and post-Heideggerian.

An important aspect of Levinas's relevance lies in his relationship to Heidegger. Without ever denying his great debt to this master, Levinas has been the first and fiercest critic of Heidegger's thought among the French philosophers of this century. Although his interpretations of Heidegger are sometimes debatable, Levinas's criticisms and his proposals for a drastic transformation of philosophy cannot be ignored. For many French authors, including Ricoeur,

Derrida, Marion, Nancy, and Chrétien, Levinas's work has become seminal in their endeavor to develop a post-Husserlian and post-Heideggerian philosophy. Levinas's discussions of the classics of philosophy provide a critical diagnosis of Western civilization. His critique has no doubt been intensified by his own experience of victimization and genocide in our enlightened but murderous century. Levinas's oeuvre offers itself as a possible guide for those who think that a certain kind of philosophical wisdom is still possible. In light of his personal experience and thought it is not surprising that this guide encompasses profound analyses of the relations of ethics, religion (especially Judaism), and philosophy.

This book presents the essentials of Levinas's philosophical thought through a representative selection of texts Levinas wrote after his rupture with Heidegger in the 1930s. The editors have added introductions and notes to each piece; to justify the selections, I note here briefly some aspects of the texts chosen which make them appropriate for this purpose. References to the publication of the French original and its translation into English are given in the first note accompanying each text.

Chapter 1, "Is Ontology Fundamental?" (1951), is Levinas's first explicit and extensive criticism of Heidegger's philosophy; the reasons why Levinas, despite his lasting recognition of and respect for Heidegger, takes leave of "the climate of that philosophy" are clearly stated and remain constant in all Levinas's later work.

Chapter 2, "Transcendence and Height" (1962), is programmatic in character. Here Levinas summarizes the main lines of argument in *Totality and Infinity* from an epistemological perspective and discusses with members of the Société française de philosophie some of the problems this argument raises.

"Meaning and Sense" (1964), chapter 3, can be read as Levinas's discourse on method; in a critical confrontation with Merleau-Ponty and Heidegger, Levinas shows how his style of thought differs from phenomenology, a philosophical method which he continues to practice as an obligatory passage to any thinking beyond phenomenology.

"Enigma and Phenomenon" (1965), chapter 4, resumes Levinas's discussion of the phenomenological method. Against Husserl and Heidegger, Levinas contends that the dimension of the phenomena cannot be the ultimate; he analyzes the enigmatic character of a revelation that is not a phenomenon and indicates how we can approach it in philosophy.

"Substitution" (1968), chapter 5, is the first English translation of the essay that Levinas heavily revised to make it the core of *Otherwise than Being*, a core to which all interpretations of his work should refer.

Chapter 6, "Truth of Disclosure and Truth of Testimony" (1972), supplements "Meaning and Sense" and "Enigma and Phenomenon." Through a critique of the Greek-European conception of truth, Levinas shows the necessity of a prophetic truth that surpasses, precedes, and transforms this conception without destroying it altogether.

Chapter 7, "Essence and Disinterestedness" (1974), is a summary of *Otherwise than Being* in which the argument and the connection between its topics is stated.

"God and Philosophy" (1975), chapter 8, answers the difficult question of how we must understand the statement in *Totality and Infinity* (p. 34) that the alterity of the Other is both "the alterity of the human Other (*Autrui*) and of the Most-High." The essay is essential for an accurate understanding of Levinas's view on the relationships between first philosophy, ethics, and religion.

"Transcendence and Intelligibility" (1984), chapter 9, is probably the clearest and most succinct statement of Levinas's thinking about thinking. In just a few pages it contains the core of his metaphilosophy.

Chapter 10, "Peace and Proximity" (1984), may be read as a conclusion that opens a way to the future. The essay indicates how Levinasian "ethics" can be developed into an account of politics. At the same time it sketches the ethical orientation according to which Europe might overcome its particularisms and move toward peace.

A number of the translations offered here are based on previously published translations. Notably, the translations of Alphonso Lingis were the basis for chapters 3, 4, 7, and 8. But all existing translations were checked and modified as needed. Robert Bernasconi and Simon Critchley revised the translations of chapters 4, 5, and 8. With Peter Atterton and Graham Noctor, Critchley translated chapters 1, 5, and 10. With Tina Chanter and Nicholas Walker, Simon Critchley translated chapter 2, and, with Tamra Wright, chapter 9. Adriaan Peperzak revised chapters 1 and 2 and, with Critchley, also revised chapters 3 and 7. Iain MacDonald translated chapter 6.

One particular difficulty which any translator of Levinas has to solve is the rendering of *Autre*, *autre*, *Autrui*, and *autrui*, Levinas's use of which is not always consistent. Among Levinas scholars it has become a convention to reserve "the Other" with a capital for all places where Levinas means the human other, whether he uses *Autrui*, *autrui*, *autre*, or *Autre*. This convention has many inconveniences, however. For example, it cannot show the difference between *Autre* when it is used to refer to God and when it refers to the human other. It also blurs the difference between "the Other" as *Autrui* (or *autrui*) and *l'Autre* in the sense of *to heteron* as opposed to "the Same" (*to auton*). Since most translators maintain the capital letter when rendering *le Même* as "the Same," that convention produces the inconsistent "the Same and the other." To avoid such anomalies we have decided to follow Levinas's unsystematic way of capitalizing *Autre* and *Autrui*.

In order to indicate the difference between *l'autre* (or *l'Autre*) and *autrui* (or *Autrui*), both of which we translate as "the other" (or "the Other"), we have added between parentheses *autrui* (or *Autrui*) when that is the word used in the French text. However, there are a few places where this convention, too, would lead to difficulties, especially when Levinas, after having analyzed the opposition between the Same and the Other in an abstract sense, states the thesis that the Other (*l'Autre*) is *Autrui*. Here *Autrui* cannot be translated by "the Other" because "the Other is the Other" would miss the point completely. In this and similar sentences we have therefore translated *Autrui* (or *autrui*) by "the human Other" (or "the human other").

Notes to the texts include those originally supplied by Levinas and others provided by the editors. Since Levinas often quotes from memory without giving explicit references, we have tried whenever possible to identify the references. We have also added explanatory notes. Most chapters contain only a few author's notes, but the texts of chapters 4, 5, and 8 are annotated extensively by Levinas himself. Levinas's notes are clearly marked, usually with the designation (EL). Critchley wrote the notes to chapters 9 and 10, Bernasconi is responsible for those to chapters 5 and 8, and Peperzak wrote the notes to chapters 1, 2, 3, 6, and 7. Bernasconi and Peperzak collaborated on the notes to chapter 4.

The introductions to chapters 1, 9, and 10 were provided by Critchley, those to chapters 4, 5, and 8 by Bernasconi, and those to chapters 2, 3, 6, and 7 by Peperzak.

The preparation of this book would have been impossible without the assistance of many friends. Besides the co-translators mentioned above, we also want to thank John Llewelyn, John Drabinski, Max Maloney, James Hanas, Christine Harris, Aron Reppmann, and Dimitri Frenkel Frank. We are especially grateful to Beth Spina, who typed and retyped various drafts of the manuscript without ever losing her gentle patience.

Adriaan T. Peperzak

ACKNOWLEDGMENTS

The editors and the publisher thank the following for permission to publish the texts in this collection: Lester Embree, editor of the forthcoming *Encyclopaedia of Phenomenology*, for a part of the preface; *Revue de Métaphysique et de Morale* and *Philosophy Today* for "Is Ontology Fundamental?"; *Bulletin de la Société Française de Philosophie* for "Transcendence and Height" with the discussion and correspondence; Kluwer Academic Publishers for "Meaning and Sense," "Enigma and Phenomenon," and "God and Philosophy," which appear in Levinas's *Collected Philosophical Papers*, and "Essence and Disinterestedness," which appears in *Otherwise than Being or Beyond Essence*; *Revue Philosophique de Louvain* for "Substitution"; *Archivio de Filosofia* and Aubier-Montaigne for "Truth of Disclosure and Truth of Testimony"; Labor et Fides for "Transcendence and Intelligibility"; and *Les Cahiers de la Nuit Surveillée* for "Peace and Proximity."

Abbreviations of Works by Levinas

ADV	*L'au-delà du verset*. Paris: Minuit, 1982.
AE	*Autrement qu'être ou au-delà de l'essence*. The Hague: Martinus Nijhoff, 1974
BV	*Beyond the Verse*. Trans. Gary D. Mole. Bloomington: Indiana University Press, 1994.
CP	*Collected Philosophical Papers*. Trans. Alphonso Lingis. The Hague: Martinus Nijhoff, 1987.
DE	*De l'existence à l'existant*. Paris: Vrin, 1947.
DF	*Difficult Freedom*. Trans. Seàn Hand. Baltimore: Johns Hopkins University Press, 1990.
DL	*Difficile liberté*. 2nd ed. Paris: Albin Michel, 1976.
DMT	*Dieu, la mort et le temps*. Paris: Grasset, 1993.
DVI	*De Dieu qui vient a l'idée*. Paris: Vrin, 1982.
EaI	*Ethics and Infinity*. Trans. Richard Cohen. Pittsburgh: Duquesne University Press, 1985.
EDE	*En découvrant l'existence avec Husserl et Heidegger*. 3rd ed. Paris: Vrin, 1974.
EE	*Existence and Existents*. Trans. Alphonso Lingis. The Hague: Martinus Nijhoff, 1978.
EeI	*Ethique et infini*. Paris: Librairie Arthème Fayard, 1982.
EN	*Entre nous: Essais sur le penser-à-l'autre*, Paris: Grasset, 1991.
HAH	*Humanisme de l'autre homme*. Montpellier: Fata Morgana, 1976.
LR	*The Levinas Reader*. Ed. Seán Hand. Oxford: Blackwell, 1989.
MT	*La mort et le temps*. Paris: Editions de l'Herne, 1991.
NP	*Noms propres*. Montpellier: Fata Morgana, 1976.
NTR	*Nine Talmudic Readings*. Trans. Annette Aronowicz. Bloomington: Indiana University Press, 1990.
OB	*Otherwise than Being or Beyond Essence*. Trans. Alphonso Lingis. The Hague: Martinus Nijhoff, 1981.
OS	*Outside the Subject*. Trans. Michael Smith. Stanford: Stanford University Press, 1993.
S	"La Substitution," *Revue Philosophique de Louvain*, 1968, pp. 487–508.
Si	"Signature," in DL, pp. 373–79.
SS	*Du sacré au saint*. Paris: Editions de Minuit, 1977.
TA	*Le temps et l'autre*. Montpellier: Fata Morgana, 1979.

TaI   *Totality and Infinity: An Essay on Exteriority*. Trans. Alphonso Lingis. The Hague: Martinus Nijhoff, 1969.

TeI   *Totalité et infini: Essai sur l'exteriorité*. The Hague: Martinus Nijhoff, 1961.

TIH   *The Theory of Intuition in Husserl's Phenomenology*. Trans. A. Orianne. Evanston: Northwestern University Press, 1973.

TIPH   *Théorie de l'intuition dans la phénoménologie de Husserl*. Paris: Félix Alcan, 1930.

TO   *Time and the Other*. Trans. Richard Cohen. Pittsburgh: Duquesne University Press, 1985.

Basic Philosophical Writings

Is Ontology Fundamental?
(1951)

Levinas is engaged here in a questioning of Heidegger's project of fundamental ontology, that is to say, his attempt, in *Being and Time*, to raise anew the question of the meaning of Being through an analysis of that being for whom Being is a question: *Dasein*.[1] In Heidegger's early work, ontology - science of Being in the Aristotelian sense - is fundamental, and Dasein is the fundament or condition of possibility for any ontology, a being whose "a priori" structure must first be clarified in an existential analysis. For Levinas, the exceptional character of Heideggerian ontology is that it presupposes the factual situation, or existential facticity, of the human being. The comprehension of Being (*Seinsverständnis*), which must be presupposed in order for Heidegger's project to begin, does not assume a merely intellectual attitude, but rather the rich variety of intentional life - emotional, practical, and theoretical - through which we relate to the Being of various beings. Thus - and this fundamental agreement with Heidegger can already be found at the basis of Levinas's critique of Husserl in his 1930 doctoral thesis, published as *Théorie de l'intuition dans la phénoménologie de Husserl* - the essential contribution of Heideggerian ontology is its critique of intellectualism: the fact that ontology is not simply a contemplative science but is grounded in a fundamental ontology of the existential engagement of human beings in the world which forms the "anthropological" preparation for the elaboration of the question of Being.

However, as Levinas's writings prior to this essay make clear (for example, the introduction to his 1947 book *De l'existence à l'existant*), although Levinas's work is to a large extent inspired by Heidegger and by the conviction that we cannot put aside *Being and Time* for a philosophy that would be pre-Heideggerian, it is also governed by what Levinas calls "the profound need to leave the climate of that philosophy" (DE 19; EE 19). "Is Ontology Fundamental?" shows the basis for this claim and demonstrates for the first time the *ethical* significance of this critique of Heidegger. The enduring importance of this essay for Levinas's subsequent work can be seen in the way its argumentation is alluded to and repeated in the analyses of *Totality and Infinity* (see "Metaphysics Precedes Ontology" [TeI 12–18; TaI 42–48] and "Ethics and the Face" [TeI 172–75; TaI 197–201]). And yet the essay has many attractions for the reader coming to it from Levinas's later work, for example the two significant allusions to Kant's ethics, and the proximity and distance of Levinas's account of the ethical relation to Hegel's dialectic of intersubjectivity ("the life and death struggle").

The central task of this essay is to describe a relation irreducible to comprehension, that is to say, irreducible to what Levinas sees as the *ontological* relation to others where alterity is reduced to the Same. Even the Heideggerian ontology that exceeds intellectualism is unable to describe this relation, because the particular being is always already understood within the horizon of Being. Thus, for Levinas, Heidegger rejoins the great Platonic tradition of Western philosophy, where in order to comprehend the particular being, it is always understood with reference to the universal *eidos*. Yet how can a relation with an entity be other than comprehension? Levinas's response is that it cannot, "unless it is the other (*autrui*)." The claim here is that the relation with the other goes beyond comprehension, that it does not affect us in terms of a concept or theme. For Levinas, this "original relation" takes place in the concrete situation of speech. In speaking or calling or listening to the other, I am not reflecting upon the other, but I am actively engaged in a noncomprehensive, nonsubsumptive relation to alterity where I focus on the particular individual in front of me and forgo the mediation of the universal. It is this event of being in relation with the other - variously described in the essay as "expression," "invocation," and "prayer" - that Levinas describes first as "religion" and then, and only on the basis of an allusion to Kant, as "ethical." This leads to a significant insight: that Levinas does not posit, a priori, a conception of ethics that then instantiates itself in certain concrete experiences; rather, the ethical (rather than "ethics") is a name that describes, a posteriori, a certain event of being in a nonsubsumptive relation with the other.

---

1. The Primacy of Ontology

Does not the primacy of ontology among the branches of knowledge rest on a most obvious evidence? Does not all knowledge of relations by which beings are connected or opposed to one another already involve the comprehension of the fact that these relations and these beings exist? To spell out the significance of this fact, i.e., to take up once more the problem of ontology (implicitly resolved by everyone, be it only under the form of forgetfulness), is, so it seems, to establish a fundamental knowledge without which all philosophical, scientific, or common knowledge remains naïve.

The dignity of contemporary ontological research results from the imperious and original character of this evidence. On the basis of it, thinkers straightaway rose above the "illuminations" of literary coteries in order to breathe afresh the air of the great dialogues of Plato and the metaphysics of Aristotle.

To question this fundamental evidence is a reckless undertaking. But to take up philosophy by such questioning is, at least, to return to its source, beyond literature and emotional problems.

2. Contemporary Ontology

The renewal of ontology by contemporary philosophy is unusual in that the knowledge of being in general - fundamental ontology - presupposes the *factual situation* of the mind that knows. A reason freed from temporal contingencies, a soul co-eternal with the Ideas, such is the self-image cultivated by a reason that has forgotten itself or is unaware of itself, a reason that is naive. Ontology, allegedly authentic,[2] coincides with the facticity of temporal existence. To comprehend being as being is to exist here below.

Not that the *here below*,[3] by the trials it imposes, elevates and purifies the soul, enabling it to become more receptive toward being. Not that the here below opens a history, the progress of which alone would make thinkable the idea of being. The *here below* gets its ontological privilege neither from the ascesis it comprises nor from the civilization to which it gives rise.[4] Already in these temporal concerns the comprehension of beings is spelled out. Ontology is not accomplished in the triumph of human beings over their condition but in the very tension where this condition is assumed.

This possibility of conceiving contingency and facticity not as facts open to intellection but as the act of intellection, this possibility of showing in the brutality of the fact and given contents the transitivity of comprehension and a "signifying intention"[5] (a possibility discovered by Husserl, but linked by Heidegger to the intellection of being in general), constitutes the great novelty of contemporary ontology. Henceforth the comprehension of being does not presuppose a merely theoretical attitude but the whole of human comportment. The whole human being is ontology. Scientific work, the affective life, the satisfaction of needs and labor, social life and death - all these moments spell out the comprehension of being, or truth, with a rigor which reserves to each a determinate function. Our entire civilization follows from this comprehension, even if this comprehension was a forgetfulness of being. It is not because of the human being that there is truth. It is because being in general is inseparable from its *openness*, because there is truth, or, if one likes, because being is intelligible, that there is humanity.[6]

The return to the original themes of philosophy - and it is in this that the work of Heidegger remains striking - does not proceed from a pious decision to return finally to who knows what *philosophia perennis* but from a radical attention given to the urgent preoccupations of the moment. The abstract question of the meaning of being qua being and the question of the present hour spontaneously reunite.

3. The Ambiguity of Contemporary Ontology

The identification of the comprehension of being with the plenitude of concrete existence risks drowning in existence. This *philosophy of existence*, which Heidegger for his part refuses, is only the counterpart, albeit inevitable, of his conception of ontology. The historical existence that interests the philosopher insofar as it is ontology is of interest to human beings and literature because it is dramatic. When philosophy and life are intermingled, we no longer know if we incline toward philosophy because it is life or hold to life because it is philosophy. The essential contribution to the new ontology can be seen in its opposition to classical intellectualism. To comprehend the tool is not to look at it but to know how to handle it. To comprehend our situation in reality is not to define it but to find ourselves in an affective disposition. To comprehend being is to exist.[7] All this indicates, it would seem, a rupture with the theoretical structure of Western thought. To think is no longer to contemplate but to commit oneself, to be engulfed by that which one thinks, to be involved.[8] This is the dramatic event of being-in-the-world.

The comedy begins with the simplest of our movements, each of which carries with it an inevitable awkwardness. In putting out my hand to approach a chair, I have creased the sleeve of my jacket. I have scratched the floor, I have dropped the ash from my cigarette. In doing that which I wanted to do, I have done so many things I did not want. The act has not been pure, for I have left some traces. In wiping out these traces, I have left others. Sherlock Holmes will apply his science to this irreducible coarseness of each of my initiatives and thereby, the comedy may well turn tragic. When the awkwardness of the act turns against the goal pursued, we are at the height of tragedy. Laius, in order to thwart the deadly predictions, will undertake precisely what is necessary for them to be fulfilled. In succeeding, Oedipus contributes to his own unhappiness like the prey that flees the noise of the hunter across a field covered in snow, thereby leaving the very traces that will be its ruin.

We are thus responsible beyond our intentions. It is impossible for the regard that directs the act to avoid the nonintended action that comes with it. We have one finger caught in the machine and things turn against us. That is to say, our consciousness and our mastery of reality through consciousness do not exhaust our relation with reality, to which we are always present through all the density of our being. Consciousness of reality does not coincide with our habitation in the world - it is here that Heidegger's philosophy has produced such a strong impression on the literary world.

But the philosophy of existence immediately effaces itself before ontology. This fact of being involved, this event in which I find myself engaged, tied as I am to what should be my object by ties not reducible to thoughts - this existence is interpreted as comprehension. From now on the transitive character of the verb to know (connaître) is attached to the verb to exist.[9] The first sentence of Aristotle's Metaphysics, "All men by nature aspire to knowledge," remains true for a philosophy that has too easily been believed to be disdainful of the intellect. Ontology does not come merely to crown our practical concerns with being, as the contemplation of the essences in Book X of the Nicomachean Ethics crowns the virtues.[10] Ontology is the essence of every relation with beings and even of every relation in being. Does not the fact that a being is "open" belong to the very fact of its being? Our concrete existence is interpreted in terms of its entry into the "openness" of being in general.[11] We exist in a circuit of understanding with reality.[12] Understanding is the very event that existence articulates. All incomprehension is only a deficient mode of comprehension. It turns out that the analysis of existence and of what is called its *haecceity* (*Da*) is only the description of the essence of truth, of the condition of the very understanding of being.[13]

4. The Other (*Autrui*) as Interlocutor

It is not on behalf of a divorce between philosophy and reason that we hold to a meaningful language. But we are entitled to ask whether reason, presented as the possibility of such a language, necessarily precedes it, or if language is not founded on a relation anterior to comprehension and which constitutes reason. The pages that follow will attempt to characterize in a very general way this relation which is irreducible to comprehension, even to that comprehension beyond classical intellectualism determined by Heidegger.

Comprehension for Heidegger ultimately rests on the *openness* of being. While Berkeleian idealism, because of the qualitative content of being, saw in the latter a reference to thought, Heidegger sees in the - in a sense formal - fact that beings (*l'étant*) are - in their work of being (*être*), in their very independence - their intelligibility.[14] This does not involve the prior dependence of a being (*l'étant*) with respect to a subjective thought but is like a vacancy awaiting its incumbent, opened by the very fact that a being is. It is thus that Heidegger describes, in their most formal structure, the articulations of vision where the relation of the subject with the object is subordinated to the relation of the object with light, which is not an object. The understanding of a being will thus consist in going beyond that being (*l'étant*) into the *openness* and in perceiving it *upon the horizon of being*. That is to say, comprehension, in Heidegger, rejoins the great tradition of Western philosophy: to comprehend the particular being is already to place oneself beyond the particular. To comprehend is to be related to the particular that only exists through knowledge, which is always knowledge of the universal.

One cannot oppose personal preference to the venerable tradition that Heidegger continues. One cannot *prefer* as the condition of ontology a relation with beings over the fundamental thesis that every relation with a being presupposes the intimacy or the forgetfulness of being. From the moment that one engages in reflection and precisely for the very reasons which since Plato subject the sensation of the particular to knowledge of the universal, one is forced, it would seem, to subject relations between beings to structures of being, metaphysics to ontology, the existentiell to the existential. How, moreover, can the *relation* with *being* be, from the outset, anything other than its *comprehension* as being (*étant*), the fact of freely letting it be inasmuch as it is being (*étant*)?

Unless it is the other (*Autrui*). Our relation with the other (*autrui*) certainly consists in wanting to comprehend him, but this relation overflows comprehension. Not only because knowledge of the other (*autrui*) requires, outside of all curiosity, also sympathy or love, ways of being distinct from impassible contemplation, but because in our relation with the other (*autrui*), he does not affect us in terms of a concept. He is a being (*étant*) and counts as such.

Here the partisan of ontology will object: to speak of beings (*étant*), is this not already to insinuate that beings concern us thanks to a revelation of being and is therefore, since situated in the opening of being, from the very outset established in the heart of comprehension? Indeed, what does the independence of a being mean, if not its reference to ontology? To relate oneself to beings qua beings means, for Heidegger, to let beings be, to comprehend them as independent of the perception which discovers and grasps them. It is precisely through such comprehension that it gives itself as a being (*étant*) and not as a mere object. Being-with-the-Other (*Miteinandersein*)[15] thus rests for Heidegger on the ontological relation.

We respond: in our relation with the other (*autrui*) is it a matter of *letting be*?[16] Is not the independence of the other (*autrui*) accomplished in the role of being summoned? Is the one to whom one speaks understood from the first in his being? Not at all. The other (*autrui*) is not an object of comprehension first and an interlocutor second. The two relations are intertwined. In other words, the comprehension of the other (*autrui*) is inseparable from his invocation.

To comprehend a person is already to speak with him. To posit the existence of the other (*autrui*) through letting be is already to have accepted this existence, to have taken account of it. "To have accepted," "to have taken account," do not come back to comprehension and letting be. Speech delineates an original relation. It is a question of perceiving the function of language not as subordinate to the *consciousness* that one has of the presence of the other (*autrui*), his neighborliness or our community with him, but rather as the condition of any conscious grasp.

Of course, it is still necessary to explain why the event of language is no longer situated at the level of comprehension. Indeed, why not broaden the notion of comprehension according to a procedure made familiar by phenomenology? Why not present the invocation of the other (*autrui*) as the characteristic proper to his comprehension?

This we hold to be impossible. For example, the handling of everyday objects is interpreted as their comprehension.[17] But in this example, broadening of the notion of knowledge is justified by the overcoming of known objects. It is accomplished in spite of everything there may be of pretheoretical engagement in the handling of "equipment." At the heart of such handling, the being (*l'étant*) is *overcome* in the very movement that grasps it. In this "beyond" necessary to presence "at hand" we see the very itinerary of comprehension. This overcoming is not only due to the preliminary appearance of the "world" each time that we concern ourselves with something manipulable, as Heidegger argues. It is delineated also in the *possession* and in the *consumption* of the object. But it is not at all like this when it is a matter of my relation with the other (*autrui*). There also, if one likes, I comprehend being in the other (*autrui*), beyond its particularity as a being (*étant*). The person with whom I am in relation I call *being*, but in so calling him, I call to him. I do not only think that he is, I speak to him. He is my *partner* in the heart of a relation which ought only have made him present to me. I have spoken to him, that is to say, I have neglected the universal being that he incarnates in order to remain with the particular being he is. Here the formula "before being in relation with a being, I must first have comprehended it as being" loses its strict application, for in comprehending being I simultaneously tell this comprehension to this being.

A human being is the sole being which I am unable to encounter without expressing this very encounter to him. It is precisely in this that the encounter distinguishes itself from knowledge. In every attitude in regard to the human there is a greeting - if only in the refusal of greeting. Here perception is not projected toward a horizon - the field of my freedom, power and property - in order to grasp the individual upon a familiar foundation. It refers to the pure individual, to a being as such. And this signifies precisely, if one wishes to speak in terms of "comprehension," that my comprehension of beings as such is already the expression that I offer him of this very comprehension.

This impossibility of approaching the other (*autrui*) without speaking to him signifies that here thought is inseparable from expression. But such expression does not consist in decanting in some manner a thought relative to the other (*autrui*) into the other's (*autrui*) mind. We know this not since Heidegger but since Socrates.[18] Nor does such expression consist in *articulating* the comprehension that I henceforth share with the other (*autrui*). Before any participation in a common content by comprehension, it consists in the intuition of sociality by a relation that is consequently irreducible to comprehension.

The relation with the other (*autrui*) is not therefore ontology. This tie to the other (*autrui*), which does not reduce itself to the representation of the Other (*autrui*) but rather to his invocation, where invocation is not preceded by comprehension, we call *religion*. The essence of discourse is prayer.[19] What distinguishes thought aiming at an object from the tie with a person is that the latter is articulated in the vocative: what is named is at the same time that which is called.

In choosing the term *religion* - without having pronounced the word *God* or the word *sacred* - we have initially in mind the meaning which Auguste Comte gives to this term in the beginning of his *Politique positive*.[20] Nothing theological, nothing mystical, lies hidden behind the analysis that we have just given of the encounter with the other (*autrui*), an encounter whose formal structure it was important to underline: the object of the encounter is at once given to us and *in society* with us; but we cannot reduce this event of sociality to some property revealed in the given, and knowledge cannot take precedence over sociality. If the word *religion* should, however, announce that the relation with human beings, irreducible to comprehension, is itself thereby distanced from the exercise of power, whereas it rejoins the Infinite in human faces, then we accept the ethical resonance of that word and all of its Kantian echoes.

Religion is the relation with a being as a being. It does not consist in *conceiving* it as a being or as an act in which a *being* is already assimilated, even if this assimilation were to succeed in disengaging it as a being, in *letting it be*. Nor does religion consist in establishing who knows what *belonging*, nor in running up against the irrational in an effort to comprehend *beings*. Is the rational reducible to power over an object? Is reason domination by which the resistance of being as such is surmounted, not in an appeal to this very resistance but as a ruse of the hunter who ensnares all that such a being contains of strength and irreducibility on the basis of its weaknesses, the abdication of its particularity, its place in the horizon of universal being? Is understanding as ruse, understanding belonging to struggle and violence over things, able to constitute a human order? Are we not paradoxically accustomed to seeking in struggle the very manifestation of spirit and its reality? But is not the order of reason constituted rather in a situation where "one chats," where the resistance of beings qua beings is not broken but pacified?

The concern of contemporary philosophy to liberate human beings from the categories adapted uniquely for things cannot therefore content itself with notions of dynamism, duration, transcendence, or freedom, as opposed to those of the static, the inert, the determined, as a description of the human essence. In order to say what is human nature, it is not so much a matter of opposing one essence to another. It is above all a matter of finding a place where the human no longer concerns us from the perspective of the horizon of being, that is to say, no longer offers itself to our powers. A being as such (and not as incarnation of universal being) can only be in a relation where we speak to this being. A being (*l'étant*) is a human being and it is as a neighbor that a human being is accessible - as a face.

5. The Ethical Signification of the Other (*Autrui*)

In relation to beings in the opening of being, comprehension finds a signification for them on the basis of being. In this sense, it does not invoke these beings but only names them, thus accomplishing a violence and a negation. A partial negation which is violence. This *partiality* is indicated by the fact that, without disappearing, those beings are in my power. Partial negation, which is violence, denies the independence of a being: it belongs to me. Possession is the mode whereby a being, while existing, is partially denied. It is not only a question of the fact that the being is an instrument, a tool, that is to say, a means. It is an end also. As consumable, it is nourishment, and in enjoyment, it offers itself, gives itself, belongs to me. To be sure, vision measures my power over the object, but it is already enjoyment. The encounter with the other (*autrui*) consists in the fact that despite the extent of my domination and his slavery, I do not possess him. He does not enter entirely into the opening of being where I already stand, as in the field of my freedom. It is not starting from being in general that he comes to meet me. Everything which comes to me from the other (*autrui*) starting from being in general certainly offers itself to my comprehension and possession. I understand him in the framework of his history, his surroundings and habits. That which escapes comprehension in the other (*autrui*) is him, a being. I cannot negate him partially, in violence, in grasping him within the horizon of being in general and possessing him. The Other (*Autrui*) is the sole being whose negation can only announce itself as total: as *murder*. The Other (*Autrui*) is the sole being I can wish to kill.

I can wish.[21] And yet this power is quite the contrary of power. The triumph of this power is its defeat as power. At the very moment when my power to kill realizes itself, the other (*autrui*) has escaped me. I can, for sure, in killing *attain* a goal; I can kill as I hunt or slaughter animals, or as I fell trees. But when I have grasped the other (*autrui*) in the opening of being in general, as an element of the world where I stand, where I have seen him *on the horizon*, I have not looked at him in the face, I have not encountered his face. The temptation of total negation, measuring the infinity of this attempt and its impossibility - this is the presence of the face. To be in relation with the other (*autrui*) face to face is to be unable to kill. It is also the situation of discourse.

If things are only things, this is because the relation with them is established as comprehension. As beings, they let themselves be overtaken from the perspective of being and of a totality that lends them a signification. The immediate is not an object of comprehension. An immediate given of consciousness is a contradiction in terms. To be given is to be exposed to the ruse of the understanding, to be seized by the mediation of a concept, by the light of being in general, by way of a detour, "in a roundabout way." To be given is to signify on the basis of what one is not. The relation with the face, speech, an event of collectivity, is a relation with beings as such, as pure beings.

That the relation with a *being* is the invocation of a face and already speech, a relation with a certain depth rather than with a horizon - a breach in the horizon - that my neighbor is the being par excellence, can indeed appear somewhat surprising when one is accustomed to the conception of a being that is by itself insignificant, a profile against a luminous horizon and only acquiring signification in virtue of its presence within this horizon. The face *signifies* otherwise. In it the infinite resistance of a being to our power affirms itself precisely against the murderous will that it defies; because, completely naked (and the nakedness of the face is not a figure of style), the face signifies itself. We cannot even say that the face is an opening, for this would be to make it relative to an environing plenitude.

Can things take on a face? Is not art an activity that lends faces to things? Does not the facade of a house regard us? The analysis thus far does not suffice for an answer. We ask ourselves all the same if the impersonal but fascinating and magical march of rhythm does not, in art, substitute itself for sociality, for the face, for speech.

To comprehension and signification grasped within a horizon, we oppose the signifyingness of the face. Will the brief indications by which we have introduced this notion allow us to catch sight of its role in comprehension itself and of all the conditions which delineate a sphere of relations barely suspected? In any case, that which we catch sight of seems suggested by the practical philosophy of Kant, to which we feel particularly close.

In what way the vision of the face is no longer vision but audition and speech; how the encounter with the face - that is, moral consciousness - can be described as the condition of consciousness *tout court* and of disclosure; how consciousness is affirmed as the impossibility of killing; what are the conditions of the appearance of the face as the temptation and the impossibility of murder; how I can appear to myself as a face; in what manner, finally, the relation with the other (*autrui*) or the collectivity is our relation, irreducible to comprehension, with the infinite - these are the themes that proceed from this first contestation of the primacy of ontology. Philosophical research, in any case, cannot be content with a mere reflection on the self or on existence. Reflection offers only the tale of a personal adventure, of a private soul, which returns incessantly to itself, even when it seems to flee itself. The human only lends itself to a relation that is not a power.

T W O

Transcendence and Height

(1962)

Shortly after the publication of *Totalité et infini: Essai sur l'extériorité* (1961), Levinas was invited to speak to the *Société Française de Philosophie*. On January 27, 1962, he presented "Transcendance et hauteur" to the members of the society.[1] The essay can be read as a succinct summary of the opening arguments of *Totality and Infinity* from an epistemological perspective. Starting from the classical debate between idealism and realism, Levinas argues that both positions are forms of a fundamental monism: both try to reduce the plurality of beings to the unity of "the Same," thus excluding the otherness of any irreducible "Other." Levinas borrows the expressions "the Same" (*le Même*) and "the Other" (*l'Autre*) from Plato, who in his dialogue *The Sophist* had shown that *to auton* and *to heteron* are basic categories, which cannot be reduced to one another or to any other category such as "being" or "nonbeing." Levinas's characterization of philosophy as the endeavor to assure the triumph of "the Same" encompasses the whole history of Western philosophy, including Heidegger's meditation on the difference between beings and being itself. Traces of another conception of philosophy can be found in some of the classic texts of that history. Descartes, in the third of his *Metaphysical Meditations*, analyzed the irreducibility of the idea of the infinite, an idea found in human consciousness together with the idea of consciousness itself. Infinity is the "feature" that immunizes the Other against any assimilation or absorption by the Same, thus guaranteeing a separation between the two that, at the same time, is a relation.

The phenomenological verification of these seemingly abstract terms and distinctions is given through an analysis of the basic relation between myself and the human Other (*Autrui*). I, who am and remain the Same, discover myself as put into question and under the command of the human Other. The law of my "selfsame" economy, my auto-nomy, is unseated and subordinated by the law of the Other. The primacy of hetero-nomy expresses the asymmetry of the relationship between the human other, which reveals itself to be infinite, and the self, which is a conscience before being a consciousness. As a philosophy of the Same, ontology must make place for a thought that begins by recognizing its a priori relation to the height which is revealed in the other's face and speech.

Argument

Since Hegel, we are accustomed to thinking that philosophy exceeds the framework of anthropology. The ontological event accomplished by philosophy consists in suppressing or transmuting the alterity of all that is Other, in universalizing the immanence of the Same (*le Même*) or of Freedom, in effacing the boundaries, and in expelling the violence of Being (*Être*).

The knowing I is the melting pot of such a transmutation. It is the Same par excellence. When the Other enters into the horizon of knowledge, it already renounces alterity. The eternal return of idealism does not result from a capricious preference for the theory of knowledge on the part of philosophers. It rests upon solid reasons which found the privilege of the Same in comparison with the Other.

Those who would like to uphold the Other or the Transcendent will find but a disappointing recourse in realism. Realism affirms the transcendent by defining it through the idea of being, but the idea of being is fundamentally adequate to and adjusted to the Same.

Now, despite the attachment of a venerable philosophical tradition to the hegemony of the Same, its reign prolongs the War and the Administration which alienate the Same. But, above all, the freedom which is set up in the Same discovers itself imprisoned by the Same. Freedom therefore seeks itself in the relation with the *wholly other*, which is not convertible into the *already known*. It does not suffice for freedom that the Transcendent reveals its meaning after the fact, in the perspective of a history congealed into destiny, in which freedom is integrated despite its novelty. Freedom, reduced to the identity of the Same, cannot repress the Desire for the *absolutely Other*.

But in order that the presence of the Other does not announce permanent war and in order that it resists the temptation of idealism, the ultimate signification of the relation between the Same and the Other must not be interpreted as an allergy. The Other resists my attempt at investiture, not because of the extent and obscurity of the theme that it offers to my consideration but because of the refusal to enter into a theme, to submit to a regard, through the eminence of its epiphany.

The Other (*l'Autre*) thus presents itself as human Other (*Autrui*); it shows a face and opens the dimension of *height*, that is to say, it *infinitely* overflows the bounds of knowledge. Positively, this means that the Other puts in question the freedom which attempts to invest it; the Other lays him- or herself bare to the total negation of murder but forbids it through the original language of his defenseless eyes.

The analysis shows that the "putting into question" of the I is not a special case of self-knowledge, for it opens the infinite process of scrupulousness which causes the I to coincide less and less with itself. The situation so little resembles war that it is ethical. So little does the Other deliver him- or herself over to me that he does not fit into the adequate idea of being but only in the inadequation par excellence of the idea of the Infinite.

In this way, we rediscover the Cartesian itinerary, which moves from the Cogito to the World by passing through the idea of the infinite. In a more general way, the priority of the idea of the infinite is asserted over the idea of being and ontology.

Exposition

1. Philosophy exceeds empirical anthropology. It does not simply appear in the inventory of historical civilizations as one of its contingent elements, like customs, institutions, techniques, arts and sciences. It is inscribed in the essence of the Soul as its deepest thrust. Philosophy supports all the others.

But, in its turn, the Soul and, in our times, the incarnate Soul, man, are interpreted as unavoidable moments in the play of Being itself. For Plato, the Soul is wedded to the Ideas, while for Plotinus it is a hypostasis. For Hegel, subjective spirit - as soul, as consciousness, and finally as subject - is ineluctably part of the History of Spirit or Being.[2] For Heidegger, man is the shepherd of Being.[3]

As an enterprise with neither profits nor loss, the being which the real strives to be does not recuperate philosophy for the same reason as it recuperates everything: phenomena, reflections, and appearances. Philosophy is essential to being qua being. The knowledge of being that produces itself in the soul or in man - truth - is a primordial event of being itself. Knowledge of being is not added from the outside, by the action of chance by which souls curious to be would germinate spontaneously in reality.

2. The philosophical event seems to suppress multiplicity and, consequently, violence. Indeed, violence comes from opposition, that is to say, from the scission of being into Same and Other. Philosophy, as André Lalande would say, assimilates every Other into the Same.[4]

But the assimilation which occurs in philosophy qua philosophy is fundamentally a search for the truth. For, generally speaking, truth means the adequation between representation and external reality. Not because, in truth, representation and reality superimpose themselves onto each other like two congruent triangles; rather, the arrival of the *being other*, within the horizon of the being which has a representation of it, is ipso facto adequation. The fact that being unveils itself, that it shines forth, that its being consists in being true, implies that the contours of being fit into the human scale and the measures of thought. Truth is the original adequation that all adequation presupposes. Indeed, the I of knowledge is at once the Same par excellence, the very event of identification and the melting pot where every Other is transmuted into the Same. It is the philosopher's stone of philosophical alchemy.

This identification constitutes its freedom, since the I returns to itself despite any other that it may encounter such that no other can restrict or impede it. This freedom may appear as a rupture of identity, in the Bergsonian renewal, for example, or in the will, the unforeseeable suddenness of which led Heidegger (in his book on Nietzsche) to say that it is the attack (*Anfall*) par excellence (in the sense in which we use the word in "apoplectic attack").[5] But this rupture does not interrupt the identity of the person (unless it leaves him insane), whereas the entry of the Other within the Same or the accord between the I and the Other - between colleagues, between comrades, between friends, between lovers - is unable to suppress the separation.

The resistance of the Other to the Same is the failure of philosophy. Nonphilosophy is the tyranny of Opinion where the Same submits to, but does not rediscover in itself, the law of the Other; it is the obscurity of the imagination where the knowing subject goes astray and loses itself - the for-itself, the Same, the I; it is the heteronomy of inclination, where the Person follows a law that it has not given to itself; it is the alienation where the person loses itself without noticing it; it is the inauthenticity where beings flee from their identity toward anonymity. Philosophical knowledge is a priori: it searches for the adequate idea and ensures autonomy. In every new development it recognizes familiar structures and greets old acquaintances. It is an odyssey where all adventures are only the accidents of a return to self.

3. The myth of a legislative consciousness of things, where difference and identity are reconciled, is the great myth of philosophy. It rests upon the totalitarianism or imperialism of the Same. Defined by the universality of the Same, idealism is found precisely in the philosophers who denounce it most harshly. If history tends to reduce the conflicts which oppose man to himself, to other people, and to things, this reduction at once signifies the mastery of man over that which initially stands in his way. All alterity breaks up. In a homogeneous or socialist society, the central concern is how to confer on the Other (*Autrui*) the status of the I and how to liberate the I itself from the alienation that comes to it from the injustice that it commits. The right of man, which must be recognized, is the right of an I. Man is conceived of as an I or as a citizen - but never in the irreducible originality of his alterity, which one cannot have access to through reciprocity and symmetry. Universality and egalitarian law result from the conflicts in which one primitive egoism opposes another. The being of the real never ceases to signify its being for me. In this sense, idealism is an egoism.

To contest that being is *for me*, not to contest that being is for the sake of man; it is not to give up on humanism, it is not to separate the absolute and humanity. It is simply to contest that the humanity of man resides in the positing of an I. Man par excellence - the source of humanity - is perhaps the Other.

4. The transcendental thinking that has emerged from the phenomenological movement no longer places the conditions for beings in the thinking subject but in the Being of beings. It wants to go beyond idealism and realism. The position of the real outside of consciousness would no longer have any meaning, on the pretext that this real has long been posited when one simply asks oneself about its existence. But has this attitude definitively refuted the

idealist myth? To all his disciples who thus claim to overcome idealism and realism, and despite his own descriptions of the *Lebenswelt*, Husserl obstinately opposes the demand for a transcendental constitution of the world.

We are looking for a way out of idealism, but we do not find it by having recourse to realism. The realism with which both Marxism and transcendental ontology are satisfied is not sufficiently realist to overcome idealism.

5. That is because the idea of being is an idea adequate in itself. Being is the theme par excellence, which straightaway measures up to the Same. The intentionality perceived by the phenomenological movement at the roots of practice and affectivity establishes throughout all forms of consciousness the common measure between consciousness and being. Consciousness as consciousness of . . . , even in action or feeling, is consciousness of being. And inversely, the adequation is so rigorous that the entire gravity of being can resolve itself in the play of consciousness, in illusion. Perhaps the manifestation of being is only appearance. Being is easily reflected and confounds itself with reflection. The shadow is taken for a prey and the prey is dropped for the shadow.[6] Descartes thought that by myself I could account for the sky and the sun despite all their magnificence.[7] Finally, the act of being, the deployment of this peculiar action that the verb *to be* designates, has been described by Heidegger in terms of its very phosphorescence, its splendor, its radiance, its manifestation, its truth. It is therefore impossible to leave the immanence of the Same by taking as the starting point the idea of Being. Subjectivity as *res cogitans* looks at the *Other* in terms of being and already invests it, without being able to encounter anything radically different, without finding there the "wholly other" of Kierkegaard and Jankélévitch[8] - even if this investment demands a history.

For the claim of realism - the recognition of another than I - to be possible, it is necessary that I myself am not originally what I remain even in my explorations of the obscure or the unknown: the peaceful and sovereign identification of the self with itself and the source of adequate ideas.

6. Moreover, the assimilation of the Other by the Same does not simply consist in knowledge which is certainly its prefiguration and, in the case of absolute knowledge, its fulfillment. The Same or the I surmounts diversity and the Non-I, which stands against it, by engaging in a political and technical destiny. In this sense, the State and the industrial society which the homogeneous State crowns and from which it emerges belong to the philosophical process.

But war and administration, that is to say, hierarchy, through which the State is instituted and maintained, alienate the Same, which they were supposed to maintain in its purity; in order to suppress violence, it is necessary to have recourse to violence. The Same does not recognize its will in the consequence of its vote. The mediation, which should have assured the triumph of the Same, is the source of a new alienation of the Same. Could this be the beginning of a dialectic? In any case, we do not see how dialectic could reach a synthesis and resolve the contradiction. The latter is not inherent in a moment of this dialectic, but in the very process of mediation. Unless the violence that the I receives from War and Administration is neglected by declaring it animal or puerile.

7. But how can the opposition of the Same and the Other not lead to the triumph of the Same? And can we avoid wanting this triumph? Does not realism - in which the Other maintains its position - sanction the permanence of conflict?

Unless one shrinks back before the apostasy into which the hierarchy of the universal order - or totalitarianism - forces the Same. Unless one considers that an *abstraction* is necessary, breaking the coherent and concrete totality like a breath of fresh air. Unless one does not think that the Same does not support the other. Unless one accords to the Same a relation with that which is above Being. Unless one contests that philosophy is truly born of an allergy. Can the Same welcome the Other, not by giving the Other to itself as a theme (that is to say, as being) but by putting itself in question? Does not this putting in question occur precisely when the Other has nothing in common with me, when the Other is wholly other, that is to say, a human Other (*Autrui*)? When, through the nakedness and destitution of his defenseless eyes, he forbids murder and paralyzes my impetuous freedom?

Putting in question does not amount to being conscious of this putting in question. The relation with the Other does not immediately have the structure of intentionality. It is not opening onto . . . , aiming at . . . , which is already an opening onto being and an aiming at being. The absolutely Other is not reflected in a consciousness; it resists the indiscretion of intentionality. It resists it to the point where its very resistance does not become converted into a content of consciousness. The relation with the Other, where, however, the Other remains absolute and absolves itself from the relation which it enters into, is not a thought that directs itself to an object which is too obscure and too great. The I is able to notice and envelop such an excess and obscurity. The resistance of the Other to the indiscretion of intentionality consists in overturn- ing the very egoism of the Same; that which is *aimed at* unseats the intention- ality which aims at it.

What is at stake is putting consciousness in question and not the conscious- ness of putting in question. At stake is a movement oriented in a way that is wholly otherwise than the grasp of consciousness and at every instant unravels, like Penelope at night, everything that was so gloriously woven during the day.[9] We are precisely going to follow the outline of this movement. Neither the notion of the greatest nor that of the most mysterious accounts for it, but rather the notions of height and infinity.

8. Instead of seizing the Other through comprehension and thereby assuming all the wars that this comprehension presupposes, prolongs, and concludes, the I loses its hold before the absolutely Other, before the human Other (*Autrui*), and, unjustified, can no longer be powerful.[10] It is not that the I becomes conscious of its nonjustification and the powerlessness of its power such that it, looking down on itself, already settles down in its good conscience, in its nonculpability, to take refuge in itself where there would remain a fragment of the world untouched by original sin. The event of putting into question is the shame of the I for its naïve spontaneity, for its sovereign coincidence with itself in the identification of the Same. This shame is a movement in a direction opposed to that of consciousness, which returns triumphantly to itself and rests upon itself. To feel shame is to expel oneself from this rest and not simply to be conscious of this already glorious exile. The just person who knows himself to be just is no longer just. The first condition of the first as of the last of the just is that their justice remains clandestine to them.

But the putting into question of this wild and naïve liberty, certain of its refuge in itself, is not reduced to this negative movement. The putting into question of the self is precisely a welcome to the absolutely other. The other does not show it to the I as a theme. The epiphany of the Absolutely Other is a face by which the Other challenges and commands me through his nakedness, through his destitution. He challenges me from his humility and from his height. He sees but remains invisible, thus absolving himself from the relation that he enters and remaining absolute. The absolutely Other is the human Other (*Autrui*). And the putting into question of the Same by the Other is a summons to respond. The I is not simply conscious of this necessity to respond, as if it were a matter of an obligation or a duty about which a decision could be made; rather the I is, by its *very position*, responsibility through and through. And the structure of this responsibility will show how the Other (*Autrui*), in the face, challenges us from the greatest depth and the highest height - by opening the very dimension of elevation.

Hence, to be I signifies not being able to escape responsibility. This surplus of being, this existential exaggeration that is called *being me* - this protrusion of ipseity into being is accomplished as a turgescence of responsibility. Putting into question is a new tension within the I. Instead of annihilating the I, putting into question binds it to the Other in an incomparable and unique way. It is not bound in the way that matter is bound up with the block of which it forms a part, or in the way in which an organ is bound up with the organism in which it functions. These mechanical and organic solidarities would dissolve the I into a totality. The I is bound up with the non-I as if the entire fate of the Other was in its hands. The unicity of the I consists in the fact that nobody can respond in its place. The putting into question of the I by the Other is not initially an act of reflection where the I surges up again in all its glory and serenity, but neither is it the entry of the I into a suprapersonal, coherent, and universal discourse. The putting into question of the I by the Other is ipso facto an election, the promotion to a privileged place on which all that is not-I depends.

This election signifies the most radical possible engagement, namely, total altruism. The responsibility that empties the I of its imperialism and egoism, albeit the egoism of salvation, does not transform it into a moment of the universal order. Responsibility confirms the I in its ipseity, in its central place within being, as a supporter of the universe. Such an engagement is happy; it is the austere and noncomplacent happiness that lies in the nobility of an election that does not know its own happiness, tempted as it is "by the slumber of the earth" ("and yet Lord, I am not happy . . .").

9. To discover within the Same such a pulsation is to identify the I with morality. Consciousness as a conscious grasp is a possession of the Other by the Same; the I dominates the Other and is in a position to withdraw itself through an *epoche* of all engagement in being which it rediscovers as an intentional object, "bracketed" and entirely at its disposal. Total self-knowledge is total immanence and sovereignty. Consequently, the impossibility of a total reflection and of a total disengagement, as affirmed by the philosophy of existence against the idealist subject, leaves that subject in the situation of *Geworfenheit*.[11] This means that no problem is fully determinate at the moment when the subject takes it up and that its freedom is already fatally compromised by commitments which were never contracted. The resultant guilt of the subject thus has no ethical significance: it results from the alienation of liberty and not from the unscrupulousness of its very exercise. Such a guilt has tragic and not ethical overtones. It is finitude.

The putting in question of the I - which coincides with the nonallergic presence of the Other - does not consist simply in its losing its natural foundation and confidence but in an elevation; consciousness finds in itself more than it can contain, the commitment is a promotion. And it is already in this sense that we propose to speak of a dimension of height that opens within being.

Before the Other (*Autrui*), the I is infinitely responsible. The Other is the poor and destitute one, and nothing which concerns this Stranger can leave the I indifferent. It attains the apogee of its existence as I precisely when everything looks at it in the Other (*Autrui*). The scandalous interference of the prophet in the affairs of the Other (*Autrui*) already constitutes the I as I. The plenitude of power through which the sovereignty of the Same maintains itself does not extend to the Other (*Autrui*) to conquer him, but to support him. But to support the burden of the Other is, at the same time, to confirm it in its substantiality, situating it above the I. The I remains accountable for this burden to the one that it supports. The one for whom I am responsible is also the one to whom I have to respond. The "for whom . . ." and the "to whom . . ." coincide. It is this double movement of responsibility which designates the dimension of height. It forbids me from exercising this responsibility as pity, for I must render an account to the very one for whom I am accountable, or as unconditional obedience in a hierarchical order, for I am responsible to the very one who orders me.

10. The Other who provokes this ethical movement in consciousness and who disturbs the good conscience of the Same's coincidence with itself compromises a surplus which is inadequate to intentionality. Because of this inassimilable surplus, we have called the relation which binds the I to the Other (*Autrui*) the *idea of the infinite*.

The idea of the infinite is not an intentionality for which the Infinite would be the object. Intentionality is a movement of the mind adjusted to being. It takes aim and moves toward a theme. In the theme, being comfortably accommodates itself. Being is the "thematizable" par excellence; the proposable, the thetic. But intentionality, which is the opening of thought onto the theme, does not overflow this theme. It does not consist in thinking more than that which is thought in it. The noema is perfectly outlined in the noesis. The idea of the infinite consists precisely and paradoxically in thinking more than what is thought while nevertheless conserving it in its excessive relation to thought. The idea of the infinite consists in grasping the ungraspable while nevertheless guaranteeing its status as ungraspable. If there were, in the idea of the infinite, an aim that was adequate to the ungraspable or the unthinkable, it would no longer be the idea of the infinite. And yet, if the ungraspable, unthinkable surplus or excess had nothing to do with thought aiming at a theme, there would no longer have been an idea of the infinite.

The infinite is not therefore the correlative of the idea of the infinite as if this idea were an intentionality. Should we say that it can affect the I by the fact that the ungraspable surplus has a symbolic presence within the adequately given? But the marvel of the symbol can explain itself only through the overturning of intentionality - by the fact that contrary to the perfect mastery of the object by the subject in intentionality, the Infinite unseats its idea. This overturning consists in the fact that the I *receives* absolutely and learns absolutely (though not in the Socratic sense) a signification that it has not itself given, a signification that precedes any *Sinngebung*. And it is this which procures an exit from the straightforward grasp and power of consciousness. Indeed, our question was: how can a putting into question or unseating of the self take place without its being simply the verification of this failure by a new act and without its being taken up by this new act, thereby already escaping from any critique? We can respond by saying that the act which is directed toward the infinite is already put into question in its primary "intention." Now, this is possible only if it turns into a morality that submits itself to the Other (*Autrui*), thus immediately taking place as obedience and submission to a height. Or, more precisely, if the submission to the Other (*Autrui*) does not rob the act of its dignity as a spontaneous movement, this is because the Other (*Autrui*) is not only *outside* but is already at a height. The idea of *height* reconciles the contradiction which opposes spontaneity to submission. The putting in question of the Same by the Other is accomplished in a positive movement, the movement of the responsibility of the I for the Other (*Autrui*) and before the Other (*Autrui*). It is a movement at once spontaneous and critical: this is expressed in a *despite itself* which is ipso facto an affirmation of itself, an impossibility of escaping from the course of events, a necessity always to go straight before oneself without in some way having the time to turn back. Such a situation is not original - it is an existence that is prevented from being at peace with itself by the tiny pebble of scrupulousness (Ricoeur showed its importance in the structure of the mind): the more it gets hold of itself, the more this existence demands of itself, dissatisfied as it is with its own satisfaction.[12] And because moral consciousness is auto-critical, i.e., because it produces its own critique in its forward movement anterior to the movement of reflection, which, as second intention, would already be dogmatic, moral consciousness is primary and the source of first philosophy.

Many of the ideas that we have developed come perhaps too late after the work of Gabriel Marcel and Buber; but our effort does not so much consist in identifying the originality of the I-Thou relation as in showing the ethical structures of this relation, in showing above all how this structure arises from the very problem of the critical commencement of philosophy and transcendence. Moral consciousness is not invoked here as a particularly commendable variety of consciousness but as the concrete form taken by a movement within the Same in the face of the Other, a movement that is more fundamental than freedom but that returns us to neither violence nor fatality.

Being is the unconcealed, the thematized - that on which thought stumbles and stops, but which it straightaway recovers. The idea of the infinite consists in the impossibility of escaping from responsibility; it consists in the impossibility of coming to rest and in the absence of any hiding place, of any interiority where the I could repose harmoniously upon itself. But this continually forward movement is precisely the way in which the subject disengages itself from the relative in responding to the absolute. A disengagement which is not that of reflection. Being is commanded, and consequently its infinite responsibility is the response to a superiority which imposes itself absolutely. All reflective self-critique already takes place after responsibility. The relation with the infinite which puts into question but which calls with such urgency that there is no time left to turn back - or to enclose oneself in the private - is not indeed a mutilated intentionality, amputated from its reflective power or too infantile for critical self-knowledge. The relation is, to a certain extent, the condition of all reflection and its movement against nature. Pure reflection cannot have the first word: how could it arise in the dogmatic spontaneity of a force which moves by itself? Reflection must be put into question from without. Reflection needs a certain kind of heteronomy. Nonetheless, pure reflection cannot have the last word, for it remains essentially naïve insofar as it is an act addressed to a theme. The most radical critique cannot be achieved in a secondary intention which would be immune from critique like a new act of naïveté.

In the progressive increase of its responsibility, without which the subject, supporting the entire weight of the Other, would have time to turn back - in the "the more I am just, the more I am guilty" of the scrupulous conscience - the I erodes the dogmatic naïveté of its good conscience.

11. The idea of being does not therefore suffice to sustain the claim of realism, if realism is equivalent to affirming an alterity outside the Same. Only the idea of the infinite renders realism possible. And here we rediscover one of the fundamental teachings of Descartes. The being that has a weight and a foundation at its disposal which distinguishes it from a phantasm of thought must in some way refer itself to the idea of the infinite. Such is perhaps the philosophical meaning of the idea of a creature as distinct from the idea of being. It is as creatures that beings are distinguished from their reflections in the I. And it is as a command, an incitement to responsibility, that the ethical revelation of the face distinguishes itself from the notorious unconcealment.[13]

12. Cartesianism takes thought outside of immanence, but not by referring itself to the idea of being, although this idea of being suggests an alterity. Descartes shatters immanence thanks to the idea of the infinite. This idea is inadequate par excellence, for it consists in some way of thinking more than it can think. Must we not consequently think that the comprehension of being is not the most intimate work of thought and does not lead us toward the ultimate secret of subjectivity? In agreement with Plato and Plotinus,[14] who dared to pose, against all good sense, something beyond being, is not the idea of being younger than the idea of the infinite? Should we not concede that philosophy cannot confine itself to the primacy of ontology, as has been taught up to now

and against which, in France, Jean Wahl and Ferdinand Alquié have vigorously protested? And that intentionality is not the ultimate spiritual relation?

Levinas's presentation of his text was followed by a discussion and correspondence.

Discussion

JEAN WAHL. We have all greatly admired Emmanuel Levinas's paper and it is obviously very difficult to put it into question, to take up an expression that we have just heard. For simultaneously we have the impression - to employ another of the speaker's words - of an epiphany, of something very clear and, in a sense, crystalline, and also of something enigmatic, as Father de Lubac has written. It is at the same time something alluring; and the epiphany of an enigma is, by itself, an enigma. From whence arises, it seems to me, the difficulty of questioning.

There were, it seems to me, three moments in your paper: a moment of the Same and of Being, a moment of the Other, and a moment of the Infinite. I believe that we were perhaps better able to understand your thinking insofar as we followed it with increasing clarity. There is something paradoxical about the place that you give to Descartes, and I believe that we must be grateful to you for this, because once one crosses the frontiers of France, we see that Descartes is very badly understood. And you orientate us toward Descartes.

The only question that I will ask is how is it possible to maintain the idea of the face and Cartesianism at the same time? It is in this tension that I see something very interesting and very attractive, but also very mysterious. And I am now going to give the floor to those who would like to present their questions to the subject of the question that has been posed. But before that, do you want to add a few words?

EMMANUEL LEVINAS. Is not the enigmatic simply the obscure? The obscurity of my paper may derive from the imprecision of the method. One could reproach it for using classical rationalist terminology and for mixing it up and dressing it up with empirical givens. But, all things considered, what is the empirical? The purely empirical is that which receives signification, not that which gives it. The situation of the I in the face of the Other is significant. It is a structure that illuminates, and consequently its analysis is not the description of an empirical fact. On the basis of this structure, which until now has most often been expressed only with pathos, I was anxious to rejoin the "language of the professors." It is quite possible that I have not succeeded in this and that I remain obscure. It would perhaps be necessary to review the detail of my analysis. But the very principle of my enterprise - giving value to the relation of infinite responsibility which goes from the I to the Other (*Autrui*) - remains.

Certainly I believe that this is our most valuable everyday experience, one that allows us to resist a purely hierarchical world. But this is an illuminating experience, metaempirical, as Jankélévitch would say. This is not pure empiricism. On the basis of this, the concern to rejoin the accepted philosophical language, full of certain terms which have obtained a privilege and which make up the "beautiful philosophical language" (Being is one of them) - this concern is legitimate. I would also like to point out that forty years ago - I neither wish nor dare to compare myself with Heidegger, for different reasons - Heidegger's language passed for a language of pathos. Max Scheler is supposed to have said one day of *Sein und Zeit* that it was a mixture of brilliance and a Sunday sermon. In Heidegger's case, he certainly has the excuse of genius. But do the illuminating insights that he brings forth lose something of their brilliance from having to serve on Sunday?

WAHL. You spoke of the State. I very much want us to criticize the State, but I also sense its utility. Without it, what would happen?

LEVINAS. With regard to the State and the oppression of the I by the State, I do not at all think of it in a Kierkegaardian sense. I do not wish to protest against all the worries that an individual may have in a State. That would be to return to the egoism against which Reason is right (*la Raison a raison*). The I that I defend against the hierarchy is the one that is necessary for going right to the Other. For me, the negative element, the element of violence in the State, in the hierarchy, appears even when the hierarchy functions perfectly, when everyone submits to universal ideas. There are cruelties which are terrible because they proceed from the necessity of the reasonable Order. There are, if you like, the tears that a civil servant cannot see: the tears of the Other (*Autrui*). In order for things to work and in order for things to develop an equilibrium, it is absolutely necessary to affirm the infinite responsibility of each, for each, before each. In such a situation, individual consciences are necessary, for they alone are capable of seeing the violence that proceeds from the proper functioning of Reason itself. To remedy a certain disorder which proceeds from the Order of universal Reason, it is necessary to defend subjectivity. As I see it, subjective protest is not received favorably on the pretext that its egoism is sacred but because the I alone can perceive the "secret tears" of the Other, which are caused by the functioning - albeit reasonable - of the hierarchy. Consequently, subjectivity is indispensable for assuring this very nonviolence that the State searches for in equal measure - but overcoming at once the particularity of the I and the Other. I am *for* the I, as existence in the first person, to the extent that its ego-ity signifies an infinite responsibility for an Other. Which amounts to saying that it is as if substance of the I is made of saintliness. It is perhaps in this sense that Montesquieu rested democracy upon virtue.

WAHL. Voltaire, when he defended this or that unjustly accused man, had not heard this paper. It was simply that Voltaire had a conscience, and not necessarily an extraordinary conscience.

LEVINAS. Are you talking about Voltaire the way he was or the way he interpreted himself? I do not know.

WAHL. He simply thought to speak in the name of many, and not metaphysically.

LEVINAS. The goal of my communication was to insist on the irreplaceable function of the I in a world of peace, but it did not mean to dispute the role of the State and hierarchy as much as it has appeared to have done. I refer to the work of Kojève, Hyppolite, and Eric Weil as much as to the more ancient wisdom that never failed to recognize the necessity of the State. But it's the fundamental contradiction of our situation (and perhaps of our condition), which I called Hypocrisy in my book,[15] that both the hierarchy taught by Athens and the *abstract* and slightly *anarchical* ethical individualism taught by Jerusalem are simultaneously necessary in order to suppress violence. Each of these principles, left to itself, only furthers the contrary of what it wants to secure. Do you not think, especially in our epoch, that we must be particularly sensitive to the value of this protest against the hierarchy and that it *demands a metaphysical explanation*?

WAHL. To open up different horizons, would M. Filliozat give us the pleasure and the honor of saying a few words?

M. FILLIOZAT. One might perhaps observe that from the practical point of view, the paper that has been given links up, in a certain sense, with the doctrine of Gandhi, which admits that the I must give way to the Other; but the foundations of these ideas are completely different. Gandhi treats the question of violence as the primary problem. On the one hand, he supposes - with the whole of Indian civilization - that the enemy of violence is not another violence: violence opposed is not the opposite of violence. On the other hand, the putting into question of the I in the presence of the Other is justified from the general Indian point of view, in any case from the point of view which Gandhi inherits, without being a philosopher himself, in a completely different way to the one that you spoke about. The I is not justified in imposing its liberty on the Other because it is not itself a valuable entity, any more than is the Other. You have posited the I as an entity. In general Indian philosophy, one posits it simply as a conglomerate of past experiences, which give rise to an individuality, but not as a being which would have rights to oppose to the Other, any more than the Other has rights. So that the question of their conflict does not reduce itself to the conflict of two beings possessing rights, but to a battle between two tigers, which are animals without conscience. Consequently, one is not justified in wanting to impose one's freedom on the other.

M. GOUHIER. The only thing that I want to say, and this is neither a criticism nor even a question, is that the whole Cartesian itinerary that you recall at the end of your paper unfolds in a perspective which began by separating speculation from action; given this situation and despite the extremely worthwhile *rapprochement* that you have made, Descartes cannot address any of your problems, which are precisely the problems of human action. For example, I believe that the formula that you used just now, "acts of violence that can be commanded by Reason," is something absolutely unintelligible: violence is to be found precisely outside of the world where Reason and Philosophy reign. Violence can never be at the service of Reason, if only because it is practiced in a world that, from the outset, has been excluded from the realm where evidence rules. What is extremely interesting in your paper is the way in which you take up this Cartesian itinerary without having made this separation, so that you pose problems that Descartes could not have encountered. However, this would presuppose a preliminary question: is it necessary to do what Descartes did or not? Is it necessary to begin by positing Philosophy as he understands it, that is, as a rational philosophy, to begin by separating, one might say, the rational from the reasonable and philosophical speculation from empirical action?

LEVINAS. There was, all the same, in my paper, an attempt to justify the transition to moral consciousness, or the primacy of the moral, on the basis of an absolute beginning, in the concern for a critique which no longer calls for further critique before being applied to the critical act itself. There was therefore an attempt very similar to that which brought Descartes to the *Cogito*. The primacy of the moral is no longer Cartesian, I agree. I simply followed the admirable rhythm of Cartesian thinking, which only rejoins the world by passing through the idea of the Infinite.

And yet, if Descartes begins with the *Cogito*, he says a little later that in fact it is the idea of God that is primary, that is, the idea of the infinite. The idea of God was prior to the *Cogito*, and the *Cogito* would never have been possible if there had not already been the idea of God. Consequently, for Descartes as well, it is in the direct act and not in the reflective act that philosophical critique begins. This is what I also wanted to retain from Descartes.

Third and finally, I come back to what was just said by Jean Wahl about the face. Practical problems are not posed in the *Meditations*. And yet, at the end of the Third Meditation - a text which I have always exploited - Descartes comes to admire the divine Majesty, as if, suddenly, he had glimpsed a face behind the arguments. One could take this as a turn of phrase, as a fine ending to a chapter, but one can also perhaps take it seriously. One then suddenly sees that the reflection upon the idea of Infinity places Descartes before something which reflects majesty and which we can call the face. I would just like to add that, as I see it, it is not a question of God encountered outside of humans. I have always spoken of the perspective of height that opens itself through the human.

Wahl. I believe that there is a fourth remark that could be added. In listening to you, I was very strongly reminded of Léon Brunschvicg. It seems to me that there are the beginnings in his work of what a Cartesian can do when faced with problems of action and, despite everything, he found the idea of generosity in Descartes. I think this idea is essentially Cartesian. And there we come back to action, even if it was initially bracketed, as M. Gouhier has said. Also in Descartes there is the idea of totality. Perhaps it is unnecessary to insist on it too much, because to do so would make Descartes into a pre-Hegel; but finally, there are, in Descartes, the ideas of totality and generosity.

M. Minkowski. First of all, I would like to defend my friend M. Levinas against himself. Toward the end of his paper he told us that he came perhaps a little too late, after Martin Buber, Gabriel Marcel, and others. But as you rightly said at the outset, my dear Levinas, if philosophical thought is forged in the crucible of the human soul, it cannot come too late, or else we would all have to pack up our bags and stop trying. And that is why, when you envisaged the possibility of the failure of philosophy, I could not follow you at all. For, basically, philosophy goes from failure to apparent failure and, through this, affirms its triumph. And that reminds me of what Jean Wahl said in his *Metaphysics* about creative interrogation. Perhaps it is not so much precise responses that count, but just this interrogation which, at bottom, proceeds from the eternal.

That said, I will make a confession which will be surprising: the notion of transcendence remains foreign to me; I cannot succeed in establishing a clear idea of what it means. It is that once transcendence is accomplished, the transcendent becomes that which is the most immanent. For transcendence posits, at the outset, the interiority of immanence. But this immanence finds itself, in my sense, equally on the other side. It has then, I believe, the very sense of the "immediate givens of consciousness," just like the vision of essences.

For my part, I will willingly refer to language. You centered your paper on the opposition of the Same and the Other. Now, in everyday life we have three terms for the Other: other, fellow human being, and neighbor (*autrui, semblable, et prochain*). On the phenomenological plane, each of them provides us with particular givens and tends to diminish the initial distance and opposition which can exist between the Same and the Other, which leads to the proximity, an immediate given, that we find in the "neighbor." Seen from this angle, it is an essential given, namely the primitive human solidarity upon which our existence rests, whatever disruptions may subsequently arise in our concrete life. This way of seeing has found a direct application in psychology and psychopathology; in particular, our affective movements, in the broad sense of the term, do not reduce themselves to isolated individual movements, which would be encountered only occasionally, but rest on the essential phenomenon of the echo or reverberation in which all affective movement finds or tries to find its natural accomplishment. I believe that it is from there that the essential notion of the "human" emerges and, in opposition to this, the inhuman. It is in starting from there, I think, that we can proceed, without going beyond the level of creative interrogation, to use Jean Wahl's excellent expression once again.

Just one more brief remark. When you speak of height, I ask myself if you have not thereby already made a concession that is too static and too spatial. The movement of elevation that you mentioned elsewhere, appears to me much closer to the primitive dynamism of existence than that of height; in the same way that expanding or opening out (*s'étendre, s'épanouir*) has a more vital importance than the mere notion of extension (*étendue*).

I thought I could offer these few remarks, as just an amateur philosopher, in any case, as a man who tries to reflect as best he can and more particularly to study the problems which arise as he goes about his tasks.

LEVINAS. I thank M. Minkowski very much for what he has contributed. However, I would say that transcendence remains essential to what I wanted to say. I regret not having succeeded in clarifying this notion. In my opinion, transcendence is only possible when the Other (*Autrui*) is not initially the fellow human being or the neighbor; but when it is the very distant, when it is Other, when it is the one with whom initially I have nothing in common, when it is an abstraction. In all this affirmation of the concrete from which philosophy today lives, one fails to recognize that the relation with the other (*autrui*) is an element of abstraction which pierces the continuity of the concrete, a relation with the Other qua Other, denuded, in every sense of the term. Consequently, it is necessary to avoid the words *neighbor* and *fellow human being*, which establish so many things in common with my neighbor (*voisin*) and so many similarities with my fellow human being; we belong to the same essence. Transcendence is only possible with the Other (*Autrui*), with respect to whom we are absolutely different, without this difference depending on some quality. Transcendence seemed to me to be the point of departure for our concrete relations with the Other (*Autrui*); all the rest is grafted on top of it. That is why the transcendent is a notion which seems to me primary.

And what you said about human solidarity seems to me to lead toward transcendence. One can, certainly, content oneself with the empirical notion of solidarity, but this idea demands further reflection. For human solidarity is after all a very strange thing. Men are absolutely different from one another; the concept of man is the only one that cannot be comprehended, since each man is absolutely different from the other. The concept of man has a single extension, and that is human fraternity. And it would be very strange after all if the term *man* designated a genus: have we ever seen individuals from a genus who enter into fraternity? And, in this sense, if the notion of solidarity is an empirical one, a notion which the sociologist has the right to deal with, it is also very mysterious and consequently demands a philosophical and phenomenological analysis.

WAHL. I think that here we have an extremely interesting opposition, for M. Minkowski thinks that men are similar to each other. I would recall the beautiful words of Terence: "I am human and nothing human is foreign to me."[16] And for Levinas, if the human is not foreign to him, it is fundamentally because there is a God. It is because of the superhuman that the human is not foreign to him. Now, I address myself anew to M. Gouhier: we find a problem here which is not Cartesian but Bergsonian. Bergson indeed thought that if there is fraternity, it is only given - I believe that this is indeed his thought - through the idea of God. Paradoxically, I think that here there is perhaps an affinity between you and Bergson. According to Bergson, one cannot go from the notion of Fatherland to that of Humanity without passing through God. In the order of closed society, there is a Fatherland; in the order of open society, there is Humanity; but there is only Humanity because there is an open religion. It is very curious that reflection on what both you and Dr. Minkowski have said should bring Bergson to mind.

But are men so different? You say that man is the concept that is least understood. I don't know. For me, it is the idea of being that is the least understood; much less so than the idea of man. The idea of man can be understood, but to formulate it thus is perhaps to lose it.

MINKOWSKI. I do not believe that we can say - and M. Wahl also made this point - that men are absolutely different from one another. It is certain that on the empirical level, this is quite true: since the beginning of the world, there have been no two men alike. But that does not at all entail that everyone is absolutely different, because if that was the case, you would not have this audience in front of you, following you with interest. There is an element of understanding and similarity which occurs and which appears to me essential.

On the other hand, on the second question, you yourself said just now that the opposition between the Other (Autrui) and the Same is a product of abstraction. Seeing that we are speaking of immediate givens and trying to attain them, why start by precisely putting an abstraction at the primary level?

LEVINAS. I did not say that the Same and the Other are two abstractions. I said that the Other (Autrui) is an abstraction for the I, for the Same. But I agree with you: all men are alike, but they are not the same. I did not at any moment want to deny the similarities between men. But the I qua I is absolutely unique, and when it is approached nonsociologically it has nothing in common with the other. It is not a question of a difference that is due to the absence or presence of a common trait; it is a question of an initial difference that is entirely self-referential. That is the I.

VILLA. Dr. Minkowski spoke of the audience listening to Levinas in order to make a point in favor of similarity. But I believe that we can say that no one here has heard his words in the same way and that each of us has had different thoughts about them, without which there would be no object to the discussion.

LEVINAS. It is still not these differences that I have in mind. You evoke differences of formation, culture, and character which distinguish men and their ways of understanding. All things considered, these are the different qualities, like color for example, which distinguish men in the same way as one table is distinguished from another. What is unique in each man - and this is ultimately a banality - is that he is I.

I respond once again to M. Wahl. I do not want to define anything through God because it is the human that I know. It is God that I can define through human relations and not the inverse. The notion of God - God knows, I'm not opposed to it! But when I have to say something about God, it is always beginning from human relations. The inadmissible abstraction is God; it is in terms of the relation with the Other (*Autrui*) that I speak of God. I do not refuse religious terms, but I adopt them in order to designate the situation where the subject exists in the impossibility of hiding itself. I do not start from the existence of a very great and all-powerful being. Everything I wish to say comes from this situation of responsibility which is religious insofar as the I cannot elude it. If you like, it is like a Jonah who cannot escape. You find yourself before a responsibility from which you cannot escape. You find yourself before a responsibility from which you cannot steal away. You are not at all in the situation of a reflective consciousness, which, in reflection, already withdraws and hides itself. This is the sense in which I would accept the word *religious*, a word I do not want to employ because it immediately becomes the source of misunderstanding. But it is this exceptional situation, where you are always in the face of the Other (*Autrui*), where there is no privacy, that I would call the religious situation. And anything that I could go on to say about God - I cannot say everything today - starts from this experience, and not the inverse. The abstract idea of God is an idea that cannot clarify a human situation. It is the inverse that is true.

WAHL. The idea of God? Is it possible that there could not be an idea of God?

LEVINAS. There can be a discourse upon God, but only if one starts from this situation.

WAHL. You employed the expression "wholly Other." This naturally evokes the name of Kierkegaard, and perhaps others. And the "wholly Other" for him is God. Is he wrong? Is the "wholly Other" found in experience, or is it rather only in and through the call of God that the "wholly Other" is revealed?

LEVINAS. It is difficult to say. I agree that these notions are connected, but ultimately my point of departure is absolutely nontheological. I insist upon this. It is not theology that I am doing, but philosophy.

As for the question of knowing, in the context of the violence that fills us all with dread, whether we can incriminate philosophy, in which the concept of man can be comprehended - I think, indeed, that it is in the world of violence that philosophy has been established as Reason and has been explicated as such. Philosophy is one of the essential adventures of reason, without which the philosophy of the absolutely dissimilar I would also present dangers, but which if left to itself would intensify the violence that it wants to combat, wherever it arises.

WAHL. If there are no further questions, we will close the meeting and thank Emmanuel Levinas very much.

Correspondence

Letter from José Etcheveria to Jean Wahl

Paris, 29th January 1962
Sir,
Thank you for having invited me to the interesting debate on Saturday evening. I very much appreciated M. Levinas's brilliant paper.

It seems to me that it is not legitimate to reduce the idea of being to the *same* and to oppose it to the idea of infinity, for in order for the latter idea to have the role that M. Levinas so rightly attributes to it, and for it always to overcome the knowledge that we have of it, it *must be*; further, *it must be being*. All that would be less than being is only being (*étant*) and depends upon being. Therefore the latter cannot be less than whatever is, for then it would not be completely, it would not be that which, from the very fact of its definition or idea, *is*. In the Cartesian perspective, which M. Levinas rightly claims, it seems to me that there is no place to distinguish between being and infinity, no more than to establish a priority of the infinite over being. This is because *God, infinity*, and *being* are different designations for the same reality - the *real* from which everything obtains its being - that the ontological argument brings about. Indeed, this argument consists in showing that being cannot not be, that to say of a thing that it is not, presupposes being, that to deny God it is first necessary to affirm him, which makes an absurdity of negation. It is through this identification with the infinite that being is placed beyond beings (*étants*), even if it manifests itself in them, and that God is distinguished from creatures, even if they only exist through him.

I am very grateful to Professor José Etcheveria for his letter, whose penetration I appreciate and which gave me a better sense of the obscurities of my paper. A few points can thus be made more precise.

One can and should distinguish between the idea of the Infinite and the idea of Being. The great philosophical tradition does not recoil before the audacity which consisted in positing the Good or the One beyond being. But this does not mean that Plato or Plotinus had placed the Good or the One in non-Being. In Descartes, the idea of the Infinite or the idea of perfect Being certainly envelops the idea of being, but also surpasses it. The idea of being is not the most ancient; and thought, history, and humanity do not begin with the understanding of being.

Can the Heideggerian overcoming of the being (*étant*) by being (*être*) be brought together with the idea of the infinite or of God in the Cartesian sense? This seems very doubtful, for the Being that transcends the being in Heidegger is not a being (*étant*), whereas God is a being and Heidegger rather reproaches metaphysics for thinking only in terms of beings (*étants*).

Is philosophy henceforth bound to Heideggerian teachings? Must Being, which transcends beings, that is to say, an impersonal and faceless power, give a meaning to the real like some *fatum*? Impious questions! They will tell us that we have understood nothing of Heidegger, that the Being of Being (*l'Etre de l'Etant*) is found beyond the personal and the impersonal as their ambivalent condition, that it is absurd to situate in relation to certain coordinates a thinking which wants to be understood as the coordination of coordinates, that words like *impersonal* or *fatum* only receive their signification on the basis of a philosophy which thinks the Being of being.

To which it is necessary to reply that respect for the person - infinite responsibility for the Other (*Autrui*) - imposes itself on thought with the power of primordial coordinates; that to seek the condition for the personal and the human is already to undermine them. Sartre, in his article "Merleau-Ponty vivant," writes about Heidegger: "when he first speaks of the *opening onto being*, I smell (*flaire*) alienation."[17] Sartre's flair does not deceive him. The poetry of the peaceful path that runs through the fields does not simply reflect the splendor of Being beyond beings. That splendor brings with it more somber and pitiless images. The declaration of the end of metaphysics is premature. This end is not at all certain. Besides, metaphysics - the relation with the being (*étant*) which is accomplished in ethics - precedes the understanding of being and survives ontology.

Meaning and Sense
(1964)

Levinas's first philosophical publication (in *Revue Philosophique de la France et de l'Etranger*, 1929) was a review article on Husserl's *Ideen*. The following year he published his dissertation on Husserl's theory of intuition (TIPH 1930). In both writings he focused on the epistemological and methodological problems of phenomenology. Having studied with Heidegger, however, he also showed how Husserl's work can be read as an ontology.

In his later work Levinas seldom concentrates on methodology as such, but all readers who take his work seriously are aware that his mode of thought shakes the foundations of philosophy as it has been practiced hitherto - even Husserlian phenomenology and Heideggerian ontology. Having been so often asked what his method was, Levinas has given two complementary answers. The first answer takes a certain distance from the modern conviction that philosophers are obliged and able to make their approach completely explicit and to justify why they choose to proceed in the way they do:

> I neither believe that there is a transparency possible in method, nor that philosophy is possible as transparency. Those who have focused on methodology during the entirety of their life wrote many books which replace more interesting books they could have written. Too bad for the march under a shadowless sun, which is deemed to characterize philosophy. (DVI 143)

The other answer insists on the necessity of passing through phenomenology and of having learned how to practice Husserlian "intentional analysis."

> The dominant trait, which marks even all those who today no longer call themselves phenomenologists is that one discovers new dimensions of meaning by going back from that which is thought to the fullness of the very thinking, without appealing to any deductive, dialectical, or other kind of implication. It is this analysis that seems to me to be the novelty of Husserl and something that is settled and remains valid for everybody outside of Husserl's own methodology. It consists in the fact that, when I turn from a theme to the "modes" by which that theme is accessible, these modes are essential for the meaning of the theme; the modes reveal an entire landscape of forgotten horizons within which the theme has a meaning that is different from the meaning it showed when we considered it in a direct concentration on it. Phenomenology does not set the phenomena up as things in themselves; it brings the *things-in-themselves* back to the horizon of their appearance, i.e., their phenomenality; it makes the very appearing behind the appearing quiddity apparent, even if this appearing does not encrust its modalities on the meaning it offers to the onlooker [...] All those who think this way [...] practice phenomenology. (DVI 140)

Levinas is, however, more than a skillful practitioner of intentional analysis, though it is not easy to characterize this "more." Like Heidegger, he passed through phenomenology, but in a way simultaneously close and very foreign to that of Heidegger. An insistence on the necessity of overcoming not only phenomenology but also ontology, the use of an ethical language to indicate the most radical step beyond ontology, and the deployment of emphasis and hyperbole are three characteristics of his procedure, but each of them demands much clarification. It is therefore fortunate that the essay "La signification et le sens," translated here as "Meaning and Sense," gives a number of precious indications about the way in which Levinas passes through and surpasses phenomenology.[1] Its text can be schematically structured according to three stages of thought.

In the first stage, Levinas explains and defends phenomenology against a positivistic form of empiricism, starting from a reflection about the distinction between metaphorical and literal languages. As always in his writings, Husserl and Heidegger are present, but this time they are accompanied by Merleau-Ponty. The essay was written under the influence of Merleau-Ponty's book *Signes* (1960), in which the cultural horizons of phenomena are emphasized and thematized. Levinas's presentation of phenomenology in this first stage does not coincide completely with that of the authors to whom he refers - and his more positive attitude toward Plato, for example, is already an indication of the difference - but it is only in the next two steps that his departure from their ways is clarified.

The second stage (mainly sections 6 and 7) introduces Levinas's own thought by introducing a "meaning" that is radically different from the meaning (*Sinn, signification*) sought by Husserlian, Heideggerian, and Merleau-Pontyan phenomenology. Levinas prefers to employ another word to describe it: not a "signification" but "le sens." In contrast with the linguistic, symbolic, and cultural meanings (*significations*), the sense - a unique sense, which is also a unique and one-way orientation that leads beyond culture - is revealed in the emergence of the Other (*Autrui*) and the confrontation with the ethical, which cannot be separated from it.

The third stage is concentrated in section 9, where Levinas briefly indicates how ethics leads to religion in the radical sense of an inescapable relationship to a nonthematizable X that has received various names, such as "He" or "the One," or "God." It is interesting to note that "La signification et la sens" incorporated the text of Levinas's paper "La trace de l'autre (The trace of the other)," which he gave in 1963, about two years after the publication of *Totalité et infini* (1961), at the Institut Supérieur de Philosophie in Leuven (Belgium). It was his first attempt to answer a fundamental question left open in that book: how is it possible that the alterity of "the Other" (*l'Autre*) "is understood as alterity of the human Other (*Autrui*) *and* as alterity of the Most High (*du Très Haut*)" (TeI 4; TaI 34, my emphasis). A later and more elaborate answer is given in the essay "God and Philosophy," chapter 8 of this volume.

---

1. Meaning and Receptivity

The reality given to receptivity and the meaning it can take on seem distinguishable. For it seems as though experience first gave contents - forms, solidity, roughness, color, sound, savor, odor, heat, heaviness, etc. - and then all these contents were animated with meta-phors, receiving an overloading through which they are borne *beyond* the given.[2]

This *metaphor* can be taken to be due to a deficiency of perception or to its excellence, according as the *beyond* involved in a metaphor leads to other contents, which were simply absent from the limited field of the perception, or is transcendent with respect to the whole order of contents or of the given.[3]

This rectangular and solid opacity would become a book only inasmuch as it bears my thought toward other data still, or already, absent - toward the author that writes, the readers that read, the shelves that store, etc. All these terms are announced, without being given, in the rectangular and solid opacity that forces itself on my sight and hands. Those absent contents confer a meaning on the given. But this recourse to absence would indicate that perception failed in its mission, which is to render present, to represent. Perception, owing to its finitude, would have failed in its vocation and would have made up for this *lack* by signifying what it could not represent. The act of signifying would be poorer than the act of perceiving. By right, reality should possess a signification from the first. Reality and intelligibility should coincide. The identity of things should bear the identity of their meaning. For God, capable of an unlimited perception, there would be no meaning distinct from the reality perceived; understanding would be equivalent to perceiving.

Intellectualism - whether it be rationalist or empiricist, idealist or realist - is bound up with this conception. For Plato, for Hume, even for contemporary logical positivists, meaning is reducible to contents given to consciousness. Intuition, in the straightforwardness of a consciousness that welcomes data, remains the source of all meaning, whether these data be ideas, relations, or sensible qualities. The meanings conveyed by language have to be justified in a reflection on the consciousness that aims at them. Every metaphor that language makes possible has to be reduced to the data, which language is suspected of abusively going beyond. The figurative meaning has to be justified by the literal meaning supplied in intuition.

Anatole France reduces the proposition "the spirit blows where it will" to its elementary meaning in *The Garden of Epicurus*.[4] He "deflates" the inflated metaphors which, unnoticed by us, would be at play in this proposition. He moves from the false prestige of language to the atoms of experience. For him, they are the atoms of Democritus and Epicurus. He wishes to go back from the flash produced by their agglomeration to the dreary downpour of the atoms that pass through space and strike our senses.

What is simplistic in this empiricism can be easily overcome without losing the essential of the intuitionist or intellectualist conception of meaning. Husserl, who, in one aspect of his work, marks the end of this notion of meaning, does continue intellectualism (and this is one of the - perhaps fertile - ambiguities of his philosophy): *he accounts for meanings by a return to the given.* Categorial intuition,[5] a notion by which he breaks with sensualist empiricism, in fact prolongs the intuitionist conception of meaning. Relations and essences are also given. Intuition remains the source of all intelligibility. Sense is given in the very straightforwardness[6] that characterizes the relationship between noesis and noema. Is not Husserl's transcendental philosophy a sort of positivism which locates every meaning in the transcendental inventory it aims to draw up? The hyletic data and the "meaning ascriptions" are minutely inventoried, as though one were dealing with an investment portfolio. Even what remains unrealized is somehow given, given in a blank, in an open "signifying" intention, and is warranted like "unpaid bills" in the noema that corresponds to this noesis. Every absence has the given as its *terminus a quo* and *terminus ad quem*. The expression of meanings serves only to fix or to communicate meanings justified in intuition. Expression plays no role in the constitution or in the understanding of these meanings.

But a metaphor - the reference to absence - can also be taken as an excellence that belongs to an order quite different from pure receptivity.[7] The absence to which the metaphor leads would then not be another given but still to come or already past. The meaning would not be the consolation for a delusive perception but would only *make perception possible*. Pure receptivity, in the sense of a pure sensible without any meaning, would be only a myth or an abstraction. Sonorous contents "without any meaning" like vowels have a "latent birth" in meanings - this is the philosophical teaching already contained in Rimbaud's famous sonnet.[8] There is no given already possessing identity; no given could enter thought simply through a shock against the wall of receptivity. To be given to consciousness, to sparkle for it, would require that the given first be placed in an illuminated horizon - like a word, which gets the gift of being understood from the context to which it refers. The meaning would be the very illumination of this horizon. But this horizon does not result from an addition of absent data, since each datum would already need a horizon so as to be able to be defined and given. This notion of horizon or *world*, conceived after the model of a context and ultimately after the model of a language and a culture - with everything that is historically adventitious and "already happened" involved - will be the locus in which meaning would then be located.

Already words are seen not to have isolable meanings, such as those in dictionaries, which one might reduce to some content or given. They could not be congealed into a literal meaning. In fact there would be no literal meaning. Words do not refer to contents which they would designate, but first, laterally, to other words. Despite the mistrust Plato shows for written language (and even, in the seventh letter, for all language),[9] he teaches in the *Cratylus* that even the names given to the gods - the proper names attached, conventionally, as signs, to individual beings - refer, through their etymology, to other words which are not proper names.[10] In addition, language refers to the positions of the one that listens and the one that speaks, that is, to the contingency of their history. To try to inventory up all the contexts of language and of the positions in which interlocutors can find themselves would be a demented undertaking. Each word meaning is at the confluence of innumerable semantic rivers.

Like language, experience too no longer appears to be made up of isolated elements, somehow lodged in a Euclidean space in which they could be exposed, each on its own, directly visible, and each signifying by itself. They signify on the basis of the "world" and of the position of the one that looks at them. We will come back to the essential role that the alleged contingency of such a position plays in language and in experience, in the theory we are now examining.

One would be wrong to take the meanings which custom attaches to words that serve to express our immediate and sensible experiences to be primary. Baudelaire's "correspondences"[11] show that sensible data overflow, through their meanings, the elements in which we take them to be contained. Mikel Dufrenne, in his fine book *The Concept of the A Priori*,[12] was able to show that, for example, the experience of spring or infancy remains authentic and autochthonous over and beyond the seasons and human ages. When another contemporary philosopher[13] speaks of "dusk" or "dawn" philosophies, the meaning of the adjectives used does not necessarily refer back to our meteorological experiences. It is much more probable that our experiences of morning and evening draw from the meaning that being as a whole has for us, a meaning which the jubilation of mornings and the mystery of twilight participate in. Then it would be more authentic to speak of a morning philosophy than of a morning briskness! But meanings are not limited to any special region of objects, are not the privilege of any content. For they arise precisely in the reference of one to another and - to anticipate already what we want to say - in the entire *gathering of Being* about him who speaks or perceives, and who also forms a part of the gathered Being. In a study of Homeric comparisons, Bruno Snell (as quoted by Karl Löwith)[14] points out that when in the *Iliad* the resistance to an attack by an enemy phalanx is compared to the resistance of a rock to the waves that assail, it is not necessarily a matter of extending to the rock, through anthropomorphism, a human behavior, but of interpreting human resistance petromorphically. Resistance is neither a human privilege nor a rock's, just as radiance does not characterize a day of the month of May more authentically than it does the face of a woman. The meaning precedes the data and illuminates them.

Here lies the essential justification and great force of Heidegger's etymologies, which, starting with the impoverished and flat meaning of a term apparently designating a content of external or psychological experience, lead toward a global situation in which a totality of experience is assembled and illuminated. The given is presented from the first qua this or that, that is, as a meaning. Experience is a reading, the understanding of meaning an exegesis, a hermeneutics, and not an intuition. *This taken as that* - meaning is not a modification that affects a content existing outside of all language. Everything remains in a language or in a world, for the structure of the world resembles the order of language, with possibilities no dictionary can arrest. In the *this as that*, neither the *this* nor the *that* is first given outside of discourse. In the example we started with, this rectangular and solid opacity does not later take on the meaning of being a book but is already signifying in its allegedly sensible elements. It contrasts with the light, with the daylight, refers to the sun that rose or the lamp that was lit, refers to my eyes also, as the solidity refers to my hand, not only as to organs which apprehend it *in* a subject and would thereby be somehow opposed to the apprehended object but also as to beings that are *alongside of* this opacity, *in the midst of* a world common to this opacity, this solidity, these eyes, this hand, and myself as a body. There never was a moment in which *meaning first came to birth out of a meaningless being*, outside of a historical position where language is spoken. And that is doubtless what was meant when we were taught that language is the house of being.[15]

Thence came, in a movement radically opposed to that which amused Anatole France, the idea of the priority of the "figurative meaning," which would not result from the pure and simple presence of an object placed before thought. The objects would become meaningful on the basis of language and not language on the basis of objects given to thought and designated by words that would function as simple signs.

2. Meaning, Totality, and Cultural Gesture

Philosophers now accord language a founding role; it would mark the very notion of culture. Its essence consists in making being as a whole shine forth, beyond the *given*. The given would take on a meaning from this totality.

But the totality that illuminates would not be the total of an addition made by a God fixed in his eternity. The totalization of the totality is not to be taken to resemble a mathematical operation. It would be a creative and unforeseeable assembling or arranging,[16] very like Bergsonian intuition in its newness and in what it owes to history. It is through this reference of the illuminating totality to the creative gesture of subjectivity that we can characterize what is original in the new notion of meaning, irreducible to the integration of contents intuitively given, irreducible also to the Hegelian totality which is constituted objectively. Meaning, as an illuminating totality necessary to perception itself, is a free and creative arrangement: the eye that sees is *essentially* in a body which is also hand and phonetic organ, a creative activity in gestures and language.[17] The "position of the one that is looking" does not introduce a relativity into the allegedly absolute order of the totality that would be projected on an absolute retina. *Of itself* a look would be relative to a position. Sight would be *by essence* attached to a body, would belong to an eye. *By essence* and not only *in fact*. The eye would not be the more or less perfected instrument in which the ideal enterprise of vision, capturing, without shadows or deformations, the reflection of being, would be realized empirically in the human species. Both the fact that the totality overflows the sensible given and the fact that vision is incarnated would belong to the essence of sight. Its original and ultimate function would not consist in reflecting being as in a mirror. The receptivity of vision should not be interpreted as an aptitude to receive impressions. A philosophy such as that of Merleau-Ponty, who guides the present analysis, was able to be astonished by the marvel of a sight essentially attached to an eye.[18] In such a philosophy the body is conceived as inseparable from the creative activity and transcendence as inseparable from the corporeal movement.

Let us go further into these notions, which are fundamental. The whole of being has to be produced in order to illuminate the given. It has to be produced before a being can be reflected in thought as an object. For nothing can be reflected in a thought before the footlights are turned on and a curtain raised on the side of being. The function of him who has to be there to "welcome the reflection" is at the mercy of this illumination. But this illumination is a process of the gathering of being. Who will operate this gathering? It turns out that the subject who is there before being to "welcome the reflection" is also on the side of being, to operate the gathering. This ubiquity is incarnation itself, the marvel of the human body.

The reversal of the gnoseological schema effected here is admirable: the work of cognition now begins on the side of the object or from behind the object, in the backstage of being. A being must first be illuminated and take on a meaning by reference to this gathering in order that a subject could welcome it. But it is the incarnate subject which, in gathering being, will raise the curtain. The spectator is an actor. Sight is not reducible to the welcoming of a spectacle; it at the same time operates in the midst of the spectacle it welcomes.

These operations to be sure in one way evoke the syntheses of the understanding which, for transcendental philosophy,[19] make experience possible. And this comparison is the more legitimate in that Kant strictly distinguished the syntheses of the understanding from intuition, as though, in the domain that concerns us here, he was refusing to identify the understanding one can have of a meaning with a vision of any sort of given, be it of some superior or sublime rank. But the transcendental operations of the understanding do not correspond to the birth of meanings in the concrete horizons of perception. It is to these horizons that Merleau-Ponty has drawn attention.[20]

The gathering of being which illuminates objects and makes them meaningful is not just an accumulation of objects. It amounts to the production of those nonnatural beings of a new type which are cultural objects - paintings, poems, melodies - but also to the effects of any linguistic or manual gesture of the most ordinary activity, which are creative in their evocation of former cultural creations. These cultural "objects" assemble into totalities the dispersion or accumulation of beings; they shine forth and illuminate, they express or illuminate an epoch, as we are indeed accustomed to say. The function of the "object as work or cultural gesture" is to collect into a whole, that is, to express, that is, to make meaning possible. And in this way there is set up a new function of *expression*, which hitherto was taken either to serve as a means of communication or to transform the world in view of our needs. The newness of this function is also due to the original ontological plane in which it is situated. As a means of communication or as a mark of our practical projects, expression wholly devolves from a thought antecedent to it; the expression moves then from the inward to the exterior. In its new function, taken on the level of a cultural "object," expression is no longer guided by an antecedent thought. The subject ventures forth by effective speaking or manual gestures into the density of the preexistent language and cultural world (which is familiar to it, but not through cognition - is foreign to it, but not through ignorance). Qua incarnate, this word and this gesture belong to that density from the start; otherwise they could not stir up and rearrange and reveal them to the "inner forum" of thought, which the venture of the cultural gesture had always already overflowed. The cultural action expresses not a preexisting thought but being, to which, as incarnate, it belongs already. *Meaning cannot be inventoried in the inwardness of a thought.* Thought itself is inserted in Culture through the verbal gesture of the body, which precedes it and goes beyond it. The objective Culture to which, through the verbal creation, it adds something new illuminates and guides it.

It is then clear that the language through which meaning is produced in being is a language spoken by incarnate minds. The incarnation of thought is not an accident that has occurred to it and has complicated its task by diverting the straightforward movement with which it aims at an object. The body is the fact that thought is immersed in the world that it thinks and, consequently, expresses this world while it thinks it. The corporeal gesture is not a nervous discharge but a celebration of the world, a poetry. The body is a feeling felt; that is, according to Merleau-Ponty, what is so wondrous about it.[21] Qua felt, it is still on this side, on the side of the subject, but qua feeling it is already on the other side, on the side of the objects; a thought that is no longer paralytic, it is a movement that is no longer blind but creative of cultural objects. It unites the subjectivity of perceiving (an intentionality aiming at an object) and the objectivity of expressing (an operation in the perceived world which creates cultural beings - language, poems, paintings, symphonies, dances - illuminating horizons). The cultural creation is not added on to receptivity but is its other side from the start. We are not the subject of the world and a part of the world from two different points of view; in expression we are subject and part at once. To perceive is both to receive and to express, by a sort of prolepsis. We know through gestures how to imitate the visible and to coincide *kinesthetically* with the gesture *seen*: in perception *our* body is also the "delegate" of *Being*.

It is visible that throughout this conception, expression defines culture; culture is art, and art or the celebration of being constitutes the original essence of incarnation. Language qua expression is, above all, the creative language of poetry. Art is then not a blissful wandering of man, who sets out to make something beautiful. Culture and artistic creation are part of the ontological order itself. They are ontological par excellence, they make the understanding of being possible. It is then not by chance that the exaltation of culture and cultures, the exaltation of the artistic aspect of culture, guides contemporary spiritual life; that, over and beyond the specialized labor of scientific research, the museums and the theaters, as in former times the temples, make communion with being possible; or that poetry passes for prayer. The artistic expression would assemble being into a meaning and thus provide the original light that scientific cognition itself would borrow from. Artistic expression would thus be an essential event that would be produced in being by artists and philosophers. It is then not surprising that Merleau-Ponty's thought seemed to evolve toward that of Heidegger.[22] Cultural meaning is taken to occupy an exceptional place between the objective and the subjective - the cultural activity disclosing being; the one that works this disclosure, the subject, invested by being as its servant and guardian.[23] Here we rejoin the schemas of the later Heidegger, but also the *idée fixe* of the whole of contemporary thought - the overcoming of the subject-object structure. But perhaps at the source of all these philosophies we find the Hegelian vision of a subjectivity that comprehends itself as an inevitable moment of the becoming by which being leaves its darkness, the vision of a subject aroused by the logic of being.

The symbolism of the meaning bound to language - and to culture as assimilated to language - can then nowise be taken to be a defective intuition, a makeshift of an experience separated from the plenitude of being, which would therefore be reduced to signs. A symbol is not the abridgement of a real presence that would preexist it; it would give more than any receptivity for the world could ever receive. The signified would surpass the given not because it would surpass our ways to capture it - since we would be without any intellectual intuition[24] - but because the signified is of another order than the given, even though it be taken as the prey of a divine intuition. To *receive the given* would no longer be the original way to relate to being.

3. The Antiplatonism of the Contemporary Philosophy of Meaning

The totality of being in which being shines forth as meaning is not an entity fixed for eternity but requires the arranging and assembling, the cultural act, of man. Being as a whole - meaning - shines forth in the works of poets and artists. But it shines forth in diverse ways in the diverse artists of the same cultures and is diversely expressed in the diverse cultures. This diversity of expression is not, for Merleau-Ponty, a betrayal of being but makes the inexhaustible riches of its event sparkle. Each cultural work traverses the whole of being yet leaves it intact. And in Heidegger being is revealed out of the hiddenness and mystery of the unsaid, which the poets and philosophers bring to speech, without ever saying everything. All the expressions which Being received and receives in history would be true, for truth would be inseparable from its historical expression; and without its expression, thought does not think anything. Whether it be of Hegelian, Bergsonian, or phenomenological origin, the contemporary philosophy of meaning is thus opposed to Plato at an essential point: the intelligible is not conceivable outside of the becoming which suggests it.[25] There exists no *meaning in itself*, which a thought would have been able to reach by jumping over the deforming or faithful but sensory reflections that lead to it. One has to traverse history or relive duration or start from concrete perception and the language established in it in order to arrive at the intelligible. All the picturesqueness of history, all cultures, are no longer obstacles separating us from the essential and the intelligible but ways that give us access to it. Even more! They are the only ways, the only possible ones, irreplaceable, and consequently implicated in the intelligible itself.

In the light of contemporary philosophy and by contrast with it, we understand better what the separateness of the intelligible world means in Plato, over and beyond the mythical sense ascribed to the realism of the Ideas: for Plato the world of meanings precedes language and culture, which express it; it is indifferent to the system of signs that one can invent to make this world present to thought. It thus dominates the historical cultures. For Plato there exists a privileged culture, which approaches it and which is capable of understanding the provisional and as it were infantile character of historical cultures; there exists a culture that would consist in depreciating the pure historical cultures and somehow colonizing the world, beginning with the land[26] in which this revolutionary culture arose - this philosophy which goes beyond cultures. There exists a culture that would consist in redoing the world in function of the intemporal order of the Ideas, as the Platonic Republic which sweeps away the allusions and deposits of history, that Republic from which the poets of the *mimēsis* are driven. For the language of these poets does not function to lead toward meanings preexisting their expression and eternal; it is not a pure account of these ideas - *haplē diegesis aneu mimēseōs*.[27] It seeks to imitate the direct discourses of innumerable cultures and of the innumerable manifestations in which each unfolds. These poets thus allow themselves to be drawn into the becoming of the particularities, peculiarities, and oddities from which the expressed thoughts would not be separable for the poets of the *mimēsis* (as for many moderns) and of which one cannot draw up a simple account. The loss or forgetting or abolition of these particularities - these idiocies - would make humanity lose inappreciable treasures of meanings, irrecuperable without the taking up of all these cultural forms, that is, without imitating them.

For contemporary philosophy, meaning is not only correlative with thought, and thought is not only correlative with a language that would make of meaning *haplē diegesis*. To this intellectualist structure of *correlation* between intellect and intelligible, which maintains the separation of the planes, is superposed a *nearness* and a *side-by-sidedness*, an alliance, *a belongingness* which unites the intellect and the intelligible on the one plane of the world, forming that "fundamental historicity" which Merleau-Ponty speaks of. The love of truth which in Plato placed pure thought in front of meaning is thus shown to be an incestuous trouble because of this consanguinity of the intellect and the intelligible, embroiled in the network of language, born in the expression from which thought is not separable. The antiplatonism of contemporary philosophy consists in this subordination of the intellect to expression: the face-to-face position of soul and idea is interpreted as a limit abstraction of a coming into contact in a common world; the intellect aiming at the intelligible would itself rest on the being which this aim only claims to illuminate. No philosophical movement better than contemporary phenomenology has brought out the transcendental function of the whole concrete density of our corporeal, technical, social, and political existence, but it has also thereby brought out the interference of the transcendental relationship and the physical, technical, and cultural relations which constitute the world in the "fundamental historicity" - in this new form of the *mixed*.[28]

We alluded above to the kinship between Bergson and phenomenology. Bergson's antiplatonism lies not only in his general revalorization of becoming;[29] it is like the phenomenological antiplatonism in that it is also found in Bergson's conception of understanding.[30] When Bergson refuses to separate the choice which the free being would have to make from the whole past of this being, when he refuses to admit that a problem which requires a decision could be formulated in abstract and intellectual terms about which just any rational being would be competent to adjudge, he situates the intelligible in the prolongation of the whole concrete existence of the individual. The meaning of the decision to be taken can be intelligible only for him who would have lived through the whole past which leads to this decision. The meaning cannot be understood directly in a fulguration which illuminates and dissipates the night in which it arises and which it leads to its denouement. The whole density of history is necessary for it.

For phenomenologists as for Bergsonians, a meaning cannot be separated from the access leading to it. *The access is part of the meaning itself.* The scaffolding is never taken down; the ladder is never pulled up. Whereas the Platonic soul, liberated from the concrete conditions of its corporeal and historical existence, can reach the heights of the empyrean[31] to contemplate the Ideas, whereas a slave, provided that he "understands Greek" which enables him to enter into relationship with the master,[32] reaches the same truths as the master, our contemporaries require that God himself, if he wishes to be a physicist, have spent his time in the laboratory, go through the weighings and measurings, the sensible perception, even the infinite series of aspects in which a perceived object is revealed.

The most recent, boldest, and most influential ethnography maintains the multiple cultures on the same plane.[33] The political work of decolonization is thus attached to an ontology - to a thought of being, interpreted in its multiple and multivocal cultural meaning. And this multivocity of the meaning of being - this essential disorientation - is perhaps the modern expression of atheism.

4. The "Economic" Meaning

In fact, to the multiplicity of meanings which come to reality from culture and cultures is opposed the fixed, privileged meaning which the world acquires in function of man's needs. Needs raise the simply given things to the rank of values. Admirably straightforward and impatient in their aim, needs give themselves the multiple possibilities of meaning only so as to choose the unique way of satisfaction. Man thus confers a unique meaning to being, not by celebrating it, but by working it. In technical and scientific culture, the ambiguity of being, like the ambiguity of meaning, would be overcome. Therefore, instead of enjoying the play of cultural meanings, one should, out of a concern for truth, liberate the words from the metaphors by creating a scientific or algorithmic terminology, insert the real, scintillating with a thousand lights for perception, into the perspective of human needs and of the action which the Real achieves or undergoes. One should reduce perception to the science which the possible transformation of the world justifies, man to the complexes exhibited by psychoanalysis, society to its economic structures. Everywhere one should find the sense beneath the meaning, beneath the metaphor, the sublimation, the literature. There would then be "serious," real meanings, put in scientific terms, oriented by needs and, in general, by economy. Economy alone would be really oriented and signifying. It alone would know the secret of a proper meaning prior to the figurative meaning. The cultural meaning, detached from this economic - technological and scientific - sense would have but the value of a symptom, the worth of an ornament suited to the needs of a game, an abusive and deceptive meaning, exterior to truth. No doubt is possible about the profoundly rationalist aspiration of this material-ism, its fidelity to the unity of sense which the multiplicity of cultural meanings would itself presuppose.

Yet the great merit of Bergson and of phenomenology will have been to have shown the metaphorical character of this identification of reality with *Wirklich-keit*.[34] The technical designation of the universe is itself a modality of culture: it reduces the Real to an "Object in general," and its interpretation of being presents this as though it were destined for the Laboratory and the Factory. The scientific and technical vision which is imposed on needs modifies them, levels them, and creates them more than it is aroused by their original straightfor-wardness and univocity. For in fact no human need exists in the univocal state of an animal need. Every human need is from the first already interpreted culturally. Only need taken at the level of underdeveloped humanity can give this false impression of univocity. Moreover, it is not certain that the scientific and technical signification of the world could "dissolve" the multiplicity of cultural meanings. We might in fact doubt that when we observe the threats that national particularisms represent for the unity of the new international society put under the sign of modern scientific and industrial development, and of the regrouping of humanity around the univocal imperatives of materialism. It is as though these particularisms themselves correspond to needs. And this to be sure takes from them the character of being simple superstructures. Finally, the forms in which this search for the unique sense of being on the basis of needs is manifested are acts aiming at the realization of a society. They are borne by a spirit of sacrifice and altruism, which no longer proceeds from these needs (unless we play on the word *need*). The needs which allegedly orient being receive their sense from an intuition which no longer proceeds from these needs. This was already the capital teaching of Plato's *Republic*: the State which is founded on the needs of men can neither subsist nor even arise without the philosophers who have mastered their needs and contemplate the Ideas and the Good.[35]

5. The Unique Sense

The impossibility of establishing the univocal meaning of being upon material-
ism (although the search for that univocal meaning is greatly to the honor of
materialism) does not itself compromise this ideal of unity, which constitutes
the force of Truth and the hope for an understanding among men. The cultural
and aesthetic notion of meaning cannot draw it from itself, nor do without it.

We are indeed told that cultural meanings do not betray by their pluralism
but only through it rise to the measure and *essence*[36] of being, that is, to its *way*
of being. Being *is* not in such a way as to congeal into a Parmenidean sphere,[37]
identical to itself, nor into a completed and fixed creation. The totality of being
envisioned from cultures could nowise be a panoramic view. There could not be
a totality in being, but only totalities. There is nothing that could encompass all
of them. They would be shielded from any judgment that would claim to be the
final judgment. We are told: being *is* historically; it requires men and their
cultural becoming in order to assemble. We are told: the unity of being at any
moment would only consist in the fact that men understand one another, in the
penetrability of cultures by one another. This penetrability could not come
about through the mediation of a common tongue that would, independently of
the cultures, convey the proper and ideal articulations of the meanings, and
thus in fact make these particular tongues useless. In this whole conception, the
penetration takes place - according to Merleau-Ponty's expression - laterally.
For a Frenchman there does exist the possibility of learning Chinese and
passing from one culture into another, without the intermediary of an *Esperanto*
that would falsify both tongues which it mediated. Yet what has not been taken
into consideration in this case is that an *orientation* is needed to have the
Frenchman take up learning Chinese instead of declaring it to be barbarian
(that is, bereft of the real virtues of language) and to prefer speech to war. One
reasons as though the equivalence of cultures, the discovery of their profusion
and the recognition of their riches were not themselves the effects of an
orientation and of an unequivocal sense in which humanity stands. One
reasons as though the multiplicity of cultures from the beginning sunk its roots
in the era of decolonization, as though incomprehension, war, and conquest did
not derive just as naturally from the contiguity of multiple expressions of being
- the numerous assemblages or arrangements which it takes on in the diverse
civilizations. One reasons as though peaceful coexistence did not presuppose
that in being there is delineated an orientation which gives it a unique sense.[38]
Must we not then distinguish the meanings, in their cultural pluralism, from
the sense, orientation, and unity of being - a primordial event in which all the
other steps of thought and the whole historical life of being are situated? Do the
cultural meanings arise as random wholes in the dispersion of the given? Do

they not take on meaning in a dialogue maintained with that which signifies *of itself* - with the other (*autrui*)? These original meanings would command the gatherings of being; it would not be these random assemblings that would already, outside of all dialogue, constitute meanings. Do not meanings require a unique sense from which they derive their very signifyingness?

The world, as soon as one moves on from the humble daily tasks, and language, as soon as one moves on from commonplace talk, have lost the *univocity* which would authorize us to expect from them the criteria of the meaningful. Absurdity consists not in non-sense but in the isolation of innumerable meanings, in the absence of a sense that orients them. What is lacking is the sense of all, the Rome to which all roads lead, the symphony in which all meanings sing, the song of songs. The absurdity lies in the pure indifference of a multiplicity. The cultural meanings put forth as ultimate are the breakup of a unity. It is not simply a matter of fixing the conditions in which the facts of our experience or the signs of our language arouse in us the feeling of understanding or appear to proceed from a reasonable intention or convey a structural order. Over and beyond these logical and psychological problems, the true meaning is at stake.

This loss of unity has been proclaimed - and consecrated against the grain - by the famous paradox, become commonplace, of the death of God.[39] The crisis of sense is thus experienced by our contemporaries as a crisis of monotheism. There was a time when a god intervened in human history by force, sovereign to be sure, invisible to the eye without being provable by reason - supernatural, consequently, or transcendental; but this intervention occurred in a system of reciprocities and exchanges. The system was sketched out starting with a man preoccupied with himself. The god transcending the world remained united to the world through the unity of an economy.[40] His effects would end up among the effects of all the other forces, get shuffled in with them and form *miracles*. God was a god of miracles, even in an age when no one expects miracles any more, a force in the world, magical despite all his morality; morality was inverted into magic and acquired magical virtues; such was a god to whom one presents oneself as a beggar. The status of his transcendence, despite the immanence of his revelation - a transcendence new with respect to the unbridgeable transcendence of the Aristotelian god[41] - the status of this transcendence of the supernatural was never established. The interventions of the supernatural god could to a certain extent be counted upon or even inflected, like the effects of other wills and other forces which presided over the events of history. When history gave the lie to this economy, this did not refute the supernatural providence any more than the deviations of the stars refuted the Ptolemaic astronomy. It even confirmed it, at the cost of some new theological "epicycles."[42]

This religion which the person required for himself, rather than feeling himself required by this religion, and this god which had entered into the circuit of economy (a religion and a god, however, which did not exhaust the message of the Scriptures) have lost much of their influence over humankind. And with them the sense of a world perfectly and very simply ordained to this god is also lost. We do not think that sense can do without God, nor that the idea of being or of the being of entities could be substituted for him, so as to bring meanings to the unity of sense without which there is no sense.

But we cannot describe sense starting with this still economic idea of God; it is the analysis of sense that must give out the notion of God which sense harbors. Sense is impossible on the basis of an Ego which exists, as Heidegger puts it, in such a way that "his very existence is at stake in his existence."[43]

6. Sense and Work

The reflection on cultural meaning leads to a pluralism which lacks a unique sense. For a moment economy and technology seemed to delineate such a sense. But if cultural meanings can be interpreted as superstructures of economy, economy in turn derives its forms from culture. The ambivalence of meanings bears witness to a disorientation. Let us note first that this ambiguity seems to respond to a certain philosophical style which is satisfied with a nonpolarized ether. Does not sense as orientation indicate a leap, an outside-of-oneself toward the *other than oneself*, whereas philosophy wants to reabsorb every Other into the Same and to neutralize alterity? A distrust of every unconsidered move, a lucidity of old age which absorbs the imprudences of youth, Action in advance recuperated in the knowledge which guides it - this is perhaps the very definition of philosophy.

Even if life precedes philosophy, even if contemporary philosophy, which means to be anti-intellectualist, insists on this priority of existence with respect to essence,[44] of life with respect to intellect, even if, in Heidegger, "gratitude" to being and "obedience"[45] are substituted for contemplation, contemporary philosophy enjoys the multiplicity of cultural meanings - and in the infinite play of art, being is relieved of its alterity. Philosophy is produced as a form in which the refusal of engagement in the Other, the waiting[46] preferred to action, indifference with regard to others, the universal allergy of the early infancy of philosophers is manifest. The itinerary of philosophy remains that of Ulysses, whose adventure in the world was only a return to his native island - a complacency in the Same, an unrecognition of the Other.

But must we renounce knowing and meanings in order to find sense? Must there be a blind orientation in order that cultural meanings take on a unique sense, and in order that being find again a unity of sense? However, does not a blind orientation represent the instinctual rather than human order, in which the person betrays his vocation of being a person in getting absorbed in the law which situates and orients him? Is it not then possible to conceive of an orientation - a sense - in being which would unite univocity and freedom? This at any rate is the goal of the analysis which we have undertaken.

First we must fix with precision the conditions for such an orientation. It can be posited only as a movement going outside of the identical toward an Other which is absolutely other. It begins in an identical, a Same, an Ego; it is not a "sense of history"[47] which dominates the ego, for the irresistible orientation of history makes the very fact of the movement senseless, since the Other would be already inscribed in the Same, the end in the beginning. An orientation which goes *freely* from the Same to the Other is a Work.

But then a Work must be conceived not as an apparent agitation of a stock which afterwards remains identical to itself, like an energy which in all its transformations remains equal to itself. Nor must the Work be conceived as a technology which through the famous negativity transforms a foreign world into a world whose alterity is converted into my idea. Both conceptions continue to affirm being as self-identical and reduce its fundamental event to thought, which is - and this is the indelible lesson of idealism - thought of itself, thought of thought.[48] An attitude, initially an attitude taken up toward the other, becomes, in Eric Weil's terminology,[49] a totality or a category. Now *the Work conceived radically is a movement of the Same toward the Other which never returns to the Same*. The Work thought through all the way requires a radical generosity of the movement which in the Same goes toward the Other. It consequently requires an *ingratitude* of the Other; gratitude would be the *return* of the movement to its origin.

On the other hand, the Work differs from a game where there is pure expenditure. It is not undertaken in pure loss. It is more serious than an identity surrounded with nothingness. The Work is neither a pure acquisition of merits nor a pure nihilism. For, like the seeker after merits, the nihilist agent immediately takes himself as his term and his goal, beneath the apparent gratuity of his action. The Work is then a relationship with the Other, who is reached without showing itself touched. It takes form outside of the "morose savoring" of failures and consolations, which for Nietzsche defines Christianity.

But a departure with no return, which, however, does not go forth into the void, would also lose its absolute *orientation* if it sought recompense in the immediacy of its triumph, if it awaited the triumph of its cause impatiently. The one-way movement of "unique sense" would be reversed and become a reciprocity. Confronting its beginning and its end, the Agent would reabsorb the work in calculations of deficits and compensations, in bookkeeping operations. It would be subordinated to thought. As an absolute orientation toward the

Other, as sense, a work is possible only in patience, which, pushed to the limit, means the Agent to renounce being the contemporary of its outcome, to act without entering into the Promised Land.[50]

The Future for which such an action acts must from the first be posited as indifferent to my death. As different from play and from computations is the Work being-for-beyond-my-death.[51] Patience does not consist in the Agent betraying his generosity by giving himself the time of a personal immortality. To renounce being the contemporary of the triumph of one's work is to envisage this triumph in a *time without me*, to aim at this world without me, to aim at a time beyond the horizon of my time, in an eschatology without hope for oneself, or in a liberation from my time.

To be *for* a time that would be without me, *for* a time after my time, over and beyond the famous "being for death," is not an ordinary thought which is extrapolating my own duration; it is the passage to the time of the Other. Should what makes such a passage possible be called *eternity*? In any case the possibility of sacrifice which goes to the limit of this passage discovers the non-inoffensive nature of this extrapolation: to be for death in order to be for that which is after me.

The work as an absolute orientation of the Same unto the Other is then like a radical youth of the generous impulse. We could fix its concept with a term from Greek, *liturgy*, which in its primary meaning designates the exercise of a function which is not only totally gratuitous but requires on the part of him who exercises it a putting out of funds at a loss.[52] For the moment all meaning drawn from any positive religion has to be removed from this term, even if in a certain way the idea of God should show its trace at the end of our analysis. On the other hand, as a work without renumeration, whose result is not allowed for in the time of the Agent and is assured only for patience, a work that is effected in the complete domination of and surpassing of my time, liturgy is not be to ranked alongside "works" and ethics. It is ethics itself.

The relationship which we have apparently just constructed is not simply constructed. The total gratuity of Action - a gratuity different from play - moves our age, even if the individuals may not be up to its height, a fact which indicates the free character of the orientation. Our age is not defined by the triumph of technology for the sake of technology, as it is not defined by art for the sake of art, and as it is not defined by nihilism. It is an action for a world to come, a going beyond one's epoch - a going beyond oneself which requires the epiphany of the Other - such is the fundamental thesis which underlies these pages. In Bourassol prison and Fort Pourtalet Léon Blum was, in December 1941, finishing a book.[53] He wrote: "We are working *in* the present, not *for* the present. How many times in meetings with the people have I repeated and commented on Nietzsche's words: Let the future and the things most remote be the rule of all the present days!" The philosophy with which Blum justifies this strange force of working, without working for the present, is not here the essential; the force of his confidence is incommensurate with the force of his philosophy. 1941! - a hole in history - a year in which all the visible gods had abandoned us, in which god was really dead or gone back into his nonrevealedness. A man in prison continues to believe in a nonrevealed future and invites men to work in the present for the most remote things, of which the present is an irrecusable denial. There is a vulgarity and a baseness in an action that is conceived only for the immediate, that is, in the last analysis, for our life. And there is a very great nobility in the energy liberated from the hold of the present. To act for remote things at the moment in which Hitlerism triumphed, in the deaf hours of this night without hours - independently of every evaluation of the "forces in presence" - is, no doubt, the summit of nobility.

7. Sense and Ethics

Sense as the liturgical orientation of the Work does not arise from need. Need opens upon a world that is *for me*; it returns to itself. Even a sublime need, such as the need for salvation, is still a nostalgia, a longing to go back. A need is return itself, the anxiety of the I for itself, egoism, the original form of identification. It is the assimilating of the world in view of self-coincidence, in view of happiness.

In the "Canticle of the Columns" Valéry speaks of a "faultless desire."[54] He is doubtless referring to Plato, who, in his analysis of pure pleasures, discovered an aspiration that is conditioned by no prior lack.[55] We are taking up this term *desire*; to a subject turned to itself, which, according to the Stoic formula is characterized by *hormē*, the tendency to persist in its being, or for which, according to Heidegger's formula, "in its existence the issue is this very existence,"[56] a subject thus defined by care for itself, which in happiness realizes its *for itself*, we are opposing the Desire for the Other which proceeds from a being already gratified and in this sense independent, which does not desire for itself. It is the need of him who no longer has needs. It is recognizable in the need for an Other who is Other (*Autrui*), who is neither my enemy (as he is in Hobbes and Hegel) nor my "complement," as he still is in Plato's *Republic*, who is set up because something is lacking in the subsistence of each individual.[57] The Desire for the Other (*Autrui*), sociality, is born in a being that lacks nothing, or, more exactly, it is born over and beyond all that can be lacking or that can satisfy. In Desire the I is borne toward the Other (*Autrui*) in such a way as to compromise the sovereign self-identification of the I, for which need is only nostalgia, and which the consciousness of need anticipates. The movement toward the Other (*Autrui*), instead of completing me or contenting me, implicates me in a conjuncture which in a way did not concern me and should leave me indifferent - why did I get involved in this business? Whence came this shock when I passed, indifferent - under the Other's (*Autrui*) gaze? The relationship with the Other (*Autrui*) puts me into question, empties me of myself and empties me without end, showing me ever new resources. I did not know I was so rich, but I no longer have the right to keep anything for myself. Is the Desire for the Other (*Autrui*) an appetite or a generosity? The Desirable does not gratify my Desire but hollows it out, and somehow nourishes me with new hungers. Desire is revealed to be goodness. There is a scene in Dostoyevsky's *Crime and Punishment* where Sonya Marmaladova looks upon Rashkalnikov in his despair, and Dostoyevsky speaks of "insatiable compassion." He does not say "inexhaustible compassion." It is as though the compassion that goes from Sonya to Rashkalnikov were a hunger which the presence of Rashkalnikov nourished beyond any saturation, increasing this hunger to infinity.

The Desire for the Other (*Autrui*), which we live in the most ordinary social experience, is the fundamental movement, a pure transport, an absolute orientation, sense. In all its analyses of language contemporary philosophy insists, and indeed rightly, on its hermeneutical structure and on the cultural effort of the incarnate being that expresses itself. Has a third dimension not been forgotten; the direction toward the Other (*Autrui*) who is not only the collaborator and the neighbor of our cultural work of expression or the client of our artistic production, but the interlocutor, he to whom expression expresses, for whom celebration celebrates, both term of an orientation and primary signification? In other words, expression, before being a celebration of being, is a relationship with him to whom I express the expression and whose presence is already required for my cultural gesture of expression to be produced. The Other (*Autrui*) who faces me is not included in the totality of being expressed. He arises behind every assembling of being as he to whom I express what I express. I find myself facing the Other (*Autrui*). He is neither a cultural signification nor a simple given. He is *sense* primordially, for he gives sense to expression itself, for it is only by him that a phenomenon as a meaning is, of itself, introduced into being.

The analysis of Desire, which it was important for us to first distinguish from need, and which delineates a sense in being, will be made clearer by the analysis of the alterity toward which Desire is borne.

The manifestation of the Other (*Autrui*) is, to be sure, produced from the first in conformity with the way every meaning is produced. The Other is present in a cultural whole and is illuminated by this whole, as a text by its context. The manifestation of the whole ensures his presence; it is illuminated by the light of the world. The understanding of the Other (*Autrui*) is thus a hermeneutics and an exegesis. The Other is given in the concreteness of the totality in which he is immanent, and which, according to Merleau-Ponty's remarkable analyses, which we have drawn upon to a large extent in the first sections of this essay, is expressed and disclosed by our own cultural initiative, by corporeal, linguistic, or artistic gestures.

But the epiphany of the Other (*Autrui*) involves a signifyingness of its own, independent of this meaning received from the world. The Other comes to us not only out of the context but also without mediation; he signifies by himself. The cultural meaning which is revealed - and reveals - as it were *horizontally*, which is revealed from the historical world to which it belongs, and which, according to the phenomenological expression, reveals the horizons of this world - this mundane meaning is disturbed and jostled by another presence that is abstract (or, more exactly, absolute) and not integrated into the world. This presence consists in coming toward us, in *making an entry*. This can be put in this way: the *phenomenon* of the Other's (*Autrui*) aspiration is also a *face* - or, again (to indicate the entry, at every moment new, into the immanency and essential historicity of the phenomenon): the epiphany of a face is a *visitation*. Whereas a phenomenon is already, in whatever respect, an image, a captive manifestation of its plastic and mute form, the epiphany of a face is alive. Its life consists in undoing the form in which all *beings* (*étant*) when they enter into immanence, that is, when they are exposed as a theme, are already dissimulated.

The Other (*Autrui*) who manifests himself in a face as it were breaks through his own plastic essence, like a being who opens the window on which its own visage was already taking form. His presence consists in divesting himself of the form which does already manifest him. His manifestation is a surplus over the inevitable paralysis of manifestation. This is what the formula "the face speaks" expresses. The manifestation of a face is the first disclosure. Speaking is before anything else this way of coming from behind one's appearance, behind one's form, an openness in the openness.

The visitation of the face is thus not the disclosure of the world. In the concreteness of the world a face is abstract or naked. It is denuded of its own image. Through the nudity of a face nudity in itself is first possible in the world.

The nudity of a face is a bareness without any cultural ornament, an absolution,[58] a detachment from its form in the midst of the production of its form. The face *enters* into our world from an absolutely foreign sphere, that is, precisely from an ab-solute, which in fact is the very name for ultimate strangeness. The signifyingness of a face in its abstractness is in the literal sense of the term extra-ordinary, outside of every order, every world. How is such a production possible? How can the coming of the Other, the visitation of a face, the absolute not be - in any way - converted into a revelation, not even a symbolism or a suggestion? How is a face not simply a *true representation*[59] in which the Other renounces his alterity? To answer, we will have to study the exceptional signifyingness of the trace and the personal "order" in which such a signifyingness is possible.

Let us for the moment attend to the sense which the abstraction or nudity of a face which breaks into the order of the world involves and the overwhelming of consciousness which corresponds to this "abstraction." Stripped of its very form, a face shivers in its nudity. It is a distress. The nudity of a face is a denuding, and already a supplication in the straightforwardness that looks at me. But this supplication is an exigency; in it humility is joined with height. The ethical dimension of visitation is thereby indicated. A true *representation* remains a possibility of appearance; the world which strikes against thought can do nothing against free thought - which is able to refuse inwardly, to take refuge in itself, to remain precisely a *free thought* before the true, to return to itself, to reflect on itself and take itself to be the origin of what it receives, to master what precedes it through memory. While free thought thus *remains the Same*, a face imposes itself upon me without my being able to be deaf to its call or to forget it, that is, without my being able to suspend my responsibility for its distress. Consciousness loses its first place.

The presence of the face thus signifies an irrecusable order, a command, which puts a stop to the availability of consciousness. Consciousness is called into question by the face. Being called into question is not the same as becoming aware of this being called into question. The "absolutely other" is not reflected in consciousness. It resists it to the extent that even its resistance is not convertible into a content of consciousness. Visitation consists in overwhelming the very egoism of the I which supports this conversion. A face confounds the intentionality that aims at it.

What is at stake here is the calling of consciousness into question and not a consciousness of a calling into question. The I loses its sovereign self-coincidence, its identification, in which consciousness returns triumphantly to itself to rest on itself. Before the exigency of the Other (*Autrui*), the I is expelled from this rest and is not the already glorious consciousness of this exile. Any complacency would destroy the straightforwardness of the ethical movement.

But the calling into question of this wild and naïve freedom for itself, sure of its refuge in itself, is not reducible to a negative movement. The calling into question of oneself is in fact the welcome of the absolutely other. The epiphany of the absolutely other is a face, in which the Other (*Autrui*) calls on me and signifies an order to me through his nudity, his denuding. His presence is a summons to answer. The I does not only become aware of this necessity to answer, as though it were a particular obligation or duty about which it would have to come to a decision; it is in its very position wholly a responsibility or a diacony, as it is put in Isaiah, chapter 53.[60]

To be an I means then not to be able to escape responsibility, as though the whole edifice of creation rested on my shoulders. But the responsibility that empties the I of its imperialism and its egoism, even the egoism of salvation, does not transform it into a moment of the universal order; it confirms the uniqueness of the I. The uniqueness of the I is the fact that no one can answer for me.

To discover such an orientation in the I is to identify the I with morality. The I before the Other (*Autrui*) is infinitely responsible. The Other who provokes this ethical movement in consciousness and puts out of order the good conscience of the Same coinciding with itself involves a surplus not adequated to intentionality. Such is desire: to burn with another fire than need, which saturation extinguishes, to think beyond what one thinks. Because of this inassimilable surplus, because of this *beyond*, we have called the relationship which links the I with the Other the idea of the Infinite.[61]

The idea of the Infinite is Desire. It paradoxically consists in thinking more than what is thought and maintaining what is thought in this very excess relative to thought - in entering into a relationship with the ungraspable while guaranteeing its status of being ungraspable. The Infinite is thus not a correlate of the idea of the Infinite, as though this idea were an intentionality that is *fulfilled* in its "object."[62] The wonder of the infinite in the finite of a thought is an overwhelming of intentionality, an overwhelming of the appetite for light which is intentionality; unlike the saturation in which intentionality subsides, that Infinite confounds its Idea. The I in relationship with the Infinite is an impossibility of stopping its forward march, the impossibility of deserting its post, as Plato says in the *Phaedo*;[63] it is, literally, not to have time to turn around. It is not to be able to escape responsibility, not to have a hiding place of inwardness where one comes back into oneself, to march forward without concern for oneself. There is an increase of exigencies on oneself: the more I face my responsibilities the more I am responsible. The putting into question of consciousness and its entry into a conjuncture of relations which contrast with disclosure is a power made of "impotencies."

Thus in the relationship with a face, in the ethical relationship, there is delineated the straightforwardness of an orientation, or sense. The *consciousness* of philosophers is essentially reflective. Or, at least, consciousness is grasped by philosophers in its moment of return, which is taken for its very birth. Already in its spontaneous and prereflexive movements they take it to cast a glance back at its origin and measure the path crossed. That is where its initial essence would lie: it is a critique, a self-mastery, an analysis and decomposition of every meaning that overflows the self. Responsibility is to be sure neither blind nor amnesiac; but across all the movements of thought in which it extends it is borne by an extreme urgency, or, more exactly, it coincides with it. What has just been described as a "lack of time to turn around" is not the accident of a clumsy or unhappy consciousness "overtaken by events" or one that "has trouble keeping up" but the utter rigor of an attitude without reflection, a primordial straightforwardness, a *sense* in being. "Where does this resistance of the unreflected to reflection come from?" Merleau-Ponty asked at Royaumont in April 1957, in connection with problems that the Husserlian theory of phenomenological reduction poses.[64] Our analysis of *sense* perhaps responds to this fundamental question, which Merleau-Ponty refused to resolve by simple recourse to the finitude of the subject, incapable of total reflection. "To turn to the truth with one's whole soul"[65] - the Platonic recommendation is not limited to a pedagogy of good sense, preaching effort, and sincerity. Does it not aim at the ultimate reticence, the most sly of all, that of a soul which, before the Good, persists in reflecting on its Self and thus arresting the movement unto the Other? Is not the force of this "resistance of the unreflected to reflection" the Will itself, prior and posterior to, alpha and omega of, every Representation? And is not the will thus at bottom humility rather than will to power? Humility is not to be confused with an equivocal negation of one's Self, already proud of its virtue, which, in reflection, it immediately recognizes in itself. This humility is that of him who does not "have time" to make a return upon himself and undertakes nothing to "negate" oneself, save the very abnegation of the rectilinear movement of the Work which goes to the infinity of the Other.

To affirm such an orientation and such a sense, to posit a consciousness without reflection beneath and above all the reflections, in short to surprise at the bottom of the ego an unequivocal sincerity and a servant's humility which no transcendental method could corrupt or absorb, is to ensure the necessary condition for a "beyond the given" which dawns in every meaning, for the *meta*phor which animates it. This is the marvel of language, whose "verbal origin" philosophical analysis will continue to denounce without destroying the evident intention that penetrates it. Whatever be its psychological, social, or philological history, the *beyond* which the metaphor produces has a sense that transcends this history; the power to conjure up illusions which language has must be recognized, but lucidity does not abolish the beyond of these illusions. It is, to be sure, the role of reflection to reduce meanings to their subjective, subconscious, social, or verbal sources, to draw up a transcendental inventory of them. But the method, though legitimate to destroy many false reputations, already prejudges an essential result: it forbids in advance any transcendent aim in meaning. Before the research, every *Other* is already converted by it into the *Same*, but in its purifying work Reflection will nonetheless itself use these notions, if only the notion of a *beyond* with respect to which immanence is situated - which without the sincerity and straightforwardness of the "consciousness without return" would have no meaning. Nothing of what is sublime does without psychological, social, or verbal sources, save sublimation itself.

This consciousness "without reflection" is not the spontaneous, simply prereflexive and naïve consciousness; it is not precritical. To discover the orientation and the unique and one-way sense in the moral relationship is precisely to posit the Ego[66] as already put into question by the Other (*Autrui*) it desires and, consequently, as criticized in the very straightforwardness of its movement. That is why the putting into question of consciousness is not initially a consciousness of the putting into question. The first is the condition for the second. How would spontaneous thought turn back if the Other, the Exterior, did not put it into question? And how, in a concern for total Critique entrusted to reflection, would the new naïveté of reflection that removes the first naïveté itself be removed? The Ego erodes its dogmatic naïveté before the Other who asks of it more than it can do spontaneously.

The "term" of such a movement, both critical and spontaneous - which is not, properly speaking, a term, for it is not an end, but the principle soliciting a Work without recompense, a liturgy - is no longer called being. Here perhaps we can catch sight of the necessity for a philosophical meditation to resort to notions such as that of the Infinite or God.

8. Before Culture

We will say, to conclude, that before Culture and Aesthetics, meaning is situated in the Ethical, presupposed by all Culture and all meaning. Morality does not belong to Culture: it enables one to judge it; it discovers the dimension of height. Height ordains being.

Height introduces a sense into being. It is already lived across the experience of the human body. It leads human societies to raise up altars. It is not because men, through their bodies, have an experience of the vertical that the human is placed under the sign of height; because being is ordained to height, the human body is placed in a space in which the high and the low are distinguished and the sky is discovered - that sky which for Tolstoy's Prince André, without any word of the text evoking colors, is all height.

It is most important to insist on the antecedence of sense to cultural signs. To attach every meaning to culture, not to distinguish between meaning and cultural expression, between meaning and the art that prolongs cultural expression, is to recognize that all the cultural personalities equally realize the Spirit. No meaning can any longer be detached from these innumerable cultures, to allow one to bear a judgment on these cultures. Universality can only be lateral according to Merleau-Ponty's expression. This universality would consist in being able to penetrate one culture from another, as one learns a language on the basis of one's mother tongue. The idea of a universal grammar and an algorithmic language built on the framework of this grammar would have to be given up. No direct or privileged contact with the world of Ideas is possible. In short, such a conception of universality expresses the radical opposition, so characteristic of our epoch, to the expansion of culture by colonization. To cultivate and to colonize should be completely separated. We would be at the antipodes of what Léon Brunschvicg[67] (and Plato, hostile to the poets of the *mimēsis*) taught us; the progress of Western consciousness would no longer consist in purifying thought of the alluvium of cultures and the particularisms of language, which far from signifying the intelligible would perpetuate the infantile. It is not that Brunschvicg could have taught us anything but generosity, but for him this generosity and the dignity of the Western world was a matter of liberating truth of its cultural presuppositions, so as, with Plato, to proceed toward meanings themselves, thus separated from becoming. The danger of such a conception is clear; the emancipations of minds can be a pretext for exploitation and violence. Philosophy had to denounce the equivocation, show meanings dawning at the horizon of cultures, and show the very excellence of Western culture to be culturally and historically conditioned. Philosophy thus had to rejoin contemporary ethnology. Platonism is vanquished! But it is vanquished in the name of the very generosity of Western thought, which, catching sight of the *abstract* man in men, proclaimed the absolute value of the person, then encompassed in its respect for the person the cultures in which these persons stand or in which they express themselves. Platonism is overcome with the very means which the universal thought issued from Plato supplied. It is overcome by this so much disparaged Western civilization, which was able to understand the particular cultures, that never understood themselves.

The saraband of innumerable and equivalent cultures, each justifying itself in its own context, creates a world which is, to be sure, de-occidentalized, but also disoriented. To catch sight, in meaning, of a situation that precedes culture, to envision language out of the revelation of the Other (which is at the same time the birth of morality) in the gaze of a human being looking at another human precisely as abstract human disengaged from all culture, in the nakedness of his face, is to return to Platonism in a new way. It is also to find oneself able to judge civilization on the basis of the ethical. Meaning, the intelligible, consists for beings in showing itself in its nonhistorical simplicity, in its absolutely unqualifiable and irreducible nakedness, in existing "prior to" history and culture. Platonism, as an affirmation of the human independently of culture and history, is found also in Husserl, in the obstinacy with which he postulated the phenomenological reduction and the constitution (at least *de jure*) of the cultural world in the transcendental and intuitive consciousness.

We are not obliged to follow him down the way he took to rejoin this Platonism, and we think we have found the straightforwardness of meaning by another method. That intelligible manifestation is produced in the straightforwardness of morality, and the Work measures the limits of the historical understanding of the world and marks a return to Greek wisdom, even though mediated by all the development of contemporary philosophy.

Neither things nor the perceived world nor the scientific world enable us to rejoin the norms of the absolute. As cultural works, they are steeped in history. But the norms of morality are not embarked in history and culture. They are not even islands that emerge from it - for they make all meaning, even cultural meaning, possible, and make it possible to judge Cultures.

9. The Trace

The notion of sense developed on the basis of the epiphany of the face, which has enabled us to affirm it as a sense "before history," poses a problem to which, in closing, we would like to outline a response.

Is not the "beyond" from which the face comes, and which fixes consciousness in its straightforwardness (*droiture*), an idea understood and disclosed in its turn?

If the extraordinary experience of Entrance and Visitation retains its signifyingness, it is because the *beyond* is not a simple background from which the face solicits us, is not "another world"[68] behind the world. The *beyond* is precisely beyond the "world," that is, beyond every disclosure, like the One of the first hypothesis of the *Parmenides*,[69] transcending all cognition, be it symbolic or signified. The One is "neither similar nor dissimilar, neither identical nor nonidentical," Plato says, thus excluding it from every revelation, even an indirect one. A symbol still brings the symbolized back to the world in which it appears. What then can be this relationship with an absence radically withdrawn from disclosure and dissimulation? And what is this absence that makes visitation possible, but which is not reducible to concealment, since this absence involves a signifyingness, a signifyingness in which, however, the Other is not convertible into the Same?

The face is abstract. This abstractness is not, to be sure, like the brute sensible datum of the empiricists. Nor is it an instantaneous cross-section of the time in which time would "cross" eternity. An instant belongs to the world. It is an incision that does not bleed. But the abstractness of the face is a visitation and a coming which *disturbs* immanence without settling into the horizons of the World. Its abstraction is not obtained by a logical process starting from the substance of beings and going from the individual to the general. On the contrary, it goes toward those beings but does not compromise itself with them, withdraws from them, ab-solves itself. Its wonder is due to the *elsewhere* from which it comes and into which it already withdraws. This coming from *elsewhere* is not a *symbolic reference* to that *elsewhere* as to a term. The face presents itself in its nudity; it is neither a form concealing, but thereby indicating, a ground nor a phenomenon that hides, but thereby betrays, a thing itself. Otherwise, the face would be one with a mask, but a mask presupposes a face. If signifying were equivalent to indicating, the face would be insignificant. And Sartre will say that the Other (*Autrui*) is a pure hole in the world[70] - a most noteworthy insight, but he stops his analysis too soon. The Other proceeds from the absolutely Absent, but his relationship with the *absolutely Absent* from which he comes *does not indicate, does not reveal*, this *Absent*; and yet the *Absent* has a meaning in the face. This signifyingness is not a way for the Absent to give itself in a blank in the presence of the face - which would again bring us back to a mode of disclosure. The relationship which goes from the face to the Absent is outside every relation and dissimulation, a third way excluded by these contradictories. How is this third way possible? But are we not still seeking that from which the face proceeds as though it were a sphere, a place, a world? Have we been attentive enough to the interdiction against seeking the beyond as a world behind our world? The order of being would still seem to be presupposed, an order which contains no other status but that of the revealed and of the dissimulated. In being, a transcendence revealed is inverted into an immanence, the extra-ordinary is inserted into an order, the Other is absorbed into the Same. In the presence of the Other (*Autrui*), do we not respond to an "order" in which signifyingness remains an irremissible disturbance, an utterly bygone past? Such is the signifyingness of a trace. The beyond from which the face comes signifies as a trace. The face is in the trace of the utterly bygone, utterly past Absent, withdrawn into what Paul Valéry calls "the deep yore, never long ago enough,"[71] which cannot be discovered in the Self by any introspection. For the face is the unique openness in which the signifyingness of the trans-cendent does not nullify the transcendence and make it enter into an immanent order; here on the contrary transcendence refuses immanence precisely as the ever *bygone* transcendence of the transcendent. In a trace the relationship between the signified and the signification is not a correlation, but *unrectitude* itself. The allegedly immediate and indirect relationship between a sign and the signified belongs to the order of *correlation* and is thus still a rectitude and a disclosure which neutralizes trans-cendence. The signifyingness of a trace places us in a "lateral" relationship, unconvertible into rectitude (something inconceivable in the order of disclosure and being), answering to an irreversible past. No memory can follow the traces of this past. It is an immemorial past - and this also is perhaps eternity, whose signifyingness obstinately throws one back to the past. Eternity is the very irreversibility of time, the source and refuge of the past.

But if the signifyingness of the trace is not immediately transformed into the straightforwardness which still marks signs, which reveal the signified Absent and bring it into immanence, it is because the trace signifies beyond being. The personal "order" to which the face obliges us is beyond being. *Beyond being is a Third Person* which is not definable by the Self, by ipseity. It is the possibility of that third direction of radical *unrectitude* which escapes the bipolar play of immanence and transcendence proper to being, where immanence always wins against transcendence. Through the trace, the irreversible past takes on the profile of a "He" (*Il*). The *beyond* from which the face comes is in the third person. The pronoun *He* expresses its unexpressible irreversibility, already escaping every revelation as well as every dissimulation, and in this sense absolutely unencompassable or absolute, a transcendence in an absolute past. The *illeity*[72] of the third person is the condition for the irreversibility.[73]

This third person, who in the face has already withdrawn from every revelation and every dissimulation, who has passed, this *illeity*, is not a "less than being" by comparison with the world in which the face enters; it is the whole enormity, the whole inordinateness, the whole infinity of the absolutely Other, which eludes treatment by ontology. The supreme presence of the face is inseparable from this supreme and irreversible absence which founds the eminence of visitation.

If the signifyingness of the trace consists in signifying without making appear, if it establishes a relationship with illeity, a relationship which, as personal and ethical, is an obligation and does not disclose, and if, consequently, the trace does not belong to phenomenology, to the comprehension of *appearing* and *dissimulating*, we can at least approach this signifyingness in another way by situating it with respect to the phenomenology it interrupts.

A trace is not a sign like any other. But it also plays the role of a sign; it can be taken for a sign. A detective examines, as revealing signs, everything in the area where a crime took place which betokens the voluntary or involuntary work of the criminal; a hunter follows the traces of the game, which reflect the activity and movement of the animal the hunter is after; a historian discovers ancient civilizations as horizons of our world on the basis of the vestiges left by their existence. Everything has a place in an order, in a world, where each thing reveals another or is revealed in function of another. But when a trace is thus taken as a sign, it is exceptional with respect to other signs in that it signifies outside of every intention of signaling and outside of every project of which it would be the aim. When in transactions one "pays by check" so that there will be a trace of the payment, the trace is inscribed in the very order of the world.

But a real trace disturbs the order of the world. It occurs by overprinting. Its original signifyingness is sketched out in, for example, the fingerprints left by someone who wanted to wipe away his traces and carry out a perfect crime. He who left traces in wiping out his traces did not mean to say or do anything by the traces he left. He disturbed the order in an irreparable way. For he has passed absolutely. To be qua *leaving a trace* is to pass, to depart, to absolve oneself.

But in this sense every sign is a trace. In addition to what the sign signifies, it is the past of him who delivered the sign. The signifyingness of a trace doubles up the signifyingness proper to a sign emitted in view of communication. A sign stands in this trace. This signifyingness lies in, for example, the writing and the style of a letter, in all that brings it about that during the emission of a message, which we capture on the basis of the letter's language and its sincerity, someone passes, purely and simply. This trace can be taken in its turn as a sign. A graphologist, an expert in writing styles, or a psychoanalyst could interpret a trace's singular signifyingness, and seek in it the sealed and unconscious, but real, intentions of him who delivered the message. But then what remains specifically a trace in the writing and style of the letter does not signal any of these intentions, any of these qualities, reveals and hides nothing. In the trace has passed a past absolutely bygone. In the trace its irreversible lapse is sealed. Disclosure, which reinstates the world and leads back to the world and is proper to a sign or a signification, is done away with in this trace.

But then is not the trace the weight of being itself outside of its acts and its language, weighing not through its presence, which fits into the world, but by its very irreversibility, its ab-soluteness? The trace would seem to be the very indelibility of being, its omnipotence with regard to all negativity, its immensity incapable of being self-enclosed, somehow too great for discretion, interiority, or a Self. And it was indeed important for us to say that the trace does not effect a relationship with what would be less than being but obliges with regard to the Infinite, the absolutely Other. But this superiority of the superlative, this height, this constant elevation to power, this exaggeration or this infinite overbidding - and, let us say the word, this divinity - are neither deducible from the being of beings or from its revelation, even if this is contemporary with a concealment, nor from "concrete duration."[74] These signify something on the basis of a past which, in the trace, is neither indicated nor signaled but yet disturbs order while coinciding neither with revelation nor with dissimulation. The trace is the insertion of space in time, the point at which the world inclines toward a past and a time. This time is a withdrawal of the Other and, consequently, nowise a degradation of duration, which, in memory, is still complete. Superiority does not reside in a presence in the world but in an irreversible transcendence. It is not a modulation of the being of beings. As He and third person it is somehow outside the distinction between being and beings. Only a being that transcends the world, an ab-solute being, can leave a trace. The trace is the presence of that which properly speaking has never been there, of what is always past. Plotinus conceived the procession from the One as compromising neither the immutability nor the ab-solute separation of the One. It is this situation, at first purely dialectical and quasi-verbal (and which is also true of the Intellect and the Soul, which remain with their principle in their higher parts, and are inclined only through their lower parts, a structure which still belongs to iconography), that the exceptional signifyingness of the trace delineates in the world. ". . . When the issue is the principle anterior to beings, that is to say, the One, this remains in itself; but although it remains in itself, no thing that is different from it produces the beings which conform to it; the One is enough to engender them [. . .] Here, the trace of the One gives birth to essence, and being is only the trace of the One."[75]

That which preserves the specific signifyingness of the trace in each trace of an empirical passage, over and above the sign it can become, is possible only through its situation in the trace of this transcendence. This position in a trace, which we have called *illeity*, does not begin in things, which by themselves do not leave traces but produce effects, that is, remain in the world. When a stone has scratched another stone, the scratch can, to be sure, be taken as a trace, but in fact without the man who held the stone this scratch is but an effect. It is as little a trace as the forest fire is a trace of the lightning. A cause and an effect, even separated by time, belong to the same world. Everything in things is exposed, even what is unknown in them. The traces that mark them are part of this plenitude of presence; their history is without a past. The trace qua trace does not simply lead to the past but is the very passing toward a past more remote than any past and any future which still are set in my time - the past of the Other in which eternity takes form, an absolute past which unites all times.

The absoluteness of the Other's presence, which has justified the interpretation of his epiphany in the exceptional straightforwardness (*droiture*) of thou-saying, is not the simple presence in which in the last analysis things are also present. Their presence still belongs to the present of *my* life. Everything that constitutes my life with its past and its future is assembled in the present in which things come to me. But it is in the trace of the Other that a face shines: what is presented there is absolving itself from my life and visits me as already ab-solute. Someone has already passed. His trace does not *signify* his past, as it does not *signify* his labor or his enjoyment in the world; it is the very disturbance imprinting itself (we are tempted to say *engraving* itself) with an irrecusable gravity.

The *illeity* of this *He* is not the *it* of things which are at our disposal and to which Buber and Gabriel Marcel rightly prefer the Thou to describe a human encounter. The movement of an encounter is not something added to an immobile face; it is in the face itself. A face is of itself a visitation and a transcendence. But the face, wholly open, can at the same time be in itself because it is in the trace of illeity. Illeity is the origin of the alterity of being in which the *in itself* of objectivity participates while also betraying it.

The God who passed[76] is not the model of which the face would be an image. To be in the image of God[77] does not mean to be an icon of God but to find oneself in his trace. The revealed God of our Judeo-Christian spirituality maintains all the infinity of his absence, which is in the personal "order" itself. He shows himself only by his trace, as is said in Exodus 33. To go toward Him is not to follow this trace, which is not a sign; it is to go toward the Others who stand in the trace of illeity. It is through this illeity, situated beyond the calculations and reciprocities of economy and of the world, that being has a sense. A sense which is not a finality.

For there is no end, no term. The Desire of the absolutely Other will not, like need, be extinguished in a happiness.

FOUR

Enigma and Phenomenon

(1965)

"Enigma and Phenomenon" marks an important stage in the transition from *Totality and Infinity* to *Otherwise than Being*.[1] Levinas draws attention to one of the changes himself. In a note he observes that he has overcome his previous reluctance to use the term *neighbor*. Previously the focus had fallen on the stranger. *Stranger* suggested itself to Levinas as a term for the Other for whom I am responsible, not least because it suggested the alterity of the Other as someone to whom I was not already in debt or with whom I was not communally bound. The introduction of the word *neighbor* alongside the word *stranger* would be relatively unimportant did it not bring with it the notion of proximity. Proximity, like neighbor, had already played a minor role in Levinas's thought. In "Enigma and Phenomenon," it was not yet the central notion that it would be in the exposition of substitution a decade later, but there are indications of the change. For example, at the end of the essay, *you* is no longer the *Vous* of *Totality and Infinity*, but *Tu*. What saves this from being a reversion to the Buberian *Du* is the *Il* of illeity that Levinas had introduced in "The Trace of the Other" and "Meaning and Sense" (chapter 3 in this volume). In "Enigma and Phenomenon," Levinas writes that a you (*tu*) is inserted between the I and the absolute He, but in terms of the development of Levinas's work one could equally say that the *Vous* of the stranger opens up into the relation of the *Tu* of the neighbor to the absolute *Il*.

The central issue of "Enigma and Phenomenon," although it is not posed as such, is the question of whether Levinas's thought is a phenomenology. The answer Levinas gives here, as elsewhere, is that he draws on phenomenology, but that the Other is not a phenomenon. The Other does not appear within the world but is an interruption or disturbance of it. In other words, the Other does not appear, but phenomenology gives access to the Other's nonappearance. The word Levinas uses here and in *Otherwise than Being* is *enigma*. It is a word that Levinas had rejected in the discussion following the lecture "Transcendence and Height" (chapter 2 in this volume). It is to explain how the enigma is retained that Levinas has recourse to Kierkegaardian subjectivity: "it is up to *me*."

Levinas sometimes seems to say that alterity is encountered in an experience. In "Enigma and Phenomenon," he is more cautious, particularly if experience is in some way thought of as an experience of the present. That is why the notion of the trace plays such an important role in the exposition. This role is particularly apparent in the fact that Levinas here changes his account of the trace in order to specifically distance it from the present. Whereas in "The Trace of the Other" and "Meaning and Sense," Levinas had written that "the trace is the presence of whoever, strictly speaking, has never been there (*été là*); of someone who is already past," in "Enigma and Phenomenon" Levinas says that "the past of the other must never have been present" and refers to "a past which was never a pure now." This shows Levinas acknowledging the characterization of ontology as dominated by the idea of presence and attempting to distance himself from it.

> In short, we still do not know if, when someone rings
> the doorbell, there is someone there or not . . .
>
> Ionesco, *The Bald Soprano*[2]

Rational Speech and Disturbance

As rational speech, philosophy is taken to move from evidence to evidence, directed to what is seen, to what shows itself, thus directed to the present. The term *present* suggests both the idea of a privileged position in the temporal series and the idea of manifestation. The idea of being connects them. As a presence, being excludes the nonbeing that marks the past and the future but assembles their residues and their germs, which, in structures, are contemporary.[3] Being is a manifestation in which uncertain memory and aleatory anticipation are moored; being is a presence to the gaze and to speech, an appearing, a phenomenon.

As a speech directed upon the present, philosophy is an understanding of being, or an ontology, or a phenomenology. In the order of its speech it encompasses and situates even what seemed first to contain this speech or overflow it, but which, when present, that is, discovered, fits into this logos, is ordered in it, even making what is discernible of the past or of the future in the present enter into it. Being and speech have the same time, are contemporary. To utter a speech that would not be anchored in the present would be to go beyond reason. Beyond what is discernible in the present, only meaningless speech would hold forth.

And yet human thought has known concepts or has, as though mad, operated with notions in which the distinction between presence and absence was not as clear-cut as the idea of being or the idea of a becoming assembled and tied about the present would have demanded. Such are the Platonic notions of the One and the Good.[4] Such is the notion of God, which a thought called faith succeeds in getting expressed and introduces into philosophical discourse. Is it not folly to ascribe plenitude of being to God, who, always absent from perception, is no longer manifest in the moral conduct of the world, subject to violence, where peace is established only provisionally and at the price of blood tribute paid to some Minotaur, the price of compromises and politics - where, consequently, the divine "presence" remains an uncertain memory or an indeterminate expectation? To endure the contradiction between the existence included in the essence of God and the scandalous absence of this God is to suffer an initiation trial into religious life which separates philosophers from believers. That is, unless the obstinate absence of God were one of those paradoxes that call to the highways.

The impossibility of manifesting itself in an experience can be due not to the finite or sensible essence of this experience but to the structure of all thought, which is correlation. Once come into a correlation, the divinity of God dissipates, like the clouds that served to describe his presence. All that could have attested to his holiness, that is, to his transcendence, in the light of experience would immediately belie its own witness already by its very presence and intelligibility, by its chain of significations, which constitute the world. To appear, to seem, is forthwith to resemble terms of an already familiar order, to compromise oneself with them, to be assimilated to them. Does not the invisibility of God belong to another game, to an approach which does not polarize into a subject-object correlation but is deployed as a drama with several personages?

But we have anticipated our conclusions. Let us fix the point of departure: the nonmanifestation, the invisibility which language sets forth. This refusal to exhibit itself does not necessarily contain a complacency for hidden abodes. The extravagance or hyperbole which language can express by the superlative of the supreme being retains the trace of a beyond-being where day and night do not divide the time that can make them coexist in the dusk of evening, the trace of a beyond borne by a time different from that in which the overflowings of the present flow back to this present across memory and hope. Could faith be described then as a glimpse into a time whose moments are no longer related to the present as their term or their source? This would produce a diachrony which maddens[5] the subject but channels transcendence. Is transcendence a thought that ventures beyond being or an approach[6] beyond thought which speech ventures to utter and whose trace and modality it retains?

But is not to glimpse into a time whose moments do not refer to the present to connect everything together again in the present of that glimpse? Already correlation or structure returns: transcendence is synchronized with speech and reenters the indestructible order of being in its undephasable simultaneity, that is, into a totality which gives it meaning. Is there nothing in the world that could refuse this primordial order of contemporaneousness, without immediately ceasing to signify? Is a truly diachronic transcendence nothing more than something to delude gratuitous imagination, opinion, and positive religions?

Everything depends on the possibility of vibrating with a meaning that is not synchronized with the speech that captures it and cannot be fitted into its order; everything depends on the possibility of a signification that would signify in an irreducible disturbance. If a formal description of such a disturbance could be attempted, it would have us speak of a time, a plot, and norms that are not reducible to the understanding of being, which is allegedly the alpha and the omega of philosophy.

The Call to Order

How could such a disturbance occur? If the Other is presented to the Same, the co-presence of the Other and the Same in a phenomenon forthwith constitutes an order. The discordance that may be produced within this order proposes itself as an invitation to the search for a new order in which this first discord would be resolved: the discordance becomes a problem. The science of yesterday, before the new facts of today, thus makes its way toward the science of tomorrow.

Bergson has taught us that disorder, like nothingness, is a relative idea.[7] For there to be an absolute disturbance, must there erupt into the Same an absolute alterity, that of the Other (*Autrui*)? Someone unknown to me rang my doorbell and interrupted my work. I dissipated a few of his illusions. But he brought me into his affairs and his difficulties, troubling my good conscience. The disturbance, the clash of two orders, ends in a conciliation, in the constitution of a new order which, more vast, closer to the total, and in this sense ultimate or original, order, shines through this conflict.

The Other (*Autrui*) can also not appear without renouncing his radical alterity, without entering into an order. The breaks in the order reenter the order whose weave lasts unendingly, a weave these breaks manifest, and which is a totality. The unwonted is understood. The apparent interference of the Other in the Same has been settled beforehand. The disturbance, the clash of two orders, then does not deserve our attention. That is, unless one is attached to abstractions. And who would admit to such bias? The disturbance was a precursor of a more concrete totality, a world, a history. That strident ringing of the bell is reabsorbed into significations; the break in my universe was a new signification that came to it. Everything is understood, justified, pardoned. And what of the surprise of that face behind the door? That surprise will be denied. Attention will be directed to the order that annuls the disturbance, the history in which men, their distress and their despairs, their wars and their sacrifices, the horrible and the sublime, are summed up. Like Spinoza, one will contest the possibility of an error that would not be borne by a partial truth and be on its way toward a whole truth.[8] An uninterrupted discourse will be exalted which death alone could stop, if the immortal intersubjectivity did not ensure it against death itself (is it indeed immortal? - one can raise this question, formerly taken to be absurd).[9] Everything that is real would thus be meaningful and every action would arise in the real as the conclusion of a reasoning, in an advance without shortcuts; a short circuit would, it seems, produce only the night of dreams.

Proximity, Expression, and Enigma

But is the disturbance produced by this abrupt coming completely reduced in the light of the new order, which, in its triumphant dawning, would absorb the unwonted visitation, as history effaces the trace of blood and tears? Across the unbreakable chain of significations, standing out against the historical conjuncture, was there not an expression, a face facing and interpellating, coming from the depths, cutting the threads of the context? Did not a neighbor approach?[10]

How did the neighbor tear himself up from the context? How could he approach and face without being forthwith petrified into a signification silhouetted against the context? Where could proximity and uprightness in a universe of mediations come from? Whence comes expression, *saying*, in this universe of significations *said*, of structures - Nature and History - visible to everyone in their display as phenomena? Would expression and proximity contain a reference to a dimension of depth?

One would be right to distrust this formula if it had to mean that phenomena *indicate* an order of "things in themselves" of which they would be signs, or which they would hide like a screen. For indications and relations reestablish a conjuncture, a simultaneity, between the indicating and the indicated terms and abolish depth. A relationship that would not create simultaneity between its terms but would hollow out a depth from which expression approaches would have to refer to an irreversible, immemorial, unrepresentable past.

But how refer to an irreversible past, that is, a past which this very reference would not bring back, like memory which retrieves the past, like signs which recapture the signified? What would be needed would be an indication that would reveal the withdrawal of the indicated, instead of a reference that rejoins it. Such is a trace, in its emptiness and desolation. Its desolation is not made of evocations but of forgettings, forgettings in process, putting aside the past. The forgettings are surprised before this "forgettingness" (*"obliviscence"*) could reverse into a bond, reconnect this absolute past to the present, and become evocative. What is this original trace, this primordial desolation? It is the nakedness of a face that faces, expressing itself, interrupting order. If the interruption is not taken up by the context interrupted, to receive a meaning from it, this is because it was already ab-solute. The context was given up before beginning, the breaking of contact took place before engagement: a face is decomposed and naked. In this defeatism,[11] this dereliction, this timidity that does not dare to dare, this solicitation that does not have the effrontery to solicit and is nonaudacity, this beggar's solicitation, expression no longer participates in the order from which it tears itself but thus faces and confronts in a face, approaches and disturbs absolutely.

But a trace would then simply be a sign of a remoteness. A trace can, to be sure, become a sign. But in a face before signifying as a sign it is the very emptiness of an irrecuperable absence. The gaping open of emptiness is not only the sign of an absence. A mark traced on sand is not a part of a path, but the very emptiness of a passage. And what has withdrawn is not evoked, does not return to presence, not even to an indicated presence.

Disturbance is a movement that does not propose any stable order in conflict or in accord with a given order; it is movement that already carries away the signification it brought: disturbance disturbs order without troubling it seriously. It enters in so subtle a way that unless we retain it, it has already withdrawn. It insinuates itself, withdraws before entering. It remains only for him who would like to take it up. Otherwise, it has already restored the order it troubled - someone rang, and there is no one at the door: did anyone ring? Language is the possibility of an enigmatic equivocation for better and for worse, which men abuse. One diplomat makes an exorbitant proposition to another diplomat, but this proposition is put in terms such that, if one likes, nothing has been said. The audacity withdraws and is extinguished in the very words that bear and inflame it. Such is the duplicity of oracles: extravagances are lodged in words that guarantee wisdom. A lover makes an advance, but the provocative or seductive gesture has, if one likes, not interrupted the decency of the conversation and attitudes; it withdraws as lightly as it had slipped in. A God was revealed on a mountain or in a burning bush, or was attested to in Scriptures. And what if it were a storm! And what if the Scriptures came to us from dreamers! Dismiss the illusory call from our minds! The insinuation itself invites us to do so. It is up to us, or, more exactly, it is up to *me* to retain or to repel this God without boldness, exiled because allied with the conquered, hunted down and hence ab-solute, thus disarticulating the very moment in which he is presented and proclaimed, unrepresentable. This way the Other has of seeking my recognition while preserving his *incognito*, disdaining recourse to a wink-of-the-eye of understanding or complicity, this way of manifesting himself without manifesting himself, we call enigma - going back to the etymology of this Greek term,[12] and contrasting it with the indiscreet and victorious appearing of a *phenomenon*.

A New Modality

What is essential here is the way a meaning that is beyond meaning is inserted in the meaning that remains in an order, the way it advances while retreating.

An enigma is not a simple ambiguity in which two significations have equal chances and the same light. In an enigma the exorbitant meaning is already effaced in its apparition. The God who spoke said nothing, passed incognito, everything in the light of phenomena gives lie to him, refutes, represses, persecutes him. The Kierkegaardian God is revealed only to be persecuted and unrecognized, reveals himself only in the measure that he is hunted - such that subjectivity, despairing in the solitude in which this absolute humility leaves it, becomes the very locus of truth. The Kierkegaardian God is not simply the bearer of certain attributes of humility; he is a way of truth which this time is not determined by a phenomenon, by the present and contemporaneousness, and is not measured by certainty. This truth is irreducible to phenomena and is hence essential in a world which can no longer believe that the books about God attest to transcendence as a phenomenon and to the Ab-solute as an apparition. And without the good reasons atheism brings forth, there would have been no Enigma. Apart from the salvation drama whose play in existence Kierkegaard, a Christian thinker, fixed and described, his properly philosophical work seems to us to lie in the formal idea of a truth persecuted in the name of a universally evident truth, a meaning paling in a meaning, a meaning thus already past and driven out, breaking up the *undephasable simultaneity* of phenomena.[13] The God "remaining with the contrite and humble" (Isaiah 57:15), on the margin, a "persecuted truth," is not only a religious "consolation" but the original form of "transcendence." He is the node of an intrigue separate from the adventure of being which occurs in phenomena and in immanence, a new modality which is expressed by that "if one likes" and that "perhaps," which one must not reduce to the possibility, reality, and necessity of formal logic, to which skepticism itself refers.[14]

Disturbance is then not the breakup of a category too narrow for the order, which this breakup would then let shine forth in the setting of a broader category. Nor is it the shock of a provisional incomprehension which will soon *become* understanding. It is not as something irrational or absurd that disturbance disturbs. For the irrational presents itself to consciousness and lights up only within an intelligibility in which it ends by being situated and defined. No one is irrational knowing that he is.

The disturbance that is not the surprise of the absurd is possible only as the entry into a given order of another order which does not accommodate itself with the first. Thus we exclude from disturbance the simple parallelism of two orders that would be in a relationship of sign to signified, of appearance to thing in itself, and between which, we have said, the relationship would reestablish the simultaneity of one single order. But it is also not a question of the meeting of two series of significations that each, with equal rights, lay claim to the same phenomenon, as when a revolution is ascribed both to economic and to political causality, or a work of art both to the biography of the artist and to his philosophy, or when, in the ambiguity of metaphors, a literal meaning is inseparable from the figurative meaning and neither vanishes nor is absorbed in the meaning that nourishes it, but the two meanings glimmer in the same dawn, both turned to the light. In both these cases the different orders are simultaneous, or have a point of contact and synchronism. The tearing up of one order from another would already be a reciprocal participation. *The difference between contents is not strong enough to break the continuous form, the unbreakable plot, in which this difference is still regulated.*

For there to be a possibility of disturbance, a fissile present is required, "destructuring" itself in its very punctuality. The alterity that disturbs order cannot be reduced to the difference visible to the gaze that compares and therefore synchronizes the Same and the Other. *Alterity occurs as a divergency and a past* which no memory could resurrect as a present. And yet disturbance is possible only through an intervention. A stranger is then needed, one who has come, to be sure, but left *before* having come, ab-solute in his manifestation. "At the same time" would not be enough for the breakup of order. In order that the tearing up from order not be ipso facto a participation in order, this tearing up, this abstraction, must, by a supreme anachronism, precede its entry into order; the past of the Other must never have been present.

This anachronism is less paradoxical than it seems. The temporal continuity of consciousness is *overwhelmed* whenever it is a "consciousness" of the Other, and "against all expectation," counter to all attention and anticipation, the "sensational" *turns back* the sensation that brings it. The - voluptuous - *acumen*, while still rising, has already fallen.[15] Self-consciousness is kept breathless with tension or relaxation, in the before or the after. In the *meanwhile* the event expected turns into the past without being lived through, without being equaled, in any present. Something takes place between the Dusk in which the most ecstatic intentionality, which, however, never aims far enough, is lost (or is recollected) and the Dawn in which consciousness returns to itself, but already too late for the event which is moving away. The great "experiences" of our life have properly speaking never been lived. Are not religions said to come to us from a past which was never a pure now? Their grandeur is due to this exorbitance exceeding the capacity of phenomena, of the present and of memory. To the voice that calls from the Burning Bush, Moses answers, "Here I am," but does not dare to lift up his eyes. The glorious theophany which makes so much humility possible will be missed because of the humility which lowers the eyes.[16] Later, on the rock of Horeb, the prophet ventures to know, but glory is refused to the boldness that seeks it. As transcendence, a pure passage, it shows itself as past.[17] It is a trace.

The enigma does not come from afar to obscure a phenomenal manifestation, as though this manifestation - proportionate to cognition, that is, rational - were interrupted by mysterious islands of the Irrational in which the double flowers of faith grow. The enigma extends as far as the phenomenon that bears the trace of the *saying* which has already withdrawn from the *said*. All the moments of historical time are fissile; the enchainment of the Story is exposed to interruption. This is nowise an anthropological particularity, since language does not come to double up phenomena, so that men could point them out to one another. The significations of Nature are but the result of a transfer of meaning from the anthropological to the natural. The human face is the face of the world itself, and the individual of the human race, like all things, arises already within the humanity of the world. This humanity is not anonymous but is the humanity aimed at in him or her who, when his or her face shines, is just him or her one had been waiting for. Human sexuality is perhaps but this expectation of an unknown, but known, face. Significations which link up cover over the traces of the *saying* that left them, as the perfect crime artist inserts the traces of his violence in the natural folds of Order. Phenomena open to disturbance, a disturbance letting itself be brought back to order: such is the ambiguity of an Enigma. A manifestation turns into an expression, a skin left desolate by an irreversible departure which immediately denies it, reverted to the state of a ridge of sand on the earth, driving out even the memory of this departure. But the earth's crust remains permeable to expression, and space, the "pure form of the sensibility" and the "object of a geometry,"[18] gapes open as a void in which the irreversible is not re-presented. Expression, saying, is not added on to significations that are "visible" in the light of phenomena, to modify them or confuse them and introduce into them "poetic," "literary," "verbal" enigmas; the significations *said* offer a hold to the *saying* which "disturbs" them, like writings awaiting an interpretation. But herein is the - in principle - irreversible antecedence of the Word with respect to Being, the irretrievable delay of the Said after the Saying. Of this antecedence, the significations which, meanwhile, suffice to themselves, bear a trace, which they forthwith contest and efface.

Subjectivity and "Illeity"

All speaking is an enigma. It is, to be sure, established in and moves in an order of significations common to the interlocutors, in the midst of triumphant, that is, primary truths, in a particular language that bears a system of known truths which the speaking, however commonplace it is, does stir up and lead on to new significations. But behind this renewal, which constitutes cultural life, the

Saying, that is, the face, is the discretion of an unheard-of proposition, an insinuation, immediately reduced to nothing, breaking up like the "bubbles of the earth," which Banquo speaks of at the beginning of *Macbeth*.[19] Yet what can an attentive ear hear, listening at the doorway of language, which by the significations of which it is made closes on its own apertures? It is perhaps reasonable to respect the decency of this closed door. This door thus both open and closed is the extra-ordinary duplicity of the Enigma. But the Enigma concerns so particularly subjectivity, which alone can retain its insinuation, this insinuation is so quickly belied when one seeks to communicate it, that this exclusivity takes on the sense of an assignation first raising up such a being as a subjectivity. Summoned to appear, called to an inalienable responsibility - whereas the disclosure of Being occurs in the knowledge and sight of universality - subjectivity is enigma's partner, partner of the transcendence that disturbs being.

How does it happen that there is subjectivity in being? Why is the silence of a breath held back produced in the bustling of the totality? In order to tear itself from the ontological weight, must not the subjectivity have to have received some most private convocation to appear from beyond being and the rational enchainment of its significations? This message is untranslatable into objective language, undefendable by coherent speech, null compared with the public order of the disclosed and triumphant significations of nature and history. It nonetheless summons with precision and urgency, because it first hollows out the dimension of inwardness. What good is inwardness, the extreme privacy of the singular ego, if it has to reflect beings or the being of beings, whose dwelling is in the light, which is of itself reason, and whose repetition in the psyche or the subjectivity would be a luxury in the economy of being? Must luxury double up the light? A quite different intrigue takes form in the I.

Phenomena, apparition in the full light, the relationship with being, ensure immanence as a totality and philosophy as atheism. The enigma, the intervention of a meaning which disturbs phenomena but is quite ready to withdraw like an undesirable stranger, unless one harkens to those footsteps that depart, is transcendence itself, the proximity of the Other as Other.

Other than Being. Being excludes all alterity. It can leave nothing outside and cannot remain outside, cannot let itself be ignored. The being of beings is the light in which all things are in relationship. Its very night is a mute and concerted hammering out of all things, the obscure labor of the totality, an uninterrupted thrust of generation, growth, and corruption. But the other distinguishes himself absolutely, by absolving himself, moving off, passing, passing beyond being, to yield his place to being. Passing beyond being: this is the supreme goodness that would belie itself if it proclaimed itself! It is, to be sure, possible to ask anew if this departure, this humility of being ab-solute, this divinity, does or does not exist. And nothing can stop this triumphant question. For how transparent is the shadow that troubles the clarity of coherent speech! How light is the voice of the "subtle silence"[20] that covers its victorious noise, how irresistible the authority of the call to order! But how empty is the space that the word that knows how to speak as though nothing had been said leaves to being.

An enigma is beyond not finite cognition but all cognition. Cognition rests on apparition, on phenomena, which the being of beings unfolds, putting all things together by light, ordering order. Taken in the light, inevitably contemporaneous, things are present even in their most secret hiding places, as though being were a game of blind-man's bluff where a blindfold over your eyes does not prevent presence from calling to you from all sides. But what in an Enigma has signifyingness does not take refuge in a sphere that is present in its own way and awaits a concept capable of finding and grasping it there. The signifyingness of an Enigma comes from an irreversible, irrecuperable past which it has *perhaps* not left since it has already been absent from the very terms in which it was signaled ("perhaps" is the modality of an enigma, irreducible to the modalities of being and certainty). We hear this way to signify - which does not consist in being unveiled nor in being veiled, absolutely foreign to the hide-and-seek characteristic of cognition, this way of leaving the alternatives of being - under the third-person personal pronoun, under the word He (*Il*). The enigma comes to us from Illeity. The enigma is the way of the Ab-solute, foreign to cognition, not because it would not shine with a light disproportionately strong for the subject's weak sight but because it is already too old for the game of cognition, because it does not lend itself to the contemporaneousness that constitutes the force of the time tied in the present, because it imposes a completely different version of time. While being designates a community, without any possible dissidence, of the totality of fate and the undephasable contemporaneousness of cognition or comprehension (even historical)[21] to which the time tied in the present lends itself, in the trace of *illeity*, in the Enigma, the synchronism falls out of tune, the totality is transcended in another time. This extravagant movement of going beyond being or transcendence toward an immemorial antiquity we call the idea of infinity. The infinite is an inassimilable alterity, a difference and ab-solute past with respect to everything that is shown, signaled, symbolized, announced, remembered, and thereby "contemporized" with him who understands. It is absolution, anachorism - unto what abode? Its abode is in the refusal to dare, in Goodness, which excludes precisely all complacency in oneself and in one's definition, is not petrified in an image, never tempts. The infinite is a withdrawal like a farewell which is signified not by opening oneself to the gaze to inundate it with light but in being extinguished in the incognito in the face that faces. For this, as we have said, there must be someone who is no longer agglutinated in being, who, at his own risk, responds to the enigma and grasps the allusion. Such is the subjectivity, alone, unique, secret, which Kierkegaard caught sight of.

Ethics

This assignation - categorical in its straightforwardness but already discrete, as though no one assigned and no one checked - summons to moral responsibility. Morality is the Enigma's way.

How is a response made?

To the idea of the Infinite only an extravagant response is possible. There has to be a "thought" that understands more than it understands, more than its capacity, of which it cannot be contemporary, a "thought" which, in this sense, could go beyond its death. To understand more than one understands, to think more than one thinks, to think of what withdraws from thought, is to desire, with a desire that, unlike need, is renewed and becomes ardent the more it is nourished with the Desirable. To go beyond one's death is to sacrifice oneself. The response to the Enigma's summons is the generosity of sacrifice outside the known and the unknown, without calculation, for going on to infinity.

If what is Desirable to Desire is infinite, it cannot be given as an end.[22] The infinite's impossibility to be an end for the Desire it arouses preserves it from contemporaneousness, precisely by reason of its infinitude. The way in which Desire goes to infinity is thus not the correlation characteristic of cognition. Even if it, with a different intentionality, should become an axiology or a praxis, the movement would still go from a subject to an object and would imitate correlation. Desire, or the response to an Enigma or morality, is an intrigue with three personages: the I approaches the Infinite by going generously toward the You, who is still my contemporary, but, in the trace of Illeity, presents himself out of a depth of the past, faces, and approaches me. I approach the infinite insofar as I forget myself for my neighbor who looks at me; I forget myself only in breaking the undephasable simultaneity of representation, in existing beyond my death. I approach the infinite by sacrificing myself. Sacrifice is the norm and the criterion of the approach. And the truth of transcendence consists in the concording of speech with acts.

"Beyond Being"

The unwonted intrigue which solicits the I and comes to a head beyond cognition and disclosure in Enigma is ethics. The relationship with the Infinite is not a cognition but an approach, a neighboring with what signifies itself without revealing itself, what departs but not to dissimulate itself. As Infinite, it cannot lend itself to the present in which this play of clarity and abscondity is enacted. The relationship with the Infinite then no longer has the structure of an intentional correlation. The supreme anachronism of a *past* that was never a *now*, and the approach of the infinite through sacrifice - is the Enigma's word. A face can appear as a face, as a proximity interrupting the series, only if it enigmatically comes from the Infinite and its immemorial past. And the Infinite, to solicit Desire, a thought thinking more than it thinks, cannot be incarnated in a Desirable, cannot, qua infinite, be shut up in an end. It solicits across a face, the term of my generosity and my sacrifice. A You is inserted between the I and the absolute He.[23] Correlation is broken.

It is then vain to posit an absolute You. The absolute withdraws from the illuminated site, the "clearing"[24] of the present, in which being is unveiled and in which speech about speech still claims, and perhaps legitimately, to be a speech about being. This speech will take pleasure in showing that order remains ever intact. But the absolute which withdraws has disturbed it: the illuminated site of being is but the passage of God. It is not a tomb in which his form would be sketched out, for the site of the Same, deserted by the absolutely Other, could never contain the infinity of alterity. He who has passed beyond has never been a presence. He preceded all presence and exceeded every contemporaneity in a time which is not a human duration, nor a falsified projection, nor an extrapolation of duration, is not a disintegration and disappearance of finite beings, but the original antecedence of God relative to a world which cannot accommodate him, the immemorial past which has never presented itself, which cannot be said with the categories of Being and structure, but is the One, which every philosophy would like to express, beyond being.[25]

FIVE

Substitution

(1968)

Levinas presented "Substitution" in 1967 as a lecture in Brussels before revising it for publication the following year in *La Revue Philosophique de Louvain*.[1] In 1974, the essay was further modified to serve as the "centerpiece" of *Otherwise than Being* (OB xli). The importance Levinas attached to the essay seems entirely justified. In "Substitution" and the companion essay, "Language and Proximity," Levinas introduced into his philosophical writings the notions of substitution, hostage, and persecution. These terms had already played a role in his confessional writings. Their introduction here must be understood as part of Levinas's attempt to avoid the traditional language of ontology, something which he conceded that he had failed to do in *Totality and Infinity*.

The novelty of "Substitution" is not restricted to the terminology it employs. "Substitution" offers a reexamination of the Western philosophical concept of identity, which Levinas associates with self-coincidence, self-possession, and sovereignty. In *Totality and Infinity* the philosophical concept of identity remained largely intact. It was as if Levinas feared that to question it might diminish the sense of one's responsibility. Even though the major thrust of *Totality and Infinity* is to say that the Other puts me in question, it was only in the analyses of fecundity toward the end of the book that the identity of the I was explicitly challenged. In "Substitution" the identity of the I is under challenge, specifically in the context of responsibility. Unlike the conventional conception of responsibility, whereby I am primarily responsible only for what I have chosen, Levinas conceives of a responsibility to which one is elected and by which one finds oneself answerable for everything and everyone, even for one's persecutors. The primary language of *Totality and Infinity* is that of the Same and the Other. This language finds its way into the "Substitution" essay, but it is not left uncomplicated, as when Levinas employs the phrase "one-for-the-other."

The text printed here is the first English translation of the 1968 version of the essay. Levinas made numerous additions and changes before republishing the essay in *Otherwise than Being*. Readers familiar with the later version may miss some of the striking formulations added there, such as the qualified endorsement of Kant's categorical imperative if only it could be freed from the details of Kant's system. They may also be struck by the absence of words such as *goodness*, *guilt*, and *expiation*, which are prominent in the later version. However, the most decisive difference is that the earlier version published here seems the more focused and, importantly for such a difficult essay, the easier of the two to follow. Even so, the translators have chosen to divide some of Levinas's larger sentences into more manageable units and to offer interpretive renderings of some of Levinas's more elliptical sentences. For a better idea of the style adopted by Levinas in his later texts, the reader is invited to consult the translation of "Peace and Proximity" (chapter 10 in this volume).

1. Principle and Anarchy

In the relationship with beings which is called consciousness, we identify these beings through the dispersion of "adumbrations"[2] in which they appear. Similarly, in self-consciousness, we identify ourselves through a multiplicity of temporal phases.[3] It is as though subjective life, in the form of consciousness, involved being's losing and rediscovering itself, so as *to possess itself* by showing itself, proposing itself as a *theme*, exposing itself in the truth. This identification is not the *counterpart* of any image. It is a *claim* of the mind, proclamation, saying, kerygma. It is by no means arbitrary, however, resting as it does on a mysterious operation of schematism,[4] through which an ideality corresponds with the dispersion of aspects and images, adumbrations or phases. Consciousness is therefore always the grasping of a being through an ideality. Even an empirical, individual being appears through the ideality of the logos. Subjectivity as consciousness is thus interpreted as an ontological event, namely, the rediscovery of being on the basis of an ideal principle or *arche* in its thematic exposition. The detour of ideality leads to a coinciding with oneself, that is, to the certainty which remains the guide and guarantee of the whole spiritual adventure of Being. That is why the "adventure" is not exactly an adventure. It is never dangerous. It is always a self-possession, sovereignty, *arche*. What arrives of the *unknown* is already disclosed, open, manifest, cast in the mold of the *known*, and can never come as a complete surprise. For the Western philosophical tradition, all spirituality is consciousness, the thematic exposition of Being, that is to say, knowledge.

In starting with *touching*, interpreted not as palpation but as caress, and *language*, interpreted not as the traffic of information but as contact, we have tried to describe *proximity* as irreducible to consciousness and thematization.[5] Proximity is a relationship with what cannot be resolved into "images" and exposed. It is a relationship not with what is inordinate with respect to a theme but with what is incommensurable with it; with what cannot be identified in the kerygmatic logos, frustrating any schematism.

Incapable of remaining in a theme and of appearing, this invisibility that becomes contact does not result from the nonsignifyingness of what is approached but rather from a way of signifying wholly other than that of exhibition from a *beyond* of the visible. Not that the "beyond" would be "further" than everything that appears, or "present in absence," or revealed by a symbol, which would again be to submit to a principle and to give oneself to consciousness. Here what is essential lies in the refusal to let oneself be domesticated or subdued by a theme. The "beyond" loses its proper signifyingness and becomes immanence as soon as the logos interrogates, invests, presents, and exposes it, although its attachment in proximity is absolute exteriority. Without any common measure with the present, proximity is always "already past," above the "now" which it troubles and obsesses. This way of passing, troubling the present, without allowing itself to be invested by the *arche* of consciousness, this striation of rays across the clarity or the exposable, we have called "trace."[6] *Anarchically*, proximity is a relationship with a singularity, without the mediation of any principle or ideality. In the concrete, it describes my relationship with the neighbor, a relationship whose signifyingness is prior to the celebrated "sense bestowing."[7] This incommensurability with regard to consciousness, emerging as a trace from *I know not where*, is neither the inoffensive relation of knowledge where everything is equivalent nor the indifference of spatial contiguity. It is the summoning of myself by the other (*autrui*), it is a responsibility toward those whom we do not even know. The relation of proximity does not amount to any modality of distance or geometrical contiguity, nor to the simple "representation" of the neighbor. It is *already* a summons of extreme exigency, an obligation which is *anachronistically* prior to every engagement. An anteriority that is older than the a priori. This formulation expresses a way of being affected that can in no way be invested by spontaneity: the subject is affected without the source of the affection becoming a theme of re-presentation. The term *obsession* designates this relation which is irreducible to consciousness.

Irreducible to consciousness, even if this relation overturns consciousness and manifests itself there - obsession traverses consciousness contrariwise, inscribing itself there as something foreign, as disequilibrium, as delirium, undoing thematization, eluding *principle*, origin, and will, all of which are affirmed in every gleam of consciousness. This movement is, in the original sense of the term, an-archic. In no way, then, is obsession to be confused with a hypertrophy of consciousness.

An-archy is not a matter of disorder as opposed to order, just as the withdrawal from a theme is not a putative return to a diffuse "field of consciousness" awaiting attention.[8] Disorder is but another order, and the diffuse can possibly be thematized.[9] Anarchy troubles being beyond these alternatives. It halts the ontological play, which, precisely as play, is consciousness in which being loses and rediscovers itself and is thereby lit up. Anachronistically *lagging* behind its present, incapable of recovering this lag and of thinking what touches it,[10] the Ego is evinced in the ascendancy of the Other over the Same to the point of interruption, leaving it speechless: an-archic, obsession is persecution. Here persecution does not amount to consciousness gone mad; it designates the manner in which the Ego is affected and a defection from consciousness. This inversion of consciousness is without doubt a passivity, but a passivity this side of all passivity, defined in terms totally different from those of intentionality, where *submission* is always also an *assuming*, that is, an experience always forestalled and sanctioned, attached once more to an origin. The intentionality of consciousness certainly does not refer solely to a voluntary intention. And yet it does retain the initiating and inchoate motif of a voluntary intention. Thought recognizes and invests its very project in the given which enters it. The given manifests itself a priori - from the first, it re-presents itself - but it does not knock at the door unannounced, allowing, across the interval of space and time, the leisure necessary for welcome. The *for itself* is thus the power that a being exercises over itself, its will and sovereignty, where it is equal to itself and in possession of itself. Domination is within consciousness as such and Hegel thought that the *I* is simply consciousness mastering itself in equality with itself, what he called "the freedom of this infinite equality."

The obsession we have recognized in proximity contrasts strongly with this view of a being possessing itself in equality with itself. How can the passivity of obsession find a place in consciousness, where everything is intentionally assumed? Consciousness is total freedom, or is ultimately that; and it is total equality, equality of self with self, but also equality to the extent that, for consciousness, responsibility is always strictly measured in terms of freedom, and thus always limited. How can there be in consciousness an undergoing, or a Passion, whose "active" source would not in any way fall into consciousness? It is important to stress this exteriority, which is neither objective nor spatial. Irrecuperable in immanence, and thus outside the order (or command) of consciousness, exteriority is obsessional, nonthematizable, and, in the sense defined above, an-archic. We might go so far as to say "extra-ordinary."

It is in a *responsibility that is justified by no prior commitment* - in the responsibility for the other (*autrui*) - an ethical situation, that the me-ontological[11] and meta-logical structure of this Anarchy is outlined, undoing the logos framing the apology through which consciousness still recovers itself and commands. This Passion is absolute in that it takes hold without any a priori. Consciousness is thus afflicted before entertaining an image of what reaches it, afflicted in spite of itself. Under these characteristics, we recognize persecution, a placing in question anterior to questioning, a responsibility beyond the logos of the response, as though persecution by the other (*autrui*) were the basis of solidarity with the other (*autrui*). How can such a Passion[12] have a place and time in consciousness?

2. Recurrence and the Hither Side

Does consciousness exhaust the notion of subjectivity? Is there not a condition in the Ego that is still tacitly reduced to consciousness? Does the Ego coincide with the *for itself* of consciousness? We have long since treated subjectivity and consciousness as equivalent concepts, without interrogating the dimension masked by the controversial notion of soul. We must ask ourselves whether the notion of the Ego can be reduced to the *for itself* of consciousness.

But to speak of the hither side of consciousness is not to turn toward the unconscious. The unconscious, in its clandestinity, rehearses the game played out in consciousness,[13] namely, the search for meaning and truth as the search for the self. While this opening onto the self is certainly occluded and repressed, psychoanalysis still manages to break through and restore self-consciousness. It follows that our study will not be following the way of the unconscious.

The reduction of subjectivity to consciousness dominates philosophical thought, which, since Hegel, has striven to overcome the dualism of being and thought by identifying, under different forms, substance and subject.[14] Philosophy itself would be the ongoing and progressive disclosure of Being to itself. Consequently, disclosure is not annexed to the being of beings, to *essence* (if the term *essence* may be used in italics as an abstract noun of action[15] for the "being of beings"), but is constitutive of this *essence* as a perpetual vigilance and self-possession. The philosophy that proposes an ontology consummates this *essence* through this proposition, through the logos, whence the idea of consciousness fulfilling the very being of beings.

The disclosure of being to itself involves a *recurrence*, which poses a problem. *Essence* is drawn out like a colorless thread woven from the distaff of the Parcae.[16] For there to be a return, must not the knot of ipseity be tied at some point? Were this not so, *essence* would continually elude itself, stretching out like a destiny. How can a jolt, an expulsion outside of the Same, an awakening and tracking down of the Same, the very play of *consciousness*, occur in the stretching out of *essence*? How can this distance with regard *to the self* and nostalgia of the self or retention of the self, according to which every present is a re-presentation, be produced? Must not all the articulations of this movement require the "rhythm" or the "pulse" of ipseity? Is not this rhythm in its turn but the disclosure of being to itself, the representation of being by itself, the identity of this "itself" being without mystery? Does not everything take place as if the disclosure of self to self came to be added to the identity of the object, an identity originating in the idealizing identification that thematizing thought bestows kerygmatically on adumbrations?[17] What is the relation between the "oneself" and the *for self* of representation? Is the "oneself" a recurrence of the same type as consciousness, knowledge, and representation, all of which would be sublimated in consciousness conceived as Mind? Is the "oneself" consciousness in its turn, or is it not a quite distinct event, one which would justify the use of separate terms: Self, I, Ego, soul?

Philosophers have for the most part described the identity of the oneself in terms of the return to self of consciousness. For Sartre, like Hegel, the *oneself* is posited as a *for itself*.[18] The identity of the *I* would thus be reducible to a turning back of *essence* upon itself, a return to itself of essence as both subject and condition of the identification of the Same. The sovereignty of the "oneself," positing itself as one being among others, or as a central being, would only be an abstraction referring back to the concrete process of Truth where this return is accomplished; referring back, consequently, to the exposition of being - lost and rediscovered - to the expatiation and stretching out of time, referring back to the logos. This approach must be placed in question.

The identity of ipseity is not due to any kind of distinguishing characteristic, a *unicum* or a *hapax*,[19] like fingerprints, and which as a principle of individuation would win for this identity a proper noun and thus a place in speech. The identity of the "oneself" is not the inertia of an individuated quiddity resulting from any incomparable quality inherent in the body or character, or the unicity of a natural or historical conjuncture.

The identity of the *oneself* is not equivalent to the identity of identification. This is so even if one seeks a source for the individual in the logos, wherein an ideal identity is proclaimed across an indefinite multiplicity of adumbrations via the schematism of discourse; and it is so even if the identity of the subject is bound to a process of identification through the structure of intentionality, be it that of immanent time in the Husserlian sense, in which is displayed not inertia but the scission of "eternal rest," nostalgia and rediscovery.[20] The oneself which lives (we are almost tempted to say, without metaphor, which palpitates) alongside the movements of consciousness or intentionality, which are said to constitute it, does not bear its identity as do identical beings, themes, or parts of discourse, where they show themselves and where it is necessary that they remain identical; that is to say, they say themselves without being unsaid. The identity of ipseity is to be distinguished from the identity which allows a being to enter into discourse, to be thematized, and to appear to consciousness.

To be sure, reflection *upon* the self is possible, but this reflection does not *constitute* the living *recurrence* of subjectivity, a recurrence without duality, but a unity without rest, whose un-rest is due neither to dispersion of exterior givens nor to the flux of time biting into the future while conserving a past. The living identity of oneself is not distinguished from the self and does not lend itself to either a synthetic activity or recollection or anticipation. To present the knot of ipseity which is tied into the straight thread of *essence* according to the model of intentionality of the *for itself*, or as an opening on the self, is to presuppose a new ipseity behind ipseity. Ipseity is an indefeasible unity that has never been separated from the self. Perhaps it is this that explains Leibniz's mysterious formula: "the ego is innate to itself."[21] The oneself guards the secret of its identification as a contraction, as an "entrance within." Unlike conscious-ness, which loses itself so as to find itself again in the retentions and protentions of its time, the oneself does not slacken the knot attaching it to the self only to tie it once more. It does not enter into the indiscreet play of concealments and unconcealments known as the phenomenon (or phenomenology, since the appearing of the phenomenon is already discourse). It is not a question of keeping or telling a secret, a concern for nondivulgence. The oneself is the irremissible identity that has no need to prove or thematize this identity. The oneself is "in itself" as one is in one's skin.

The fulcrum where the return of being to itself as knowledge or Mind is produced thus indicates the singularity par excellence. To be sure, this singu-larity may appear in an indirect language as a proper noun, as a *being*, situated at the threshold of generality, characteristic of every signification, whereby it is capable of referring to *essence*. But, as an original nonquiddity - no one - clothed as a being by a pure borrowing that masks its nameless singularity by bestowing it with a role, the fulcrum of the mind is a personal pronoun. If the return to self of knowledge, which is consciousness, the original truth of being, can be accomplished, this is because the recurrence of ipseity has already been produced. An inversion in the process of *essence* is a move *outside the game* that being plays in consciousness. It is precisely a withdrawal *in itself*, an exile *in itself*, without foundation in anything else, a noncondition. It is a withdrawal without spontaneity, and thus always already over, always already past. Ipseity is not an abstract point, a center of rotation, identifiable by way of the trajectory traced by a movement of consciousness. It is here and now identified without having to identify itself in the present, nor having to "decline" its identity, already older than the time of consciousness.

The identity of singularity does not issue from the identification of a being within *essence*.[22] It does not result from a synthesis of phases, nor, as identity, is it modified by the erosion of aging. An identity unutterable, shameful, and hence unjustifiable - these negative qualifications of subjectivity pertaining to the *oneself* do not hallow some ineffable mystery. They confirm a unity of the self which is presynthetic, prelogical, and (in some way) atomic, precluding the splitting up or separation of the self from itself, preventing it from showing itself (since no longer under a mask) and from being named otherwise than by a pro-noun. This prevention is the positivity of the One. But how this unity can be a tension, irreducible to the function carried out by the oneself in the ontology accomplished by consciousness, where, through the one-self, it operates its return upon itself - this is the question.

The oneself does not rest in peace under its identity. And yet its unrest is neither a splitting nor a process which levels difference. Its unity is not simply attached to some content of ipseity, like an indefinite article which substantifies even verbs in "nominalizing" and thematizing them. Here, unity precedes every article and every process. It is, in a sense, the content itself. The oneself, a unity in both form and content, is a singularity this side of the distinction between the particular and the universal.

This relation is not a pure and simple repetition of consciousness where being gathers itself, as the sea gathers the waves that lap the shore. It is a relation without a disjunction of the terms that are in relation, a relation which does not lead back to the intentional opening upon the self. The ego is *in itself* not like matter is in itself, which, perfectly wedded to its form, is what it is. The ego is in itself like one is in one's skin, that is to say, cramped, ill at ease in one's skin, as though the identity of matter weighing on itself concealed a dimension allowing a withdrawal this side of immediate coincidence, as though it concealed a materiality more material than all matter. The ego is an irritability, a susceptibility, or an exposure to wounding and outrage, delineating a passivity more passive still than any passivity relating to an effect. This *hither side* of identity is not reducible to the *for itself*, where a being recognizes itself in its difference beyond its immediate identity. Here we are obliged to speak of the irremissibility and the anguish (in the etymological sense of the term) of this *in itself* of the Oneself.[23] This anguish is not the existential "being-toward-death" but the constriction of an "entry within," which is not a flight into the void but a passage into the fullness of the anxiety of contraction.[24] Such is the relation in which a being is immolated without taking leave of itself - without becoming ecstatic. Unable to take a distance from itself, it is hunted down in itself, on the hither side of resting in itself and of self-coincidence. This recurrence, which could certainly be called negativity (albeit a negativity prior to discourse as the indisputable homeland of dialectical negativity) - this recurrence of contraction - is the Self.

The negativity of the *in itself* (in the dual sense of *an sich* and *in sich*) has none of the openness of nothingness, but is a passage into fullness. Behind the distinction between rest and motion, between being *at home with oneself* and adventure, between equality and difference, this negativity brings to mind the formulae of the *Parmenides* describing the moment where the One "being in motion . . . comes to rest, and when being at rest . . . changes to motion," and where "it must itself be in no time at all" (156c). This "strange kind of nature," which "is interposed between motion and rest" (156d),[25] is not a break in time dynamically preserving a potential contradiction between present and future, or between present and past. Nor is it an extratemporal ideality governing temporal dispersion. Both of these in their own way imply the ontological adventure. This "strange kind of nature" is a *hither side* outside of all dialectical germination and all reference (even references to references, growing like an "itch"). Absolutely sterile and pure, completely cut off from adventure and reminiscence. No-place. A wrong time or between time (or bad-time)[26] - nonbeing, but on this side of being and nothingness thematizable as being.

The expression "in one's skin" is not simply a metaphor for the *in itself*. It relates to a recurrence in the dead time or the *between-time* separating inspiration and expiration, the diastole and systole of the heart beating softly against the lining of one's own skin. The body is not merely an image or a figure; above all, it is the in-oneself and contraction of ipseity.[27]

The fundamental concept of ipseity, while tied to incarnation, is not a biological concept. (Indeed, must not the original meaning of the "lived body" be sought in the "in itself" conceived as "in one's skin"?) The ontological (or me-ontological) movement of contraction takes us further. It outlines a schema in corporeality which permits us to attach the biological to a higher structure. Let us indicate this briefly for the moment: negativity without the void of nonbeing, negativity entangled in its own impossibility, outside of all initiative, an incredible withdrawal into fullness, without any detachment from self, is an impossibility of slipping away, a responsibility anterior to any free commitment. The oneself is a responsibility for the freedom of others.

3. The Self and Persecution

To return to our initial development, we wish to know if the passive folding back upon the self of ipseity (which, though it does not have the virtue of being an *act* of folding back, still makes possible the act of consciousness returning to itself) coincides with the an-archic passivity of obsession. Is not obsession a relationship with the outside, prior to the act that would open up the outside? Obsession is a total passivity, more passive still than the passivity of things. Things as "prime matter" bear the weight of the kerygmatic logos, which gives this matter its characteristics. Through falling under the directives of this saying, matter takes on a meaning and shows itself as this or that, i.e., a thing. This fall (or case), this pure submission to the logos, without considering the proposition whereby the thing becomes a narrative to which the logos belongs, is the essence of the accusative. The logos that informs prime matter in calling it to order is an accusation or a category. Obsession, however, is anarchic. It accuses me on the hither side of prime matter seized by the category, still modeled on what remains of obduracy, or potency, in the matter. As a potential being, prime matter remains a power which form takes into account. It is not by chance that Plato speaks of the indestructibility of matter or that Aristotle views matter as a *cause*.[28] Such is the truth appropriate to the order of *things*. Western philosophy, arguably reification itself, has remained faithful to this order. It does not know the absolute passivity, this side of activity and passivity, conveyed by the idea of creation.[29] Philosophers have always been inclined to think of creation in terms of ontology, that is, in terms of a preexisting and indestructible matter.

In obsession, the accusation corresponding to the category is transformed into an absolute accusative in which the ego proper to free consciousness is caught up. Without foundation, prior to every will, the obsessional accusation is a persecution. It strips the Ego of its self-conceit and its dominating imperialism. The subject is in the accusative, without recourse in being, expelled from being, that is to say, in itself. In itself one. The recourse that being would offer the Ego brought back to itself would be the splitting of absolute unity, as in the first hypothesis of the *Parmenides*, where the existence of the One would be the negation of the One. The return of the Ego to the Self through obsession is not a self-reflection, a contemplative turning back on the self, but the reduction of the ego to the self. It is a return of the Ego to the passivity of the self, an anarchic passivity whose active source is not thematizable. Subjectivity in this sense is not a for-itself but an in-itself. In the approach, the subject does not detach itself from itself so as to recover itself. It is not like the instant which, through retention and protention in the temporality of consciousness, redis-covers itself already separated from itself. In the obsessive approach, the subject is not detached from itself so as then to become its own object and to have care for the self. It is an intrigue other than of egoism. In itself, the ego is divested of the ego that recovers and masks it. For, in the ego, the One is already contaminated by being, an exasperated and intrusive being. In its persecution, the ego returns to the self, not to reflect on the self but to denude itself in the absolute simplicity of identity. The absolutely individuated identity of the interior, in-itself, without recourse to any system of references. To be sure, this identity cannot be individuated as the "pole" of a self-identifying conscious-ness, nor even as an existence which, in its existence, would care for itself.[30] The reflexive pronoun "itself," or the self, remains the great secret to be divulged. The return upon the self proper to reflection already implies the initial recur-rence of the "itself."

Obsessed with responsibilities which do not result from decisions taken by a "freely contemplating" subject, consequently accused of what it never willed or decreed, accused of what it did not do, subjectivity is thrown back on itself - in itself - by a persecuting accusation. Concretely, this means to be accused of what others do and to be responsible for what others do. It is to be pushed to the limit, responsible for the very persecution undergone. Subjectivity is subject to the limitless passivity of an accusative that is not a mere declension derived from a nominative. Everything begins here in the accusative. Such is the exceptional condition - or noncondition - of the Self (even in our Latin grammars). Backed up against itself, because the self is in itself without recourse to anything, in itself as one is in one's skin (and this incarnation is not metaphorical, since to be in one's skin is an extreme way of being exposed, different from things). Does not the self take hold of itself through the very impossibility of slipping away from its identity, an identity toward which it is driven back by persecution? Does not a beginning dawn in this passivity?

Certainly. But how can the passivity of the self become a "hold on oneself"? Leaving aside a play on words, does this not presuppose an activity, a hidden and clandestine freedom, behind the absolutely an-archic passivity of obsession? Indeed, has any progress been made in the study so far?

4. Substitution

In speaking of the in-itself of persecuted subjectivity have we been faithful enough to the an-archy of passivity? In speaking of the recurrence of the ego to the self have we freed ourselves sufficiently from the postulates of ontological thinking, where eternal being always assumes what it undergoes and, whatever the nature of this undergoing, always reappears as the *principle* of what happens to it? It is perhaps here that ontological thinking ultimately differs from the thought which speaks of the creature rather than of being. Does not this thought, in its absolute diachrony, in the noninstant of creation, where the self called to being is not there to hear the call which it obeys, conceive an unlimited and anarchic passivity of the creature? In the absolute passivity of the creature, the Self is thought to the very end: the total passivity of the Self, suggested by the idea of creation, is a recurrence to the self, on this side of the self. *A* does not come back to *A*, as in an identity, but withdraws behind its point of departure. Must we not speak of a responsibility that is not assumed? Far from recognizing itself in the freedom of consciousness losing and rediscovering itself, slackening the order of being so as to reintegrate it in a free responsibility, the responsibility of obsession implies an absolute passivity of a self that has never been able to depart from itself so as to return within its limits and identify itself by recognizing itself in its past; an absolute passivity whose contraction is a movement this side of identity. Responsibility for the other does not wait for the freedom of commitment to the other. Without ever having done anything, I have always been under accusation: I am persecuted. Responsibility is not a return to self but an irremovable and implacable crispation, which the limits of identity cannot contain. In obsession, the self's responsibility is, as it were, a deficit. Its recurrence breaks open the limits of identity, the *principle* of being that lies in me, the intolerable resting in oneself proper to definition. Such is the ego's responsibility for what it did not will, that is to say, responsibility for others. This anarchy of self-recurrence, beyond the predictable play of action and passion in which the identity of being is maintained, is a passivity that is undergone in proximity. On this side of the limits of identity, the passivity of self-recurrence is not, however, an alienation. What can it be if not a substitution for others? In its passivity without the *arche* of identity, ipseity is a hostage. The word "I" means to be answerable for everything and for everyone.

In this substitution whereby identity is inverted, a passivity more passive still than all passivity, beyond the passivity of the identical, the self is freed from itself. This freedom is not that of a free initiative, an absolution which, in substituting for others, escapes relationship with them. At the extreme of passivity, it escapes passivity or the inevitable limitation to which every term in a relation is subject. In the incomparable relation of *responsibility*, the other is not merely a contestation but is supported by what it contests. Here we observe the overdetermination of ontological categories, transforming them into ethical notions. In this most passive passivity, the *Self* is freed from every Other and from itself.

In contrast to Hegel and the tradition, in which the ego is equal to itself (and thus a return of being to itself through the concept),[31] the affirmation called forth by obsession, from the an-archic passivity of the self, can be stated only in terms of inequality. Yet inequality cannot be taken to mean an inadequation of the apparent being with respect to a profound or sublime being, nor is it a return toward an original innocence (such as the inequality of the ego to itself spoken of by Nabert).[32] Rather, it signifies the passage of the identical to the other in substitution, which makes possible sacrifice.

The upsurge of the oneself in persecution, the anarchic passivity of substitution, is not some event whose history we might recount but a conjunction which describes the ego. It is the very gravity of being, a gravity which is perhaps the first meaning imported to being, over and above the simple "that's how it is." Being is recast as the unity of the universe insofar as it rests on the self: subject to being and subject to every being. The self bears the weight of the world; it is responsible for everyone. The subject is the one who, as in *Lamentations* 3:30, "presents his cheek to he who strikes him and is filled with shame." Here it is not a question of humiliating oneself, as if suffering were in itself, in its empirical essence, a magical power of atonement. But because, in suffering, in the original traumatism and return to self, where I am responsible for what I did not will, absolutely responsible for the persecution I undergo, outrage is done to me. The self is what in being inverts the work, upright, imperturbable, and without exemption, inverts the unfolding of the *essence* of being. Being in-itself, backed up against the self, to the point of being substituted for all that drives you into this non-Place, is the way in which the ego is in-itself, or "beyond essence."

Contrary to Eugen Fink and Jeanne Delhomme, both of whom demand an unconditional freedom without responsibility, a freedom of play, we discern in obsession a responsibility not resting on any free commitment, that is, a responsibility without freedom,[33] a responsibility of the creature; a responsibility of one who comes too late into being to avoid supporting it in its entirety. This way of being, without prior commitment, responsible for the other (*autrui*), amounts to the fact of human fellowship, prior to freedom.

Being takes on a meaning and becomes a universe not because there exists among thinking beings a being pursuing ends, a being thereby structured as an Ego. There is abandonment, obsession, responsibility, and a Self because the trace of the Infinite (exceeding the present, turning its *arche* into anarchy) is inscribed in proximity.[34] The noninterchangeable par excellence, the I, substitutes itself for others. Nothing is a game. Thus being is transcended.

The ego is not merely a being endowed with certain so-called moral qualities, qualities it would bear as attributes. Its exceptional unicity in the passivity of the Passion of the self is the incessant event of substitution, the fact of being emptied of its being, of being turned inside out, the fact of *nonbeing*. In speaking of an *event*, we do not mean to reduce the being which is the Ego to the *act of substituting itself*, which would be the *being* of this *being*. Substitution is not an act but contrary to the act; it is a passivity inconvertible into an act, on this side of the act-passivity alternative. It is the ex-ceptional, which cannot serve as the grammatical *category* of Noun or Verb, the recurrence that can only be stated as an *in itself*, or as an *inside-out of being*, or as *nonbeing*. Nonbeing is a matter of bearing the burden of the misery and failure of the other, and even the responsibility that the other can have for me. To be a "self" is always to have one degree of responsibility more.[35] The responsibility for the other (*autrui*) is perhaps the concrete event designated by the verb "not to be," in an attempt to distinguish it both from nothingness and from the product of the transcendental imagination.

It is through the condition of being a hostage that there can be pity, compassion, pardon, and proximity in the world - even the little there is, even the simple "after you sir." All the transfers of sentiment which theorists of original war and egoism use to explain the birth of generosity[36] (it isn't clear, however, that there was war at the beginning; before wars there were altars) could not take root in the ego were it not, in its entire being, or rather its entire nonbeing, subjected not to a category, as in the case of matter, but to an unlimited accusative, that is to say, persecution, self, hostage, already substituted for others.

The ego is not a being which is capable of expiating for others; it is this original expiation which is involuntary because prior to the initiative of the will. It is as though the Ego's unity and unicity were already the hold over the self exerted by the gravity of being, abandoned by the unrepresentable withdrawal of the Infinite. This hold over the self is the Self, outside of any place where its load may be set down, a nonlocation where the "I" is an other (but without the alienation Rimbaud speaks of).[37] *In itself*, this side of identity and the autonomy of auto-affection, subjectivity is not a substance; it is in itself through the absolute passivity that comes to it anarchically from the Other and where we are perhaps justified in rejecting the activity-passivity alternative in order to speak of expiation.

It is from subjectivity understood as a self, from the *excidence*[38] and dispossession of contraction, whereby the Ego does not appear but immolates itself, that the relationship with the other is possible as communication and transcendence. This relation is not simply another quest for certainty, a self-coincidence paradoxically claimed to be the basis of communication. Consequently, all one can say of communication and transcendence is their incertitude. As an adventure of subjectivity which is not governed by the concern to rediscover oneself, an adventure other than the coinciding of consciousness, communication rests on incertitude (here a positive condition) and is possible only as deliberately sacrificed. Communication with the other (*autrui*) can be transcendence only as a dangerous life, as a fine risk to be run.[39] These words receive their full weight when, instead of merely designating a lack of certainty, they express the gratuity of sacrifice. In speaking of a fine risk to be run, the word *fine* has not been given sufficient thought. In their antithesis to certainty, indeed to consciousness, these terms take on a positive meaning and are no longer makeshift expressions.

The ethical language we have resorted to does not derive from a special moral experience which would be independent of the description hitherto developed. It proceeds from what Alphonse de Waelhens called nonphilosophical experiences,[40] arising from the very meaning of the approach that cuts across knowledge, from the face that cuts across the phenomenon. Phenomenology is able to follow the reversion of thematization into an-archy in the description of the approach. Ethical language succeeds in expressing the paradox in which phenomenology suddenly finds itself, since ethics, beyond politics, features at the level of this reversion. Beginning with the approach, the description refers to the neighbor who bears the trace of a withdrawal ordering it as a face. The signifyingness of the trace in respect of behavior is a signifyingness whose anarchic insinuation should not be forgotten and confused with indication, that is, with the monstration of the signified in the signifier, with the itinerary taken by theological and edifying thinking in deducing too readily the truths of faith, whereby obsession is contained as a principle in a theme and the very an-archy of its movement is annulled.[41] The trace in which the face is ordered is not reducible to a sign, for the sign and its relation to the signified are synchronous in a theme. The approach is not the thematization of any relation but that very relation which resists thematization inasmuch as it is an-archic. To thematize it is already to lose it and to depart from the absolute passivity of self. The passivity which is this side of the passivity-activity alternative, a passivity more passive than any inertia, is expressed in ethical terms: accusation, persecution, responsibility for others. The persecuted one is expelled from its place and has nothing left but itself, has nothing in the world upon which to rest its head. Accused beyond any fault, persecuted, one is unable to offer a self-defense in language, because the disqualification of the apology is the very characteristic of persecution, so that persecution is the precise moment where the subject is reached or touched without the mediation of the logos.[42]

5. Before Freedom

In coming to the end of our discussion we may ask ourselves whether we have not been so imprudent as to affirm that the first word of the mind, that which makes all the others possible, including the words *negativity* and *consciousness*, is an unconditional *Yes* of submission. A *Yes* of submission which negates truth and all the highest values!

An unconditional *Yes* certainly, but not a naïve one: a *Yes* older than naïve spontaneity. We still reason as though the ego had been present at the creation of the world and as though the world, henceforth in its charge, had issued from an act of free will. Such are the presumptions of philosophers, the presumptions of idealists. Indeed, it is for this that Scripture reproaches Job. No doubt he could have understood his misfortunes had they been the result of his faults. But he never wanted to do evil! His so-called friends thought as he did: in an orderly world one is responsible only for one's *own* actions. Ergo, Job must have been guilty of an oversight. But the meaning of the world is not inscribed in being as a theme that exhibits itself in this world. Job does not have at his disposal all that is required for deliberating in matters of justice. Entering too late into a world created without him, he is responsible over and above what he experiences. And yet, in the same way, he is *better* for not being a mere effect of this world. The distinction between the free and the nonfree is not therefore ultimate. Prior to the Ego taking a decision, the *outside of being*, where the Ego arises or is accused, is necessary. This occurs not through freedom but through an unlimited susceptibility, anarchical and *without assumption*, which, unlike the susceptibility of matter determined by the energy of a cause, is overdetermined by a valuing.[43] The birth of the Ego in a gnawing remorse, which is precisely a withdrawing into oneself; this is the absolute recurrence of substitution. The condition, or noncondition, of the Self is not originally an auto-affection presupposing the Ego but is precisely an affection by the Other, an anarchic traumatism this side of auto-affection and self-identification,[44] a traumatism of responsibility and not causality..

A disengagement outside (or this side) of being is not the result of an inconsequential game played out in some corner of being where the ontological plot is relaxed. An exit made possible by the weight exerted at a single point by the remainder of its substance: responsibility. It is this responsibility for the creature that constitutes the "self." Responsibility for the creature, for that which the ego had not been the author. To be a "self" is to be responsible before having done anything. It is in this sense to substitute oneself for others. In no way does this represent servitude, for the distinction between master and slave already assumes a preestablished ego.

To say that subjectivity begins in the person, that the person begins in freedom, that freedom is the primary causality, is to blind oneself to the secret of the self and its relation to the past. This relation does not amount to placing oneself at the beginning of this past so as to be responsible within the strict limits of intention, nor to being the simple result of the past. All the suffering and failure of the world weighs on that point where a singling out occurs, an inversion of being's *essence*. A point is subject to everything. The impossibility of slipping away is the very singling out of the subject. The notion of hostage overturns the position that starts from presence (of the ego to the self) as a beginning of philosophy. I am not merely the origin of myself, but I am disturbed by the Other. Not judged by the Other, but condemned without being able to speak, persecuted. But we have shown that it is necessary to go further: to be substitutable for the persecutor; whence the idea of responsibility preceding freedom.

Of course, the notion of the subject to which the analysis of proximity leads us does not coincide with the notion of Mind, but the notion of soul does not correspond either. It is Me who is a substitution and sacrifice and not another, not the Other (*Autrui*), in whom I would like to discover a soul identical to my own. To say that the soul should sacrifice itself for others would be to preach human sacrifice. To say that the ego is a substitution is not to proclaim the universality of a principle, the "essence" of an Ego, but, quite the contrary, it is to restore to the soul its egoity, which supports no generalization. From this situation, the way by which the logos attains to the essence of the ego, passes through the third party.[45]

Modern antihumanism, which denies the primacy that the human person, a free end in itself, has for the signification of being, is true over and above the reasons it gives itself.[46] It makes a place for subjectivity positing itself in abnegation, in sacrifice, and in substitution. Its great intuition is to have abandoned the idea of person as an end in itself. The Other (*Autrui*) is the end, and me, I am a hostage.

Shall we say that the world, with all its sufferings and all its failings, weighs on the ego because the ego is a free consciousness, capable of sympathy and compassion? Shall we say that only a being which is free is susceptible to the weight of the world that it takes upon itself? Let us suppose for a moment that the ego is free and capable of deciding in favor of solidarity with others. At least it will be recognized that this freedom has no time to assume this urgent weight and that, consequently, it appears collapsed and defeated under its suffering. In the impossibility of evading the neighbor's call, in the impossibility of distancing ourselves - perhaps we approach the other (*autrui*) in contingency, but henceforth we are not free to distance ourselves from him or her - the assumption of the suffering and failings of the other (*autrui*) in no way goes beyond passivity: it is passion. This condition, or noncondition, of the hostage will therefore be nothing less than the primary and essential modality of freedom and not an empirical accident of the Ego's freedom (in itself proud).

Certainly - but this would be another paper - my responsibility for everyone can manifest itself while also limiting itself. The ego may be called, in the name of this unlimited responsibility, to be concerned also with itself. The fact that the other, my neighbor, is also a third in relation to another, likewise a neighbor, is the birth of thought, of consciousness, of justice, and of philosophy. The unlimited and initial responsibility that justifies this concern for justice, for the self, and for philosophy can be forgotten. In this forgetfulness, consciousness is pure egoism. But the egoism is neither first nor last. The impossibility of escaping God - the adventure of Jonas - dwells in the depths of myself as a self, as an absolute passivity. (I pronounce the word *God* without suppressing the intermediaries that lead to this word and, as it were, the anarchy of its entrance into discourse, just as phenomenology announces concepts without ever destroying the scaffoldings by which they are reached. Here, at least, God is not merely a value among values.) This passivity is not simply the possibility of death within being, the possibility of impossibility,[47] but is an impossibility anterior to this possibility, an impossibility of slipping away, an absolute susceptibility, a gravity without any frivolity, the birth of a meaning in the obtuseness of being, a "being able to die," submitted to sacrifice.

Truth of Disclosure and Truth of Testimony
(1972)

"Vérité du dévoilement et vérité du témoignage," a dense and difficult text, can be read as a summary of the first sections of "Subjectivity and Infinity" (chapter 5 of *Autrement qu'être*, AE 167–94; OB 131–52).[1] Following his habitual method, Levinas begins by giving a sketch of the point of view he will try to overcome. In order to represent the conception of truth that has prevailed from the ancient Greeks up to our days, he discusses Aristotle, Brentano, and Husserl. As his wording shows, however, Heidegger, although not explicitly mentioned, is very present, especially through his conception of truth and *Erschlossenheit* as analyzed in *Being and Time* § 44.

The philosophical tradition has understood truth as self-manifestation of being to consciousness, a representational or gathering disclosure of being for which human subjectivity is only a means. Within the horizon of this conception, meaning can be found only in the dis-covering or un-veiling of being in its synchronic presence to the mind. Testimony, in the sense of the "confession of a subject's experience or knowledge," must then be considered a secondary, lower, or degraded form of access to truth. Its subjective character awakens suspicions, and a critique of testimony is necessary in order to ascertain to what extent it manifests the truth of being. Can it be understood as an allegory of conceptual truth? Can we interpret it as a concrete schematization of truth, in a manner analogous to art works?

Testimony cannot convey the highest level of truth unless it is supported by a primordial relation that is not the correlation between consciousness and being. But how is it possible to go beyond or to precede this correlation, which is the basis not only of all phenomenology but also of the entire Western attitude and culture?

At this point Levinas refers to other publications in which he showed that the human "psychism" is not primarily consciousness but rather a relation to the nonrepresentable: conscience, responsibility for the other, obsession, and alienation (but an alienation that constitutes identity). This preconscious relation is the primordial or "preoriginal" testimony which testifies to the nonrepresentable infinite as that which precedes and surpasses being. The truth of testimony belongs to the "glory" of the Infinite. But this formulation does not refer to some private, secret, or mystical experience; instead it exhibits me as being-for-the-other (and not for my self in the interiority of an encompassing Cogito). Even against my wish or will, my Saying already testifies to the Infinite, which reveals itself in giving me the breath for this very Saying. Inspiration is the condition for all Saying and human life as such. This, and not the inner adventure of a self-contained soul, is the "secret" of all prophecy: to speak in obedience to the "law" of inspiration.

1. Truth and Being

The *true* as a synonym for the *real*, as a presentation *in the original* of disclosed being, assumes the indifference of the presented being with regard to its thematization by consciousness and, in a certain manner, its security with respect to the subjective fantasies that would project themselves onto its discovered aspect, onto its nudity.

The term *objectivity* (which, today, it is perhaps wrong to identify with the result of a process of reification, for it is in its place in every awareness, be it the awareness of becoming, of relation, of a norm, or of life and oneself) expresses this indifference, and thereby the very being of that which is. But this indifference - or this security, this objectivity - does not appear as an attribute that qualifies the disclosed realities, nor as a modality of relations among the terms that constitute the real, nor as the character of the configuration of all these terms in a system. Indifference *signifies* when being is referred to consciousness, the claim of which - to affect in any way whatsoever the order which, through consciousness, shows itself - being would, precisely, impugn.

Yet everything happens as though the signifyingness or the intelligibility of the relations among terms or relations, the arrangement of the structures of being among themselves, the intelligibility of the thematized system, were precisely the very way of impugning the interference of the gaze in being as made manifest to it. The indifference of the disclosed with respect to consciousness is not, indeed, evenly apportioned in the theme, and is dependent upon intelligibility. Signifyingness and the brilliance of appearing go, in a certain manner, together. A shadow is cast over the terms if they are taken outside the relation, over the relations and structures taken outside the system in which they are implicated; it is cast over them when, still isolated or already abstract, terms and relations have yet to take their place in conjuncture, when the structures have yet to be secured in a system. An order made manifest, in which the terms of the structures or the elements of a system are held together as abstractions, despite its thematization, offers some resistance to the light, and is not made wholly manifest. The structure is, indeed, intelligible or rational or signifying, whereas the terms on their own have no meaning. It is *in* the relation that the terms acquire a brilliance that finds itself tarnished as soon as they are separated from it.

A *lag* between the fact of *being thematized* and the fact of *being made manifest in intelligibility* can thus be adduced, a *passage* from thematization to manifestation within intelligibility. In the movement from the one to the other, a hesitation, a time, a certain risk, good or bad fortune, can be made out - the necessity of an effort for the structures to be secured. This event or this becoming within intelligibility itself can be called subjectivity. But then subjectivity thinks itself fully on the basis of objective intelligibility, come to celebrate a noon without shadows where, without proper density, it does not even cast its own shadow. Disappearing into the intelligibility or the objectivity of structures, the subject becomes aware of itself as called forth by intelligibility. Rational, theoretical consciousness in all its purity!

The truth correlative to being - in which the subject, a pure welcome reserved for the nudity of disclosed being, effaces itself *before* that which manifests itself, and in which effort, inventiveness, and genius are all just the means, ways, and detours by which being is dis-covered, by which its phases come together and its structures are secured - remains, within the thought that issued from Greece, the foundation of every notion of truth.

The truth resulting from the subject's engagement in the world and history through labor, cultural creation, and political organization, whereby the subjectivity of the subject shows itself to be humanity, finitude, care for its being thrown in anticipation of its end - this truth remains the truth of disclosed being.[2] The reflections of being in the humanity of the subject, its effects on this humanity, let themselves, precisely, be thematized. The experience of one who has lived, "been around," "got on in years," translates into objective propositions of experience as such, already offering itself to the human sciences. Everything happens as though, behind the human, lies the subject that effaces itself *before* the being of its humanity, letting it link up, come together, and disclose itself. Representation governs the notion of truth, and thereby every meaning is governed by ontology.

Husserl's famous proposition regarding the *Urdoxa*, residing at the basis of all intentionality - even nontheoretical intentionality - and allowing, *before any reflection on the act of valuation or acting will*, the transformation of the axiological and practical noematic sense into the doxical, into a meaning that is a pure position of being, establishes the priority of truth understood as disclosure and thereby the priority of the *gathering together* (of the ensemble) of the *synchrony of being*, in relation to every other way of signifying.[3] By taking up Brentano's thesis in this form - for Brentano every psychical act was either a representation or founded upon representation - Husserl finds himself affirming not so much the privilege contemplation would enjoy with respect to action (for, as has been rightly noted, within the Husserlian ideal of knowledge, it is easy to discern an ongoing task: the necessity of manual intervention in the laboratory and in the writing indispensable to the transmission of results obtained to other researchers in order to further the task - not to mention incidental digressions - the necessity of walking "around the thing," etc.) but rather the priority or ultimacy of *meaning*: *being*, in all its synchrony, in its nudity without mystery, in its immanence to knowing. In accordance with the tradition running from Aristotle to Heidegger! Every meaning and every psychism, all spirituality, lead back to dis-covery, gathering together, synchronous appearing, even if intentional correlation does not remain the ultimate structure. The priority of the doxical thesis in its Husserlian formulation establishes the priority of the truth of being and the universality of immanence.

Every confession of truths comes back to a prior disclosure of being, that is to say, situates within the limits of being every sensible thought, and subordinates sense to being. Language either refers to this previous discovery or contributes to it, receiving, in this case, transcendental status; but language in no way would know how to signify beyond being. Testimony - the confession of some knowledge or of an experience by a subject - can be conceived only in relation to the disclosed being which remains the norm; it brings about only indirect truths about being, or about the relations man has with being. These truths are evidently inferior, secondhand, and uncontrollable, distorted by the very fact of their transmission: "self-effacing subjectivity," by circulating information, is capable of bad faith and lying. The critique of testimony - by whatever method (the proliferation and comparison of testimonies, investigation into the credibility of the witness, etc.) - is necessary to draw out the truth (since the question is suppressed).[4]

In its most elevated meaning, testimony can doubtless be understood as the schematization of the abstract concept of being in the concreteness of the subject. Art would testify to the truth according to such a schematism. But once again, the structure of discovery reappears in the schema. The disclosure of being governs testimony. The concreteness of the subject or being, investigated by the critic or the historian or the philosopher, is schematized and placed on the side of being. Before being, the subject of knowledge effaces itself.

2. The Meaning of a "Beyond Being"

Does the truth of testimony illuminate only by way of borrowed light? The truth of testimony is certainly irreplaceable everywhere the subject is not just the instance that welcomes the manifestation of being but also the exclusive sphere of "subjective experiences," the enclosed and private domain that opens itself to universality and inspection only through the story that the subject makes of these. But do saying[5] and testimony contribute only a means of communication and intersubjective control to the experience of subjective being?

The conception of the subjectivity of the subject held by the Western tradition assumes that the manifestation of being is the starting point of all sense. In effect, the notion of the soul has been purified over the course of the

history of philosophy of any connotation other than that which evokes consciousness or thematizing contemplation. The importance that the concept of
intentionality has taken on in recent times marks the culmination of this trend.
Is not calling into question such a structure of the psychism to hint at a role for
testimony - and for the Saying itself - that would be more directly "veritative"
than that which they play when transmitting or communicating ontological
experiences? Far from being subordinated to the disclosure of being, are they
not the source of a meaning signifying otherwise? Do they not allow a glimpse
of a sensible adventure that would not be played out within the limits of being?
An intrigue from beyond being? One could doubtless ask whether an intrigue
that takes shape beyond being is not a contradiction in terms. But has not the
notion of the Good or the One beyond Being already been ventured?[6] And is the
concept of transcendence reducible simply to the absurd position of a being
behind the scenes in a hinter-world?

At first glance, it would seem so. Do not mind and the manifestation of being
go together? Subjectivity, in the form of consciousness and, ultimately, intentionality, is quasi-raised by the event of manifestation. Since being, by its
essence, appears, consciousness is consciousness of . . . , whereby all that might
escape presentation, all that might signify beyond the synthesis of the present,
presents itself, is put together, and synchronized. Nothing changes if the notion
of "consciousness of . . ." is expanded to describe it as *access* to being. The
exteriority of being presupposed in this manner of speaking is already borrowed from the gathering together of being in a theme that "consciousness
of . . ." gives itself. "Access to being" expresses a notion just as tautological as
manifestation of being or ontology. The subjective is understood strictly in
terms of manifestation.

3. The Psychism as Inspiration

Cannot the psychism be thought of as a relation with the unrepresentable? As
a relation with a past on the hither side of every present and every representation, not belonging to the order of presence? I have shown in another study[7] the
meaning of the subjectivity included in the everyday and extra-ordinary event
of my responsibility toward other humans, that is, of my responsibility for the
freedom of others, for a destiny that escapes my will. The freedom of the other
(*autrui*) will never have been able to originate in my own, that is to say, will
never have been able to fit into the same present, will never have been able to
be - or to become again - contemporary with my freedom, or be representable
to me. "The unlimited responsibility in which I find myself comes from the
hither side of my freedom, from a nonpresent par excellence, from the
nonoriginal, from the anarchic, from the hither side of or from beyond es-

sence."[8] Initially approached from responsibility for the other human - beginning from human solidarity or fraternity - the subject *would be alienated in the depths of its identity* - an alienation that would not empty the Same of its identity, but which would constrain it in the unimpugnable summons of me by the other, where no one could stand in for me. *The soul is the other within me*, a sickness of identity, its being out of phase, its diachrony, gasping, shuddering. But *is not the one-for-the-other meaning itself?* A signifyingness of meaning more ancient than manifestation of being, the one-for-the-other, "possession" of the same by the other in responsibility, the other in the same - the soul is already a touch mad, psychism already psychosis. The psychism of the soul is alterity within identity, animation, inspiration. Thought through to the end, the one-for-the-other is no anodyne formal relation, but rather all the gravity of the body, its *conatus* extirpated and capable of giving: *the very possibility of giving,* the for-the-other of subjectivity, nonsubstance, nonquietude. Exposure to the other, but not the exposure of skin to gaze; rather, the vulnerability to which sensibility is reducible before entering, by way of "sensations," in gnoseological play. A sensibility perhaps, coming back to the for-the-other of maternity, on the hither side of being; coming back to the maternity that is the very gestation of the other in the same, of the other in the same that would be the psyche itself.

The union of body and soul, impossible for Descartes without supernatural intervention (because sought by him on the basis of the rationality of representation, of the gathering together, and of the synchrony of terms - the soul being already understood as a thematizing thought), is, as the animation of the same by the other, the one-for-the-other of meaning, the signifyingness of meaning, intelligibility itself. The other within the same, worrying me as responsibility, as the summons of me by the other, does not open the door of non-sense through this exceptional alienation but constrains an irreplaceable subject to substitution. A subjectivity of human flesh and blood more passive in its extra-dition to the other than the passivity of the effect in a causal chain; as tearing-away-from-oneself-for-the-other in giving-to-the-other-the-bread-from-one's-mouth, identity here indicts itself neither in the confirmation of self by self, nor by self-coincidence, nor by repose in itself, but precisely by the *accusation* that summons me, the unique me, that summons me and not the Ego in me; an accusation that summons me without there being anyone to answer in my stead. As Dostoyevsky writes, "every one of us is guilty before all, for everyone and everything, and I more than others. . . ."[9]

4. Testimony

The one-for-the-other of subjectivity, unlike the generosity of a voluntary act (which would, all things considered, resuscitate intentionality, representational and taking initiatives), but all at once like extradition to the other. Responsibility for the other does not amount to a beginning: my relation with another freedom does not fit into a free decision. The two freedoms cannot be gathered in a presence. Responsibility for the other precedes every decision, it is before the origin. An-archy. Here, the without-beginning is nevertheless not the bad infinity of the extrapolation of the present by pure negation, since responsibility moves positively toward the other. A responsibility in which obligation increases in obedience while culpability augments with saintliness - an infinity which therefore is not simply that of a *Sollen*, which is asymptotic with its Ideal located at infinity, at the infinity of the bad infinite. A glorious Infinite.[10] The infinite would not know how to enter into appearance - to become a phenomenon - to become a theme without letting itself be contained, without accepting limits in immanence. This refusal to appear is thus, positively, the very responsibility for the other, anterior to every memorable present, coming from a past that was never present, that was never the freedom of a subject, ordering me to the other, to the first to come along, to the neighbor, without showing itself to me, but entering me by the simple effect of traumatism, by breaking and entering. My responsibility for the other is precisely this relation with an unthematizable Infinity. It is neither the experience of Infinity nor proof of it: it *testifies* to Infinity.

This *testimony* is not appended to a "subjective experience" in order to proclaim the ontological "conjuncture" disclosed to the subject. This testimony belongs to the very glory of the Infinite. The infinity of responsibility happens precisely as the dissipation of every secret, as the rupture of every interiority, wherein the subject, protected from obsession with the other, might escape. The glory of the Infinite is the egress of the subject from the dark corners of its *reserve*, which might offer an escape route from the summons of the other - like the thickets of Paradise wherein after sinning Adam hid, hearing the voice of God "moving through the garden from the way whence comes the day."[11] Glory is the response to the summons without any possible evasion, a surprise to the respondent himself, but by which, driven out, he develops sincerity or Saying. Indeed, sincerity is not an attribute of the Saying. It is the Saying that, unencumbered by any possessions in being, achieves the extradition of sincerity.[12] No Said recovers sincerity, and none is adequate to it. Saying without said, apparently a talking for nothing, a sign given to the other, "as simple as 'hello,'" and, within the Saying, a sign given of this giving of a sign - the pure transparency of a confession - testimony.

The Saying as testimony precedes all saying. The Saying, before stating a Said - and even the Saying of a Said - is the approach of the other and already testimony. The vocative neither harbors nor expresses its ultimate meaning. In the sign given in every proposition said to the other (for whom I am responsible and before whom I am responsible), I expose myself to the summons of this responsibility as though placed under a blazing sun that eradicates every residue of mystery, every ulterior motive, every loosening of the thread that would allow evasion - already sincere, testifying to the Infinite, not in relating it as a fact, but in unfolding, by the rupture of silence, its very glory, in breaking open the secret of Gyges,[13] the invisible-seeing-subject (*sujet-voyant-invisible*).

The glory of the Infinite does not, therefore, come to affect me as would a representation, nor as would an interlocutor in a "dialogue," before *which* or before *whom* I locate myself. It commands me from my own mouth. Interiority is precisely this reversal: the eminently exterior or the transcendent, by reason of this eminence, disproportionate to the present of the theme, not being able to be "contained," nor being able to appear, nor coming from an interlocutor, concerns me and surrounds me as a commandment speaking from my mouth. A commandment pronounced from the mouth of the one it commands - exceptional structure, and certainly unique. The very exception to the rule of Being. There is no testimony but that of the Infinite.

This is no psychological wonder but the modality according to which the Infinite comes to pass, signifying through the one to whom it signifies, ordering through the one to whom it orders. Not just an incomprehensible inconsistency or ruse of the Infinite resorting to the medium of humans to reveal itself, and to their psalms to glorify itself - but the very way in which the Infinite passes the finite, or the way in which it comes to pass.

That the Infinite comes to pass in the Saying is what lets the Saying be understood as irreducible to one psychological act among others, by which - we know not why - man would double and surpass his thoughts. True, one can show how and why a Saying must be the Saying of a Said, the exchange of information corresponding to "vital necessities." But the Saying without the Said, a sign given to the Other (*Autrui*), is not appended, as information, to a prior "experience" of the Infinite, as though there could be an experience of the Infinite. In the Saying, by which the subject, driven out, leaves its clandestinity, the Infinite comes to pass. Language, a sign given to the other, is sincerity or veracity, according to which glory is glorified. The Infinite thus has glory only through subjectivity, through the human adventure of the approach of the other, through substitution for the other, through the expiation of the other.

That the way in which the Infinite passes the finite should have an ethical sense does not issue from a project of constructing the "transcendental foundation" of ethical experience. The ethical is the field wherein the very paradox of an Infinite in relation to the finite is significant, without faltering in this relation. Testified to - and not thematized - in the sign given to the other, the Infinite signifies on the basis of responsibility for the other (*autrui*), of the one-for-the-other, of a subject supporting everything - subject to everything -

that is, suffering for everyone, but bearing the burden of everything without ever having had the chance to decide whether to take on this burden, gloriously amplifying itself to the extent that it is imposed. An obedience that precedes any hearkening unto the commandment. The possibility of finding, anachronously, the order within obedience itself, and of receiving the order from oneself - this reversal of heteronomy into autonomy is the very way in which the Infinite comes to pass - all of which the metaphor of inscribing the law in consciousness expresses in a remarkable manner, reconciling autonomy and heteronomy (in an ambivalence, of which diachrony is the very meaning, and which, in the present, is ambiguity). An inscription of the order in the *for-the-other* of obedience; an anarchic affection that slips into me "like a thief," through the nets extended by consciousness; a traumatism that surprised me absolutely; the order *has never been represented*, for it has never presented itself - not even in the past that comes forth in remembrance - to the point that it is I who says only - and after the fact - this unheard-of obligation. An ambivalence that is the exception and the subjectivity of the subject, its very psychism, the possibility of inspiration: to be the author of what was, *without my knowledge*, inspired in me - to have received, whence we know not, that of which I am the author. In the responsibility for the other, we are at the heart of this ambiguity of inspiration. The unheard-of saying is enigmatic in its an-archic response, in my responsibility for the other. This ambiguity within the subject is the trace of the infinite, alternately beginning and intermediary, the diachronic ambivalence that makes ethics possible.

5. Testimony and Prophecy

One can call prophecy this reversal whereby the perception of the *order* coincides with the meaning of this order, made up by the one who obeys it. Thus prophecy would be the very psychism of the soul: the other within the same; and all of man's spirituality would thereby be prophetic. The infinite does not announce itself in the testimony as a theme. In the sign given to the other whereby I am torn away from the secret of Gyges, in the Saying without the Said of sincerity, in my "here I am"[14] - immediately present in the accusative - I testify to the Infinite. The Infinite is not *before* the witness but rather as though it were outside presence or on the "reverse side" of presence, already past, beyond the grasp: an ulterior motive too elevated to thrust itself to the fore. "Here I am in the name of God," without directly referring myself to a presence. The sentence in which God comes forth, for the first time, and mingles with words, cannot be expressed: "I believe in God." Testifying to God does not consist in stating this extra-ordinary word or phrase, as though glory could be located within a theme, could be made into an essence of being. A sign given to the other of this very giving of a sign, "here I am" signifies me in the name of God, in the service of men, without my having anything by which to identify myself, save the sound of my voice or the movement of my gestures - the saying itself. A recurrence that is not a reflection on oneself. It is just the opposite of the return to the self, of self-consciousness. Recurrence is sincerity, effusion of the self, "extradition" of the self to the neighbor. One might, at the limit, pronounce the word *prayer* here - testimony, kerygma, confession, humility; but what is essential therefore lies - what a disappointment for those friends of the truth that thematizes being and for those of the subject that effaces itself before being! - in the fact that the responses are only heard in the demands, that the "provocation" that comes from God is in my invocation, that gratitude is already gratitude for that state of gratitude. The transcendence of revelation lies precisely in the fact that the epiphany comes, in the Saying, from the one who receives the revelation. The order that orders me leaves me no possibility of putting things right side up - of returning to the exteriority of the infinite as one returns to the exteriority of a theme. It is in prophecy that the Infinite eludes objectivation and dialogue and signifies as *illeity* in the third person, but according to a "tertiality" different from that of the third man, from the third that interrupts the face-to-face of the welcome to the other man, and by which justice arises.

The Infinite ordains the "neighbor" for me without exposing itself to me, especially as proximity draws in. An order that was not the *cause* of my response, nor even a question that would have preceded it in a dialogue; an order that I find in my response itself, in the "here I am" that brought me out of the shadows, where my responsibility could have been eluded, which, consequently, belongs to the very glory to which it testifies. *Illeity* is that direction of the "I know not whence," of that which comes without showing itself, of the nonphenomenon and, consequently, of the nonpresent, of a past that was never a present, of an order to which I am subjected before hearing it or that I hear in my own saying. The anachronism of the prophet more paradoxical, according to the retrievable time of recollection, than the prediction of the future. "Before they call, I will answer,"[15] a phrase to be understood literally: in approaching the neighbor, I am always late for the appointed time. But this singular obedience, without agreement or understanding, this allegiance prior to any oath - responsibility prior to engagement - is, precisely, the *other-in-the-same*, inspiration, prophecy - the pneuma of the soul.

I can, certainly, also give myself the God testified to as a Said. An extraordinary expression, the only one not to extinguish the Saying in the Said; a Said unique in its genre, fitting neither into grammatical categories as a word (neither a proper nor a common noun), nor into the rules of logic as meaningful (an excluded third of being and nothingness). But a *Said* that receives its meaning from testimony and which thematization betrays in theology by introducing it into a system of language, into the order of the Said, wherein its expression immediately inter-dicts itself (*s'inter-dit*). Thematization, certainly indispensable - for the meaning itself to take shape - a sophism inevitably committed wherever philosophy arises - but a betrayal that philosophy must reduce. A reduction that continually must be attempted because of the trace of sincerity that the words themselves bear. A testimony borne by every saying as sincerity, even when it is a Saying of a Said that the Said dissimulates; but a dissimulation that the saying always seeks to unsay (*dédire*) - which is its ultimate veracity. In the game that activates the cultural keyboard of language, sincerity and testimony signify through the very ambiguity of every said, through the greeting[16] it offers to the other (*autrui*) - the resounding "in the name of God" of all language. But prophecy, through its ambiguities, is not the last resort of a lame revelation. It belongs to the glory of the Infinite. That the prophecy should be able to take on the appearance of a subjective Saying, arising in the subject or in the influences to which the subject is submitted - to begin with, those influences stemming from the subject's physiology - there lies the enigma - the ambiguity - of transcendence. Transcendence would vanish in the very proof we would like to give of it; the Infinite would enter into conjunction with the subject who discloses it. Transcendence is obliged to interrupt the essence of being, to reach the world even while signifying the beyond of being. It needs ambiguity - a frontier at once ineffaceable and finer than the outline (*le tracé*) of an ideal line.

SEVEN

Essence and Disinterestedness
(1974)

This text constitutes the first chapter of *Autrement qu'être ou au-delà de l'essence* (1974) and summarizes the argument of that book. Levinas had presented this material in lecture form and an earlier version was published under the title "Au-delà de l'essence" (Beyond essence) in the *Revue de Métaphysique et de Morale* (1970).[1] The word *essence*, or, as Levinas later wrote, *essance*, refers both to Plato's *ousia* (being) and to Heidegger's being (*Sein*) with an "active" and "transitive" meaning. The expressions "otherwise than being," "beyond being" and "beyond essence" are all translations of Plato's *epekeina tēs ousias*, which characterizes "the good" in *Republic* 509 b9. Levinas appeals to Plato in order to overcome what he calls Heidegger's "ontology." He wants to show that the ontological difference between being (*Sein*) and beings (*Seiendes*) is not the ultimate matter of philosophy and that another difference is more profound and original, or rather - as he often writes - "preoriginal." Some of the provisional formulae for naming this difference are given in the "Preliminary Note" to *Otherwise than Being or Beyond Essence*: philosophy should "recognize in subjectivity a deranging ex-ception of the conjunction of *essence, beings* and '*difference*'" and "hear a God not contaminated by being" (AE x; OB lxi-lxii). How the exceptional structure of human subjectivity is connected with a nonontological meaning of "God" can only be shown through a philosophical analysis of the ways in which "the good" leaves traces in human history. To be in the trace of the good is not a question of choice, and autonomy is not the source of justice. Ethics befalls humans from beyond essence.

A full commentary on this dense and difficult text would need many pages. If "Philosophy and the Idea of Infinity" (CP 47–60) is the outline while "Transcendence and Height" is a summary of *Totality and Infinity*, we may see "Essence and Disinterestedness" as a succinct statement of the position at which Levinas arrived through his investigations between 1961 and 1974.

There is something to be said, Novalis wrote, in favor of passivity. It is significant that one of Novalis's contemporaries, Maine de Biran, who wished to be the philosopher of activity, will remain essentially the philosopher of two passivities, the lower and the higher. But is the lower lower than the higher?

—Jean Wahl, *Traité de métaphysique*

1. Being's "Other"

If transcendence has meaning, it can only signify the fact that the *event of being*, the *esse*, the *essence*,[2] passes over to what is other than being. But what is *being's other*? Among the five "genera" of the *Sophist*, a genus opposed to being is lacking, even though since the *Republic* there had been a question of what is beyond essence.[3] And what can the *fact* of passing over mean here, where the passing over, ending at being's other, can only undo its facticity during such a passage?

Passing over to being's *other*, otherwise than being. Not *to be otherwise*, but *otherwise than being*. And neither not-being. Passing over is not here equivalent to dying. Being and not-being illuminate one another and unfold a speculative dialectic, which is a determination of being. Or the negativity which attempts to repel being is immediately submerged by being.[4] The void that hollows out is immediately filled with the mute and anonymous rustling of the *there is*[5] as the place left vacant by one who died is filled with the murmur of the attendants. Being's essence dominates not-being itself. My death is insignificant - unless I drag into my death the totality of being, as Macbeth wished at the hour of his last combat. But then mortal being, or life, would be insignificant and ridiculous even in the "irony with regard to oneself" to which it could, if really necessary, be likened.

To be or not to be - that is not the question of transcendence. The statement of being's *other*, of the otherwise than being, claims to state a difference over and beyond that which separates being from nothingness - the very difference of the *beyond*, the difference of transcendence. But one immediately wonders if in the formula "otherwise than being" the adverb *otherwise* does not inevitably refer to the verb *to be*, which has simply been avoided by an artificially elliptical turn of phrase. Then what is signified by the verb *to be* would be ineluctable in everything said, thought, and felt. Our languages woven about the verb *to be* would not only reflect this undethronable royalty, stronger than that of the gods; they would be the very purple of this royalty. But then no transcendence other than the factitious transcendence of worlds behind the scenes,[6] of the Heavenly City gravitating in the skies over the terrestrial city, would have meaning. The being of beings and of worlds, however different among them-selves they may be, weaves among incomparables a common fate; it puts them in conjunction, even if the unity of being that assembles them is but an analogical unity.[7] Every attempt to disjoin the conjunction and the conjuncture only emphasizes them. The *there is* fills the void left by the negation of being.

2. Being and Interestedness

The essence thus works as an invincible persistence in essence, filling up every interval of nothingness which would interrupt its exercise. *Esse* is *interesse*; essence is interestedness.[8] Interestedness does not appear only to the Spirit surprised by the relativity of its negation or to humans resigned to the meaninglessness of their death; interestedness is not reducible to just this refutation of negativity.[9] It is confirmed positively to be the *conatus* of beings.[10] And what else can positivity mean but this *conatus*? Being's interestedness takes dramatic form in egoisms struggling with one another, each against all, in the multiplicity of allergic egoisms which are at war with one another and are thus together. War is the chronicle or the drama of the essence's interestedness. No entity can await its hour. They all clash, despite the difference of the regions to which the terms in conflict may belong. Essence thus is the extreme synchronism of war. Determination takes shape and is already undone by the clash. It is done and undone in a swarming. Here is extreme contemporaneousness or immanence.

Does not essence revert into its other by peace, in which Reason, which suspends the immediate clash of beings, reigns? Beings become patient and renounce the allergic intolerance of their persistence in being; do they not then dramatize the *otherwise than being*? But this rational peace, a patience and length of time, is calculation, mediation, and politics. The struggle of each against all becomes exchange and commerce. The clash of each against all, in which each comes to be with all, becomes the reciprocal limitation and determination of some matter. But the persisting in being, interestedness, is maintained by the future compensation which will have to equilibrate the concessions patiently and politically consented to in the immediate. The beings remain always assembled - present - in a present that is extended, thanks to memory and history, to the totality determined like matter, a present without fissures or surprises, from which becoming is expelled; a present largely made up of re-presentations, due to memory and history. Nothing is gratuitous. The mass remains permanent and interestedness remains. Transcendence is factitious and peace unstable. It does not resist interests. And the ill-kept commitment to recompense virtue and chastise vices, despite the assurances of those who claim it was made for a deadline more distant than the distance that separates the heaven from the earth, will accredit strange rumors about the death of God or the emptiness of the heavens. No one will believe in their silence.

True, commerce is better than war, for in Peace the Good has already reigned. And yet we must ask if even the difference that separates essence in war from essence in peace does not presuppose that *exhaustion of the spirit*, or the spirit holding its breath, in which since Plato what is beyond the essence is thought and said.[11] And we must now ask if this exhaustion or holding back is not the extreme possibility of the Spirit, bearing a meaning that comes from beyond Essence.

3. The Saying and the Said

Is the inescapable fate in which being immediately includes the statement of
being's *other* not due to the hold the *said* has over the *saying*, to the *oracle* in
which the said is immobilized? Then would not the bankruptcy of transcendence be but that of a theology that thematizes the *transcending* in the logos,
assigns a term to the passing of transcendence, congeals it into a "world behind
the scenes," and installs what it says in war and in matter, which are the
inevitable modalities of the fate woven by being in its interestedness?

It is not that the essence qua persistence in essence, qua *conatus* and
interestedness, would be reducible to a wordplay. Saying is not a play. Antecedent to the verbal signs it conjugates, to the linguistic systems and the semantic
glimmerings - a foreword preceding languages - it is the proximity of one to the
other, the commitment of an approach, the one for the other, the very
signifyingness of signification. (But is approach to be defined by commitment
and not rather commitment by approach? Perhaps because of current moral
maxims in which the word *neighbor* occurs, we have ceased to be surprised by
all that is involved in proximity and approach.)[12] The original or preoriginal
saying[13] - what is put forth in the foreword[14] - weaves an intrigue of responsibility. It sets forth an order graver than being and antecedent to being. By
comparison, being appears like a play. Being is play or *détente*, free from
responsibility, where everything possible is permitted. But is play free of
interest? Right away a stakes, money or honor, is attached to it. Does not
disinterestedness, without compensation, without eternal life, without the
pleasure (or agreeableness) of happiness, complete gratuity, indicate an extreme gravity and not the fallacious frivolity of play? By anticipation let us ask:
does not this gravity, where being's *esse* is inverted, refer to this preoriginal
language, the responsibility of one for the other, the substitution of one for the
other, and the condition (or the uncondition) of being hostage which thus takes
form?

In any case, this preoriginal saying changes into a language in which saying
and said are correlative of one another and the saying is subordinated to its
theme. It can be shown that even the distinction between being and beings is
borne by the amphibology of the said, though this distinction and this
amphibology are not thereby reducible to verbal artifices. The correlation of the
saying and the said, that is, the subordination of the saying to the said, to the
linguistic system and to ontology, is the price that manifestation demands. In
language qua said, everything is translated before us, be it at the price of a
betrayal.[15] Such a language is ancillary[16] and thus indispensable. At this very
moment language is serving a research conducted in view of disengaging the

otherwise than being or *being's other* from the themes in which they already show themselves, unfaithfully, as being's *essence* - but in which they do show themselves. Language permits us to utter, be it by betrayal, this *outside of being*, this *ex-ception* to being, as though being's other were an event of being. Being, its cognition, and the said in which it shows itself signify in a saying which, relative to being, forms an exception; but it is in the said that both this exception and the birth of cognition show themselves. But the fact that the exception shows itself and becomes truth in the said cannot serve as a pretext to take as an absolute the apophantic vicissitude of the Saying, which is ancillary or angelic.[17]

As ancillary or angelic vicissitude, however sublime it be, the apophantic form of the saying is only mediating. For thematization, in which being's essence is translated before us, together with theory and thought, its contemporaries, do not attest to some failing of the Saying. They are motivated by the preoriginal vocation of the Saying, by responsibility itself. We will see more of this.[18]

But the Saying does not exhaust itself in apophansis. The apophansis presupposes the language that answers with responsibility, and the gravity of this response is beyond the measure of being. The impossibility of declining responsibility is reflected only in the scruple or remorse which precedes or follows this refusal. The reality of the real takes no notice of scruples. But, though naturally superficial, essence does not exclude the recesses of responsibility in the way that being excludes nothingness. The gravity of the responsible saying retains a reference to being, and the nature of this reference must be made clearer. Moral impossibility is not of lesser gravity; it does not situate responsibility in some low tension zone, at the confines of being and nonbeing. As gravity of the *otherwise* than being, it just showed its affinity with ethics, be it in a still confused way. We have been seeking the *otherwise than being* from the beginning, and as soon as it is conveyed before us it is betrayed in the said that dominates the saying which states it. A methodological problem arises here, namely whether the preoriginal element of Saying (the anarchic, the nonoriginal, as we designate it)[19] can be led to betray itself by showing itself in a theme (if an an-archeology is possible), and whether this betrayal can be reduced; whether one can at the same time know and free the known of the marks which thematization leaves on it by subordinating it to ontology. Everything shows itself at the price of this betrayal, even the unsayable. In this betrayal the indiscretion with regard to the unsayable, which is probably the very task of philosophy, becomes possible.

When stated in propositions, the unsayable (or the an-archical) espouses the forms of formal logic,[20] the beyond being is posited in doxic theses and glimmers in the amphibology of *being* and *beings* - in which beings dissimulate being. The *otherwise than being* is stated in a saying that must also be unsaid in order to thus tear the *otherwise than being* from the said in which it already comes to signify but a *being otherwise*. Does the beyond being, which philosophy states and states by reason of the very transcendence of the *beyond*, fall inextricably into the forms of the ancillary statement?

Can this *saying* and this *unsaying* be assembled, can they be at the same time? In fact, to require this simultaneity is already to reduce being's *other* to *being* and *not being*. We must stay within the extreme situation of a diachronic thought.[21] Skepticism, at the dawn of philosophy, set forth and betrayed the diachrony of this very conveying and betraying. To conceive the *otherwise than being* requires, perhaps, as much audacity as skepticism shows, when it does not hesitate to affirm the impossibility of statements while venturing to *realize* this impossibility by the very statement of this impossibility. If, after the innumerable "irrefutable" refutations which logical thought sets against it, skepticism has the gall to return (and it always returns as the legitimate child of philosophy), it is because, in the contradiction which logic sees in it, the "at the same time" of the contradictories is missing; because a secret diachrony commands this ambiguous or enigmatic way of speaking; and because, in general, signification signifies beyond synchrony, beyond essence.[22]

4. Subjectivity

To state the otherwise than being we must articulate the breakup of a fate that reigns in essence, whose fragments and modalities, despite their diversity, belong to one another, that is, do not escape the same order, do not escape Order, as though the bits of the thread cut by the Fates were then knotted together again. This effort will look beyond Freedom. Freedom, an interruption of the determinism of war and matter, does not yet escape the destiny of essence and takes place in time and in the history which assembles events into an *epos* and synchronizes them, revealing their immanence and their order.[23]

The task is to conceive of the possibility of a wrenching from essence.[24] To go where? Toward what region? To stay on what ontological plane? But the wrenching from essence contests the unconditional privilege of the question "where?" It signifies a nonplace (*non-lieu*).[25] The essence claims to recover and cover over every ex-ception - negativity, nihilation, and already since Plato, nonbeing, which "in a certain sense is."[26] It will then be necessary to show that the exception of the "other than being," beyond not-being, signifies subjectivity or humanity, the *oneself* (*le soi-même*) which repels the annexations by essence. The ego is an incomparable unicity; it is outside of the community of genus and form and does not find any rest in itself (*soi*), either; it is troubled and does not coincide with itself (*soi*). The outside of itself, the difference from oneself (*soi*) of this unicity, is nonindifference itself and the extraordinary recurrence of the pronominal or the reflexive, the *self* (*se*) - which no longer surprises us because it enters into the current flow of language in which things show *themselves*, suitcases fold and ideas are understood.[27] A unicity without place, without the ideal identity a being derives from the kerygma[28] that identifies the innumerable aspects of its manifestation, without the identity of the ego that coincides with itself, a unicity withdrawing from essence - such is man.

The history of philosophy, during some flashes, has known this subjectivity that, as in an extreme youth, breaks with essence. From Plato's One without being to Husserl's pure Ego, transcendent in immanence, it has known the metaphysical wrenching from being, even if, betrayed by the Said as by the effect of an oracle, the exception restored to the essence and to fate immediately fell back into the rules and led only to worlds behind the scenes. The Nietzschean man above all. For Husserl's transcendental reduction, will a putting between parentheses suffice - a type of writing, of committing oneself with the world, which sticks like ink to the hands that push it off? One must go all the way to the nihilism of Nietzsche's poetic writing, reversing irreversible time in a whirlwind to the laughter which refuses language.

The philosopher finds language again in the abuses of language of the history of philosophy, in which the unsayable and what is beyond being are conveyed before us. But negativity, still correlative with being, will not be enough to signify the *other than being*.

5. Responsibility for the Other (*Autrui*)

But how, at the still temporal breaking point where being *takes place* (*se passe*), would being and time fall into ruins so as to disengage subjectivity from its essence?[29] Do not the falling into ruins and the disengagement last; do they not occur in being? The *otherwise than being* cannot be situated in any eternal order extracted from time that would somehow command the temporal series. Kant has shown the impossibility of that in the antithesis of the fourth Antinomy.[30] It is then the temporalization of time, in the way it signifies being and nothingness, life and death, that must also signify the *beyond being and not being*; it must signify a difference with respect to the couple being and nothingness. Time is essence and monstration of essence. In the temporalization of time the light comes about by the instant's falling out of phase with itself -which is the temporal flow, the differing of the identical. The differing of the identical is also its manifestation. But time is also a recuperation of all gaps, through retention, memory, and history. In its temporalization, in which, thanks to retention, memory, and history, nothing is lost, everything is presented or represented, everything is consigned and lends itself to inscription, or is synthesized or, as Heidegger would say, gathered, in which everything is crystallized or sclerosized into substance - in the recuperable temporalization, without time lost, without time to lose, and where the being of substance takes place - there must be signaled a lapse of time that does not return, a diachrony refractory to all synchronization, a transcending diachrony.

The meaning of this signaling will have to be clarified. Can it preserve a relationship across the break of the diachrony, without, however, restoring to representation this "deep pastness"[31] as a past that had slipped away without signifying a "modification" of the present and thus a commencement, a principle that would be thematizable and therefore would be the origin of every historical or recallable past? Can it, on the contrary, remain foreign to every present, every representation, and thus signify a past more ancient than every representable origin, a preoriginal and anarchical *past*? The signaling of this preoriginal past in the present would not again be an ontological relation.

But if time is to show the ambiguity of *being* and the otherwise than being, its temporalization is to be conceived not as essence but as Saying. Essence fills the said, or the epos of the Saying; but the Saying, in its power of equivocation, that is, in the enigma whose secret it keeps, escapes the epos of essence that includes it and signifies beyond in a signification that hesitates between this beyond and the return to the epos of essence. This equivocation or enigma is the inalienable power in Saying and a modality of transcendence.[32] Subjectivity is the very knot and unknotting[33] - the knot or unknotting of essence and essence's other.

But how is the saying, in its primordial enigma, said? How is time temporalized such that the diachrony of transcendence, of the other than being, is signaled? How can transcendence withdraw from *esse* while being signaled in it? In what concrete case is the singular relationship with a past produced, which does not reduce this past to the immanence in which it is signaled and leaves it be past, not returning as a present nor a representation, leaves it be past without reference to some present it would have "modified," leaves it be a past, then, which can not have been an origin, a preoriginal past, an anarchical past?

A linear regressive movement, a retrospective back along the temporal series toward a very remote past, would never be able to reach the absolutely diachronous preoriginal which cannot be recuperated by memory and history. But it may be that we have to unravel other intrigues of time than that of the simple succession of presents. Men have been able to be thankful for the very fact of finding themselves able to thank; the present gratitude is grafted onto itself as onto an already antecedent gratitude. In a prayer in which the worshiper asks that his prayer be heard, the prayer as it were precedes or follows itself.

But the relationship with a past that is on the hither side of every present and every re-presentable, not belonging to the order of presence, is included in the extraordinary and everyday event of my responsibility for the faults or the misfortune of others, in my responsibility that answers for the freedom of the other (*autrui*), in the astonishing human fraternity in which fraternity, conceived with Cain's sober coldness, would not by itself explain the responsibility between separated beings it calls for. The freedom of the other (*autrui*) could never begin in my freedom, that is, abide in the same present, be contemporary, be representable to me. The responsibility for the other (*autrui*) cannot have begun in my commitment, in my decision. The unlimited responsibility in which I find myself comes from the hither side of my freedom, from an "anterior to every memory," an "ulterior to every accomplishment," from the nonpresent par excellence, the nonoriginal, the anarchical, prior to or beyond essence. The responsibility for the other (*autrui*) is the locus in which is situated the nonplace of subjectivity, where the privilege of the question "Where?" no longer holds. The time of the *said* and of *essence* there lets the preoriginal saying be heard, answers to transcendence, to a diachrony, to the irreducible gap that opens here between the nonpresent and every representable divergency, which in its own way - a way to be clarified - makes a sign to the responsible one.

6. Essence and Signification

But is not the relationship with this preoriginal a recuperation? Let us look into this more closely. The response of the responsible one does not thematize the diachronical as though it were retained, remembered, or historically reconstructed. It cannot thematize or comprehend. Not out of weakness; no capacity corresponds to what could not be contained there. The nonpresent is incomprehensible by reason of its immensity or its "superlative" humility or, for example, its goodness, which is the superlative itself. The nonpresent here is invisible, separated (or holy) and thus a nonorigin, anarchical. The impossibility of thematization could be due to the goodness of the diachronic. The Good cannot become present or enter into a representation. The present is a beginning in my freedom, whereas the Good does not give itself to freedom; it has chosen me before I have chosen it. No one is good voluntarily. We can see the formal structure of nonfreedom in a subjectivity which does not have time to choose the Good and thus is penetrated by its rays unbeknownst to itself. But subjectivity sees this nonfreedom redeemed, exceptionally, by the goodness of the Good. The exception is unique. And if no one is good voluntarily, no one is enslaved to the Good.[34]

Immemorial, unrepresentable, invisible, the past that can do without the present, the pluperfect past, falls into a past that is a gratuitous lapse. It cannot be recuperated by reminiscence, not because of its remoteness but because of its incommensurability with the present. The present is essence that begins and ends, beginning and end assembled in a thematizable conjunction; it is the finite in correlation with a freedom. Diachrony is the refusal of conjunction, the nontotalizable and, in this sense, infinite. But in the responsibility for the Other (*Autrui*), for another freedom, the negativity of this anarchy, of this refusal of the present, of appearing, or the immemorial, commands me and ordains me to the Other (*Autrui*), to the first one on the scene, and makes me approach him, makes me his neighbor. It thus diverges from nothingness as well as from being. It provokes this responsibility against my will, that is, by substituting me for the Other (*Autrui*) as a hostage. All my inwardness is invested in the form of a despite-me-for-another. Against my will for-another, that is signification par excellence and the sense of the oneself (*soi-même*), of the *self* (*se*), that accusative that derives from no nominative; it is the very fact of finding oneself while losing oneself.

What is exceptional in this way of being signaled is that I am ordered toward the face of the other. In this order, which is an ordination, the nonpresence of the infinite is not a figure of negative theology. All the negative attributes, which state the beyond of essence, become positive in responsibility, a response answering to a nonthematizable provocation and thus a nonvocation, a trauma. This response answers before any consciousness and any present, but it does answer, as though the invisible that can do without the present left a trace by the very fact of doing without the present. That trace lights up as the face of a neighbor, in the ambiguity of the one *before whom* (or *to whom*, without any paternalism) and *for whom* I answer. For such is the enigma or ex-ception of a face, judge and accused.

What is positive in responsibility, outside of essence, conveys the infinite. It inverses relationships and principles, reverses the order of interestedness: to the extent that responsibilities are taken on they multiply. This is not a *Sollen* commanding the infinite pursuit of an ideal.[35] The infinity of the infinite lives the wrong way round (*à rebours*). The debt increases to the extent that it is paid. This divergency perhaps deserves the name glory.[36] The positivity of the Infinite is the conversion into responsibility, into approach of the other (*autrui*). The Infinite is nonthematizable, gloriously exceeding every capacity and manifesting, as it were in reverse, its exorbitance in the approach of a neighbor, obedient to its measure. Subjectivity, prior to or beyond the free and the nonfree, obliged with regard to the neighbor, is the breaking point where essence is exceeded by the Infinite.

It is the point of rupture but also of connection; the glow of the trace is enigmatic, equivocal. It is so in still another sense, which distinguishes it from the appearing of phenomena. It cannot serve as the point of departure for a demonstration, which inexorably would bring it into immanence and essence. The trace is sketched out and effaced in the face in the equivocation of a saying. In this way it modulates the modality of the Transcendent.[37]

The infinite then cannot be tracked down like game by a hunter. The trace left by the Infinite is not the residue of a presence; its very glow is ambiguous. Otherwise its positivity would not preserve the infinity of the infinite any more than negativity would.

The infinite wipes out its traces not in order to trick him who obeys but because it transcends the present in which it commands me and because I cannot deduce it from this command. The infinite who orders me is neither a cause acting straight on nor a theme, already dominated, if only retrospectively, by freedom. This detour from the face and the detour with regard to this detour in the enigma of a trace we have called illeity.[38]

Illeity lies outside the "thou" and the thematization of objects. A neologism formed with *il* (he) or *ille*, it indicates a way of concerning me without entering into *conjunction* with me. To be sure, we have to indicate the element in which this *concerning* occurs. If the relationship with illeity were a relationship of consciousness, "he" would designate a theme, as the "thou" in Buber's I-thou relation probably does.[39] For Buber has never brought out in a positive way the spiritual element in which the I-thou relationship is produced. The illeity in the beyond-being is the fact that its coming toward me is a departure which lets me accomplish a movement toward the neighbor. The positivity of this departure, that which makes this departure, this diachrony, be more than a term of negative theology, is my responsibility for the others. Or, one may say, it is the fact that the others show themselves in their face. There is a paradox in responsibility, in that I am obliged without this obligation having begun in me, as though an order slipped into my consciousness like a thief, smuggled itself in, like an effect of one of Plato's wandering causes.[40] But this is impossible in a consciousness and clearly indicates that we are no longer in the element of consciousness. In consciousness this "who knows where" is translated by an anachronical overwhelming, the antecedence of responsibility and obedience with respect to the order received or the contract. It is as though the first movement of responsibility could not consist in awaiting or even in welcoming the order (which would still be a quasi-activity) but in obeying this order before it is formulated. Or as though it were formulated before every possible present, in a past that shows itself in the present of obedience without being recalled, without coming from memory, being formulated by him who obeys in his very obedience.

But this is still perhaps a very narrative, epic, way of speaking. Am I the interlocutor of an Infinity lacking in straightforwardness and giving its commands indirectly by the very face to which it ordains me? The illeity, which does not simply designate an oblique presentation to a squinting look, may indeed first signify such a disposition of personages. But we must go all the way. The infinite does not signal itself to a subjectivity, a unit already formed, by its order to turn toward the neighbor. In its *being* subjectivity undoes *essence* by substituting itself for the other (*autrui*). Qua one-for-another, it is absorbed in signification, in saying or the verb form of the infinite. Signification precedes essence. It is not a stage of cognition calling for the intuition that would fulfill it, nor the absurdity of nonidentity or of impossible identity. It is the glory of transcendence.

Substitution is signification. Not a reference from one term to another, as it appears thematized in the Said, but substitution as the very subjectivity of the subject, interruption of the irreversible identity of the essence. It occurs in the taking in charge which is incumbent on me without any possible escape. Here the unicity of the ego first acquires a meaning - where it is no longer a question of the Ego, but of me.[41] The subject which is no longer an ego but which I am cannot be generalized; it is not a subject in general; we have moved from the Ego to me who am me and no one else.[42] Here the identity of the subject comes from the impossibility of escaping responsibility, from the taking charge of the other. Signification, saying - my expressivity, my own signifyingness qua sign, my own verbality qua verb - cannot be understood as a modality of being; disinterestedness suspends essence. As a substitution of one for the other, as me, as human, I am not a transubstantiation, a change from one substance into another, I do not shut myself up in another identity, I do not rest in a new avatar. As signification, proximity, saying, separation, I do not fuse with anything. Must we give a name to this relationship of signification grasped as subjectivity? Must we pronounce the word *expiation* and conceive the subjectivity of the subject, the otherwise than being, as an expiation? That would perhaps be bold and premature. At least we can ask if subjectivity qua signification, qua one-for-the-other, is not traceable back to the vulnerability of the ego, to the incommunicable, nonconceptualizable, sensibility.

7. Sensibility

Man is not to be conceived in function of being and not-being, taken as ultimate references. Humanity, subjectivity - the excluded middle, excluded from everywhere, a nonplace - signify the breakup of this alternative, the one-in-the-place-of-the-other, substitution, signification in its signifyingness qua sign, prior to essence, before identity. Signification, prior to being, breaks up the assembling, the recollection or the present of essence. On the hither side of or beyond essence, signification is the exhaustion of the spirit expiring without inspiring, disinterestedness and gratuity or gratitude; the rupture of essence is ethical.

This beyond is said and is translated in discourse by a Saying out of breath or retaining its breath, the extreme possibility of the spirit, its very *epochē*, by which it *says* before resting in its own theme and therein allowing itself to be absorbed by essence. This rupture of identity, this changing of being into signification, that is, into substitution, is the subject's subjectivity, or its subjection to everything, its susceptibility, its vulnerability, that is, its sensibility.

Subjectivity, place and nonplace of this rupture, takes place (*se passe*) as a passivity more passive than all passivity. To the diachronic past, which cannot be recuperated by representation effected by memory or history - a past that is incommensurable with the present - corresponds or answers the unassumable passivity of the self. *Se passer* - to take place by passing itself - a precious expression in which the *self* figures as in a past that bypasses itself, as in aging without "active synthesis." The response which is responsibility, an incumbent responsibility for the neighbor, resounds in this passivity, this disinterestedness of subjectivity, this sensibility.

Vulnerability, exposure to outrage, to wounding, passivity more passive than all patience, passivity of the accusative form, trauma of accusation suffered by a hostage to the point of persecution, putting into question the identity of the hostage who substitutes himself for the others: all this is the Self, a defecting or defeat of the Ego's identity. And this, pushed to the limit, is sensibility, sensibility as the subjectivity of the subject. It is a substitution for another, one in the place of another, expiation.[43]

Responsibility for the Other (*Autrui*), in its antecedence to my freedom - to the present and to representation - is a passivity more passive than all passivity, an exposure to the other without this exposure being assumed, an exposure without holding back, exposure of exposedness, expression, Saying. It is the frankness, sincerity, veracity of Saying. Not Saying dissimulating itself and protecting itself in the Said, just giving out words in the face of the other, but saying uncovering itself, that is, denuding itself of its skin, sensibility on the surface of the skin, at the edge of the nerves, offering itself unto suffering - and thus wholly sign, signifying itself. Substitution, at the limit of being, ends up in Saying, in the giving of signs, giving a sign of this giving of signs, expressing itself. This expression is antecedent to all thematization of the said, but it is not a babbling or a still primitive or childish form of saying. This stripping beyond nudity, beyond forms, is not the work of negation and no longer belongs to the order of being. Responsibility goes beyond being. In sincerity, in frankness, in the veracity of this Saying, in the uncoveredness of suffering, being is altered. But this saying remains, in its activity, a passivity; more passive than all passivity, for it is a sacrifice without reserve, without holding back, and therefore nonvoluntary - the sacrifice of a hostage designated who has not chosen himself to be hostage, but, possibly, elected by the Good, in an involuntary election not assumed by the elected one. For the Good cannot enter into a present or be put into a representation. But being Good it redeems the violence of its alterity, even if the subject has to suffer through the augmentation of this ever more demanding violence.

8. Being and Beyond Being

The proximity of one to the Other is here thought outside of ontological categories in which, for different reasons, the notion of the *other* also figures, whether as an obstacle to freedom, intelligibility, or perfection; or as a term that confirms a finite being, mortal and uncertain of itself, by recognizing it; or as a slave, collaborator or God able to succor. Everywhere proximity is conceived ontologically, that is, as a limit or complement to the accomplishment of the adventure of essence, which consists in persisting in essence and unfolding immanence, in remaining in an Ego, in identity. Proximity remains a distance diminished, an exteriority conjured. The present study sets out not to conceive proximity as a function of being. The *otherwise than being*, which, to be sure, is understood in being, differs absolutely from essence, has no genus in common with essence, and is said only in the exhaustion that pronounces the extraordinary word *beyond*. Alterity counts in it outside any qualification of the other for the ontological order and outside any attribute. It figures as what is near in a proximity that counts as sociality, which "excites" by its pure and simple alterity. We have sought to analyze this relation without resorting to the categories that dissimulate it, by conceiving it in terms of proximity qua saying, contact, sincerity of exposure, a saying prior to language, but without which no language, as a transmission of messages, would be possible.

The way of thinking proposed here does not fail to recognize being or treat it, ridiculously and pretentiously, with disdain, as the fall from a higher order or Disorder. On the contrary, it is on the basis of proximity that being takes on its just meaning. In the indirect ways of illeity, in the anarchical provocation which ordains me to the other, is imposed the way which leads to thematization and becoming conscious. Becoming conscious is motivated by the presence of the third alongside the neighbor approached. The third is also approached; and the relationship between the neighbor and the third cannot be indifferent to me when I approach. There must be justice among incomparable ones. There must then be a comparison between incomparables and a synopsis, a togetherness and contemporaneousness; there must be thematization, thought, history, and writing. But being must be understood on the basis of *being's other*. From the perspective of the signification of the approach, to be is to be *with* the other (*autrui*) for or against the third, with the other (*autrui*) and the third against oneself; it is to be for justice against a philosophy that does not see beyond being and reduces, by an abuse of language, the Saying to the Said and all meaning to interest. Reason, to which the virtue of arresting violence is ascribed, issuing in the order of peace, presupposes disinterestedness, passivity, or patience. In this disinterestedness - when, as a responsibility for the other, it is also a responsibility for the third - the justice that compares, assembles, and conceives, the synchrony of being and peace, takes form.

9. Subjectivity Is Not a Modality of Essence

The problem of transcendence and God and the problem of subjectivity irreducible to essence, irreducible to essential immanence, go together.

Without reverting to the truism that all reality that is in any way recognizable is subjective, a truism that goes with the one that says that everything that is in any way recognized presupposes the comprehension of being, Kant, by distinguishing in his solution of the Antinomies the temporal series of experience from the in-temporal (or synchronic?) series conceived by the understanding, has shown in the very *objectivity* of an object its *phenomenality*: a reference to the fundamental incompletion of the succession and hence to the subjectivity of the subject.[44]

But is subjectivity thus thought in its irreducibility? Hegel and Heidegger try to empty the distinction between the subject and the being of its signification. In reintroducing time into being, they denounce the idea of a subjectivity irreducible to essence and, beyond the object inseparable from the subject, reduce their correlation and the anthropological dimension understood in these terms to a modality of being. In his introduction to the *Phenomenology of Spirit*, in treating as a "pure presupposition" the thesis that knowing is an instrument to take hold of the Absolute (a technological metaphor) or a medium through which the light of truth penetrates the knower (a dioptic metaphor), Hegel denies that there is a radical break between subjectivity and the knowable. It is in the heart of the Absolute that the *beyond* takes on meaning; essence, understood as the immanence of knowing, is taken to account for subjectivity, which is reduced to a moment of the concept, of thought or of absolute essence. In a remark at the end of his *Nietzsche*, Heidegger says that the "current term *subjectivity* immediately and too obstinately burdens thought with deceptive opinions that take as a destruction of objective being any reference from being to man and especially to his egoity."[45] Heidegger tries to conceive subjectivity in function of being, of which it expresses an "epoch":[46] subjectivity, consciousness and the Ego presuppose *Dasein*, which belongs to essence as the modality in which essence manifests itself, while the manifestation of essence is what is essential in essence;

experience and the subject having the experience constitute the very manner in which at a given "epoch" of essence, essence is accomplished, that is, is manifested. Every overcoming as well as every revaluation of being in the subject would still be a case of being's essence.

Our inquiry concerned with the *otherwise than being* catches sight in the very hypostasis of a subject - in its subjectification - an ex-ception, a nonplace on the hither side of the negativity which is always speculatively recuperable, an *outside* of the absolute which can no longer be stated in terms of being. Nor even in terms of beings, which one would still suspect modulate being and thus heal the break marked by the hypostasis. The subject already resists this ontologization when it is conceived as a Saying. Behind every statement of being as being, the Saying overflows the very being it thematizes in stating it to the Other (*Autrui*). It is being which is understood in the - first or last - word, but the last Saying goes *beyond* the being thematized or totalized. Irreducible to being's essence is the substitution in responsibility, signification or the one-for-another, or the defecting of the Ego beyond every defeat, going countercurrent to a *conatus*, or goodness. In it the other (*autrui*) is imposed quite differently from the reality of the real: he imposes himself because he is other, because this alterity is incumbent on me with a whole charge of indigence and weakness. Can substitution and goodness still be interpreted as a "movement" or a modality of being's essence? Would it still move in the light of being? But is the vision of a face in the light of being? Is not vision here immediately a taking charge? The intention *toward the other* (*envers autrui*), when it has reached its peak, turns out to belie intentionality. *Toward the other* (*autrui*) culminates in a *for the other* (*autrui*), a suffering for his suffering, without light, that is, without measure, quite different from the purely negative blindness of Fortune, which only seems to close its eyes so as to give its riches arbitrarily. Arising at the apex of essence, goodness is *other* than being; it no longer keeps accounts. It is not like negativity, which conserves what it negates, in its history. It destroys without leaving souvenirs, without transporting into museums the altars raised to the idols of the past for bloody sacrifices, it burns the sacred groves in which the echoes of the past reverberate. The ex-ceptional, extra-ordinary, transcendent character of goodness is due to just this break with being and its history. To reduce the good to being, to its calculations and its history, is to nullify goodness. The ever possible sliding between subjectivity and being, of which subjectivity would be but a mode, the equivalence of the two languages, stops here. Goodness gives to subjectivity its irreducible signification.

The human subject - me - called on the brink of tears and laughter to his responsibilities, is not an avatar of nature or a moment of the concept or an articulation of "being's presence to us," that is, of its *parousia*.[47] It is not a question of assuring the ontological dignity of man, as though essence sufficed for dignity, but, on the contrary, of contesting the philosophical privilege of being, of inquiring after what is beyond or on its hither side. To reduce man to self-consciousness and self-consciousness to the concept, that is, to History, to deduce from the Concept and from History the subjectivity and the "I" in order to find meaning for the very singularity of "that one" in function of the concept, by neglecting, as contingent, what may be left irreducible after this reduction and what residue there may be after this deduction, is - under the pretext of not caring about the ineffectiveness of "good intentions" and "the beautiful soul" and preferring "the labour of the concept" to the facilities of psychological naturalism, humanist rhetoric and existentialist *pathos*[48] - to forget what is better than being, that is, the Good.

The beyond being, *being's other* or the *otherwise than being*, here situated in diachrony and expressed as infinity, has been recognized as the Good by Plato. It matters little that Plato made of it an idea and a source of light. The beyond being, showing itself in the said, always shows itself there enigmatically, that is, it is there already betrayed. Its resistance to gathering, conjunction and conjuncture, to contemporaneousness, immanence, and the present of manifestation, signifies the diachrony of responsibility for the other (*autrui*) and of a deep pastness,[49] more ancient than all freedom, which commands it while, in this very sentence, they are synchronized. This diachrony is itself an enigma: the beyond being does and does not revert to ontology; as soon as it is pronounced, the beyond, the infinite, becomes and does not become the meaning of being.[50]

10. The Itinerary

The different concepts that come up in the attempt to say transcendence echo one another. The necessities of thematization in which they are said ordain a division into chapters, although the themes in which these concepts present themselves do not lend themselves to linear unfolding and cannot be really isolated from one another without projecting their shadows and their reflections on one another. Perhaps the clarity of the exposition does not suffer here only from the clumsiness of the expounder.

The exposition is worked out between the present argument, which introduces it, and the final chapter, which, in the guise of a conclusion, elucidates it in a different way.[51] It aims to bring out the subjectivity of the subject by starting from reflections on truth, time, and being in the amphibology of being and beings borne by the Said; it will then present the subject, in Saying, as sensibility from the first animated by responsibilities (chapter 2). Then it will set out to show proximity to be the meaning of sensibility (chapter 3), substitution as the *otherwise than being* at the heart of proximity (chapter 4); and as a relation between the subject and the Infinite, in which the Infinite *comes to pass* (*se passe*, chapter 5). In bringing out substitution in the Saying which is in responsibility, it will then have to justify, starting with this *Saying* which is in substitution, of the order of the *Said*, thought, justice and being, and understand the conditions in which philosophies, in the Said, in ontology, can signify *truth*. It will do so by linking to the alternating fate of skepticism in philosophical thought - in turn refuted and returning - the alternatings or the diachrony, resisting the gathering of the *otherwise than being* or transcendence and its exposition.

Is the itinerary whose stages we have just indicated sufficiently reliable? Is its beginning indeed accessible? Will the reproach not be made that this movement is not sufficiently warned of the dangers on the way and has not provided itself with means to ward them off? No doubt it is not completely free from pre-philosophical experiences, and many of its tracks will appear beaten, many of its thrusts imprudent. But a fine risk is always worth taking in philosophy. That the beginning of the silent discourse of the soul with itself can be justified only by its end is a still optimistic conception of philosophical discourse which a genius, and a synthetic genius, such as Hegel, can permit himself, assured as he is of being able to complete the cycle of thought.[52] Hegel will ask, no doubt rightly, if a preface in which the project of a philosophical enterprise is formulated is not superfluous or even obscuring, and Heidegger will contest the possibility of an introduction where the movement begins in being instead of coming from man, where it is not a question of leading man to the present of being, but where being is in the presence of man in *parousia*. Should we not think with as much precaution of the possibility of a conclusion or a closure of the philosophical discourse? Is not its interruption its only possible end? More modestly, Husserl will have taught us that every movement of thought involves a share of naïveté, which, in the Hegelian enterprise, lies at least in its pretention to include the Real. Husserl will have taught us that the reduction of naïveté immediately calls for new reductions, that the grace of intuition involves gratuitous ideas, and that, if philosophizing consists in assuring oneself of an absolute origin, the philosopher will have to efface the trace of his own footsteps and unendingly efface the traces of the effacing of the traces, in an interminable methodological standstill. Unless the naïveté of the philosopher calls, beyond the reflection on oneself, for a critique exercised by *another* philosopher, whatever be the imprudences that the latter will have committed in his turn, and the gratuity of his own saying. Philosophy thus arouses a drama between philosophers and an intersubjective movement which does not resemble the dialogue of teamworkers in science, not even the Platonic dialogue which is the reminiscence of a drama rather than the drama itself. It is sketched out in a different structure; empirically it is realized as the history of philosophy in which new interlocutors always enter who have to say again, but in which the ancients take up the floor to answer in the interpretations they arouse, and in which, nonetheless, despite this lack of "certainty in one's movements" or because of it, no one is allowed a relaxation of attention or a lack of strictness.

God and Philosophy
(1975)

"God and Philosophy" is a far-ranging work that perhaps more than any other single essay serves as a summary of Levinas's mature thought.[1] Levinas sets out to show not only that the intelligibility of transcendence lies outside ontological structures but also that it bears an ethical sense or direction. The question of rational discourse about God which Levinas addresses in the first section is introduced in support of the claim that Western philosophy has been "a destruction of transcendence," albeit with a few exceptions.

Levinas had long allowed himself to be guided by two of those exceptions. The first was Plato's use of the phrase "beyond being" (*epekeina tes ousias*) to refer to the good; the second was Descartes's proof of the existence of God in the Third Meditation, which Levinas had explored in "Philosophy and the Idea of Infinity" in 1957 and used four years later to give structure to his first major work, *Totality and Infinity*. In "God and Philosophy," both models are appealed to, but more attention is given to the second. This is because Levinas finds in Descartes's account of a thought greater than I can contain a model of how transcendence breaks open the unity, immanence, and presence of the subject as ordinarily conceived by philosophy. Attaching to the Cartesian model a signification it does not bear in Descartes's presentation of it, Levinas claims that this transcendence has an ethical meaning. The argument is that the structure of transcendence is exemplified not by religious experience but by the ethical.

"God and Philosophy" opens with an implicit reference to Derrida's 1964 essay on Levinas, "Violence and Metaphysics." Derrida had quoted a Greek as saying, "If one has to philosophize, one has to philosophize; if one does not have to philosophize, one still has to philosophize (to say it and think it). One always has to philosophize" (see note 2). At the same time, Derrida quoted some remarks by Levinas which indicated his agreement with this formulation. Derrida's purpose was to establish that Levinas could not break free of the Western philosophical tradition, contrary to some of his more dramatic claims to that effect. At the close of "God and Philosophy" Levinas responded by contradicting Derrida directly: "not to philosophize would not be 'to philosophize still.'" This is important to Levinas because he insists that the ethical demand that the Other makes on me, so breaking up my subjectivity, comes from beyond philosophy. This is the way Levinas chooses to resist Derrida's description of the Greek *logos* as having the power to encompass whatever stands outside it.

The Priority of Philosophical Discourse and Ontology

1. "Not to philosophize is still to philosophize."[2] The philosophical discourse of the West claims the amplitude of an all-encompassing structure or of an ultimate comprehension. It compels every other discourse to justify itself before philosophy.

Rational theology accepts this vassalage. If, for the benefit of religion, it reserves a domain from the authority of philosophy, one will know that this domain will have been recognized to be philosophically unverifiable.

2. The dignity of being the ultimate and royal discourse belongs to Western philosophy because of the strict coinciding of thought, in which philosophy resides, and the idea of reality in which this thought thinks. For thought, this coinciding means not having to think beyond what belongs to "being's move" ["*geste d'être*"], or at least not beyond what modifies a previous belongingness to "being's move," such as formal or ideal notions. For the being of reality, this coinciding means: to illuminate thought and the conceived by showing itself. To show oneself, to be illuminated, is just what having meaning is, what having intelligibility par excellence is, the intelligibility underlying every modification of meaning. Then we should have to understand the rationality of "being's move" not as some characteristic which would be attributed to it when a reason comes to know of it. That a thought comes to know of it is intelligibility. Rationality has to be understood as the incessant emergence of thought from the energy of "being's move" or its manifestation, and reason has to be understood out of this rationality. Meaningful thought, and thought about being, would be pleonasms and equivalent pleonasms, which, however, are justified by the vicissitudes and privations to which this identification of the thought of the meaningful and of being is de jure exposed.

3. Philosophical discourse therefore should be able to include God - of whom the Bible speaks - if this God does have a meaning. But as soon as he is conceived, this God is situated within "being's move." He is situated there as the *being* (*étant*) par excellence. If the intellectual understanding of the biblical God, theology, does not reach to the level of philosophical thought, this is not because it thinks of God as *a being* without first explicating the "being of this being," but because in thematizing God it brings God into the course of being. But, in the most unlikely way - that is, not analogous with an idea subject to *criteria* or subject to the demand that it show itself to be true or false - the God of the Bible signifies the beyond being, transcendence. It is not by chance that the history of Western philosophy has been a destruction of transcendence. Rational theology, fundamentally ontological, strives to take account of transcendence in the domain of being by expressing it with adverbs of height applied to the verb being; God is said to exist eminently or par excellence. But does the height, or the height above all height, that is thus expressed belong to ontology? And does not the modality which this adverb expresses, borrowed from the dimension of the sky over our heads, modify the verbal meaning of the verb to be to the point of excluding it from the thinkable as something inapprehendable, excluding it from the *esse* showing itself, that is, showing itself meaningfully in a theme?

4. One can also, to be sure, claim that the God of the Bible does not have meaning, that is, is not properly speaking thinkable, this would be the other term of the alternative. "The concept of God is not a problematical concept; it is not a concept at all," writes Mme. Delhomme in a recent book,[3] continuing a major tradition of philosophical rationalism which refuses to accept the transcendence of the God of Abraham, Isaac, and Jacob among the concepts without which there would be no thought. What the Bible puts above all comprehension would have not yet reached the threshold of intelligibility!

The problem which is thus posed, and which will be ours, is whether the meaning that is equivalent to the *esse* of being, that is, the meaning which is meaning in philosophy, is not already a restriction of meaning. Is it not already a derivative or a drifting of meaning? Is not the meaning equivalent to essence - to being's move, to being qua being - first broached in presence, which is the time of the same? This supposition can be justified only through the possibility of going back from this allegedly conditioned meaning to a meaning which could no longer be put in terms of being or in terms of beings. We must ask if beyond the intelligibility and rationalism of identity, consciousness, the present, and being - beyond the intelligibility of immanence - the signifyingness, rationality, and rationalism of transcendence are not understood. Over and beyond being does not a meaning whose priority, translated into ontological language, would have to be called *antecedent* to being, show itself? It is not certain that in going beyond the terms and beings one necessarily relapses into speaking of opinion or faith. In fact, in staying or wanting to be outside of reason, faith and opinion speak the language of being. Nothing is less opposed to ontology than opinion and faith. To ask, as we are trying to do here, if God can be exposed in a rational discourse which would be neither ontology nor faith is implicitly to doubt the formal opposition, established by Yehouda Halevy and taken up by Pascal, between the God of Abraham, Isaac, and Jacob, invoked in faith without philosophy, and the god of philosophers.[4] It is to doubt that this opposition constitutes an alternative.

The Priority of Ontology and Immanence

5. We said that, for Western philosophy, meaning or intelligibility coincide with the manifestation of being, as if the very business of being led to clarity, in the form of intelligibility, and then became an intentional thematization in an experience. Pressing toward or waiting for it, all the potentialities of experience are derived from or susceptible to such thematization. Thematic exposition concludes the business of being or truth. But if being *is* manifestation, if the exertion of being amounts to this exhibition, the manifestation of being is only the manifestation of this "exertion," that is, the manifestation of manifestation, the truth of truth. Philosophy thus finds in manifestation its matter and its

form. In its attachment to being, to beings or the being of beings, it would thus remain a movement of knowledge and truth, an adventure of experience between the clear and the obscure. It is certain that this is the sense in which philosophy is the bearer of the spirituality of the West, where spirit is taken to be coextensive with knowing. But knowing - or thought, or experience - is not to be understood as a kind of reflection of exteriority in an inner forum. The notion of reflection, an optical metaphor taken from thematized beings and events, is not the proper trope for knowing. Knowing is only understood in its proper essence when one begins with consciousness, whose specificity is lost when it is defined with the concept of knowing, a concept which presupposes consciousness.

It is as a modality or modification of *insomnia* that consciousness is consciousness of . . . , a gathering into being or into presence, which, at a certain depth of vigilance where vigilance has to clothe itself with justice, is essential to insomnia.[5] Insomnia, wakefulness or vigilance, far from being definable as the simple negation of the natural phenomenon of sleep, belongs to the categorial, antecedent to all anthropological attention and stupor. Ever on the verge of awakening, sleep communicates with vigilance; while trying to escape, sleep stays tuned in, in an *obedience to the wakefulness* which threatens it and calls to it, which *demands*. The categorial proper to insomnia is not reducible to the tautological affirmation of the same, dialectical negation, or the ecstasy of thematizing intentionality. Here being awake is not equivalent to *watching over* . . . , where already the identical, rest, sleep, is sought after. It is in consciousness alone that the *watching*, already petrified, bends over toward a content which is identified and gathered into a presence, into a "move of being," and is absorbed in it. Insomnia as a category - or as a metacategory (but the *meta* becomes meaningful through it) - does not get inscribed in a table of categories from a determining activity exercised on the other as *given* by the unity of the Same (and all activity is but the identification and crystallization of the Same against the other, upon being affected by that other), in order to ensure to the other, consolidated into a being, the gravity of being. Insomnia - the wakefulness in awakening - is disturbed in the core of its formal or categorial *equality* by the *other*, which tears away at whatever forms a nucleus, a substance of the Same, identity, a rest, a presence, a sleep. Insomnia is disturbed by the other who breaks this rest, breaks it from this side of the *state* in which equality tends to establish itself. The irreducible categorial character of insomnia lies precisely in this: the other is in the Same and does not alienate the same but awakens it. Awakening is like a demand that no obedience is equal to, no obedience puts to sleep; it is a "more" in the "less." Or, to use an obsolete language, it is the spirituality of the soul, ceaselessly aroused from its state of soul, in which *wakefulness* itself already closes over upon itself or falls to sleep, resting within the boundaries it has as a state. We find here the passivity of Inspiration, or the subjectivity of the subject aroused, sobered up, out of its being. There is a formalism in insomnia, a formalism more formal than that of any defining, delimiting, confining form, more formally formal than that of a form that closes into a presence and an *esse*, filling with content. Insomnia is wakefulness, but a wakefulness without intentionality - dis-interested. Its indeterminateness does not call for a form, is not a materiality. It is a form that does not *terminate* the drawing out of a form in it, and does not condense its own emptiness into a content. It is uncontained - Infinity.

6. Consciousness has already broken with this dis-interestedness. It is the identity of the Same, the presence of being, the presence of presence. We must think of consciousness beginning with the emphasis of presence.[6] Presence is only possible as a return of consciousness to itself, outside of sleep - and consciousness thus goes back to insomnia. That is so even though this return to itself, in the form of self-consciousness, is only a forgetting of the Other which awakens the Same from within, and even if the freedom of the same is still only a waking dream. Presence is only possible as an incessant taking up of presence again, an incessant re-presentation. The incessance of presence is a repetition, its being taken up again an apperception of representation. Re-presentation is not to be described as a taking up again (*re-prise*). Re-presentation is the very possibility of a return, the possibility of the *always*, or of the presence of the present. The unity of apperception, the "I think," which is discovered and acquired its role in re-presentation, is not a way to make presence purely subjective. The synthesis effected by the unity of the *I think* behind experience constitutes the act of presence, presence as an act, or presence in act. This encompassing movement is accomplished by the unity formed into a nucleus in the "I think," a synopsis which is a structure necessary for the actuality of the present. The "activity of the mind," the operative concept of transcendental idealism, is not based on an empirical experience of the deployment of intellectual energy. It is rather the extreme purity - to the point of tension - of the presence of presence, which is Aristotle's being in act, a presence of presence, an extreme tension breaking up *presence* into an "experience of a subject," where precisely presence returns upon itself and is filled up and fulfilled. The psychic nature of consciousness is this emphasis of being, this presence of presence, a presence outdoing itself, without loopholes, without hedging, any possible forgetting in the folds of what would be only implicit and could not be unfolded. The "incessance" is an explication without any possible shading off; it refers to an awakening that would be lucidity, but also to a watching over being, an attention to . . . , and not an exposedness to the other (and already a modification of the formalism without intentionality of insom-

nia). It is always true that because of consciousness nothing can be dissimulated in being. Consciousness is a light which illuminates the world from one end to the other; everything which goes off into the past is recalled or recovered by history. Reminiscence is the extreme consciousness which is also the universal presence and the universal ontology; whatever is able to fill the field of consciousness was, in its time, received or perceived, had an origin. Through consciousness the past is only a modification of the present. Nothing can happen and nothing could have happened without presenting itself, nothing could be smuggled by without being declared, without being shown, without being inspected as to its truth. Transcendental subjectivity is the figure of this presence; no signification precedes that which I give to myself.

Thus the process of the present unfolds through consciousness like a "held note" held in its *always*, in its identity of being the same, in the simultaneity of its moments. The process of the subjective does not come from the outside; the presence of the present involves consciousness. And philosophy, then, in search of the transcendental operations of the apperception of the *I think*, is not some unhealthy and accidental curiosity; it is representation, the reactualization of representation, that is, the emphasis of presence, being's remaining-the-same in the simultaneity of its presence, in its always, in its immanence. Philosophy is not merely the knowledge of immanence; it is immanence itself.[7]

7. Immanence and consciousness, as gathering up the manifestation of manifestation, are not disturbed by the phenomenological interpretation of affective states or of the voluntary psyche, which puts in the very heart of consciousness the emotion or the anxiety which upset its imperturbability - nor by that interpretation that starts from fear or trembling before the sacred, and understands them as primary lived states. It is not accidental that the axiological and practical strata in Husserl cover over a representational ground.

The axiological and the practical strata remain in experience - experiences of values, or experiences of the willed qua willed. The representational ground, which Husserl brings out in them, consists, moreover, less in some serenity of the theoretical intention than in the identification of the identical in the form of ideality, in the assembling, in the representation in the form of a presence, a lucidity which allows nothing to escape.[8] In short, it consists in immanence.

8. But let us take note of this: the interpretation of affectivity as a modification of representation, or as founded on a representation, succeeds in the measure that affectivity is taken at the level of a tendency, or concupiscence, as Pascal would say - at the level of an aspiration which can be satisfied in pleasure or, when unsatisfied, remains a pure lack which causes suffering. Beneath such an affectivity is found the ontological activity of consciousness - wholly investment and comprehension, that is, presence and representation (of which

the specifically theoretical thematization is but a modality). This does not exclude the possibility that, in another direction besides that of a tendency going to its term, there break out an affectivity which breaks with the form and the purpose of consciousness, and leaves immanence, is a transcendence. We are going to try to speak of this "elsewhere."

9. A religious thought which appeals to religious experiences allegedly independent of philosophy already, inasmuch as it is founded on experience, refers to the "I think," and is wholly connected on to philosophy. The "narration" of religious experience does not shake philosophy and cannot break with presence and immanence, of which philosophy is the emphatic completion. It is possible that the word God has come to philosophy out of religious discourse. But even if philosophy refuses this discourse, it understands it as a language made of propositions bearing on a theme, that is, as having a meaning which refers to a disclosure, a manifestation of presence. The bearers of religious experience do not conceive of any other signification of meaning. Religious "revelation" is therewith already assimilated to philosophical disclosure; even dialectical theology maintains this assimilation. That a discourse can speak otherwise than to say what has been seen or heard on the outside, or previously experienced, remains unsuspected. From the start then a religious being interprets what he lived through as an experience. In spite of himself he already interprets God, of whom he claims to have an experience, in terms of being, presence and immanence.

Then the first question has to be: can discourse signify otherwise than by signifying a theme? Does God signify as the theme of the religious discourse which names God - or as the discourse which, at least to begin with, does not name him, but says him with another form of address than denomination or evocation?

The Idea of the Infinite

10. The thematization of God in religious experience has already dodged or missed the inordinate intrigue that breaks up the unity of the "I think."[9]

In his meditation on the idea of God, Descartes, with an unequaled rigor, has sketched out the extraordinary course of a thought that proceeds on to the breakup of the *I think*. Although he conceives of God as a being, he conceives of him as an eminent being or being that *is* eminently. Before this rapprochement between the idea of God and the idea of being, we do indeed have to ask whether the adjective *eminent* and the adverb *eminently* do not refer to the elevation of the sky above our heads, and whether they do not go beyond ontology. Be that as it may, interpreting the immeasurability of God as a superlative case of existing, Descartes maintains a substantialist language. But for us this is not what is unsurpassable in his mediation. It is not the proofs of God's existence that matter to us here but the breakup of consciousness, which is not a repression into the unconscious but a sobering up or an awakening, jolting the "dogmatic slumber" which sleeps at the bottom of every consciousness resting on its object. The idea of God, the *cogitatum* of a *cogitatio* which *to begin with* contains that *cogitatio*, signifies the noncontained par excellence. Is not that the very absolution of the absolute? It overflows every capacity; the "objective reality" of the *cogitatum* breaks up the "formal reality" of the *cogitatio*. This perhaps overturns, in advance, the universal validity and primordial character of intentionality. We will say that the idea of God breaks up the thought, which is an investment, a synopsis, and a synthesis and can only enclose in a presence, re-present, reduce to presence or let be.

Malebranche knew how to gauge the import of this event; there is no idea of God, or God is his own idea.[10] We are outside the order in which one passes from an idea to a being. The idea of God is God in me, but God already breaking up the consciousness which aims at ideas, and unlike any content. This difference is certainly not an emergence, which would be to imply that an inclusion of God in consciousness had been possible, nor some sort of escaping the realm of consciousness, which is to imply that there could have been *comprehension*. And yet there is an idea of God, or God is in us, as though the being-not-includable were also an ex-ceptional relationship with me, as though the difference between the Infinite and what ought to include and comprehend it were a nonindifference of the Infinite to this impossible inclusion, a nonindifference of the Infinite to thought. There is a putting of the Infinite into thought, but this is wholly different from what is structured as a comprehension of a *cogitatum* by a *cogitatio*. This putting is an unequaled passivity, because it is unassumable. (It is perhaps in this passivity - beyond all passivity - that we should recognize awakening.) Or, conversely, it is as though the negation of the finite included in In-finity did not signify any sort of negation resulting from the formal structure of negative judgment but rather signified the *idea of the Infinite*, that is, the Infinite in me. Or, more exactly, it is as though the psyche in subjectivity were equivalent to the negation of the finite by the Infinite, as though - without wanting to play on words - the *in* of the Infinite were to signify both the *non* and the *within*.[11]

11. The actuality of the *cogito* is thus interrupted by the unincludable, not thought but undergone in the form of the idea of the Infinite, bearing in a second moment of consciousness what in a first moment claimed to bear it. After the certainty of the *cogito*, present to itself in the Second Meditation, after the "halt" which the last lines of this meditation mark, the Third Meditation announces that "in some way I have in me the notion of the infinite earlier than

the finite - to wit, the notion of God before that of myself." The idea of the Infinite, *Infinity in me*, can only be a passivity of consciousness. Is it still consciousness? There is here a passivity which cannot be likened to receptivity. Receptivity is a collecting that takes place in a welcome, an assuming that takes place under the force of the blow received. The breakup of the actuality of thought in the "idea of God" is a passivity more passive still than any passivity, like the passivity of a trauma through which the idea of God would have been put into us. An "idea put into us" - does this stylistic turn suit the subjectivity of the cogito? Does it suit consciousness and its way of holding a content, which is to always leave some traces of its grasp on it? Does not consciousness, in its present, get its origin and its contents from itself? Can an idea be put into a thought and abjure its letters patent of Socratic nobility, its immanent birth in reminiscence, that is, its origin in the very presence of the thought that thinks it, or in the recuperation of this thought by memory? But in the idea of the Infinite there is described a passivity more passive still than any passivity befitting consciousness: there is the surprise or susception of the unassumable, more open still than any openness - wakefulness - but suggesting the passivity of someone created.[12] The putting into us of an unincludable idea overturns that presence to self which consciousness is, forcing its way through the barrier and checkpoint, eluding the obligation to accept or adopt all that enters from the outside. It is then an idea signifying with a signifyingness prior to presence, to all presence, prior to every origin in consciousness and thus an-archical, accessible in its trace. It signifies with a signifyingness from the first older than its exhibition, not exhausting itself in exhibiting itself, not drawing its meaning from its manifestation, and thus breaking with the coinciding of being with appearance in which, for Western philosophy, meaning or rationality lie, breaking with synopsis. It is more ancient than the rememberable thought which representation retains in its presence. What can this signification more ancient than exhibition mean? Or, more exactly, what can the antiquity of a signification mean? In exhibition, can it enter into another time than that of the historical present, which already annuls the past and its dia-chrony by re-presenting it? What can this antiquity mean if not the trauma of awakening - as though the idea of the Infinite, the Infinite in us, awakened a consciousness which is not awakened enough? As though the idea of the Infinite in us were a demand, and a signification in the sense that an order is signified in a demand.

Divine Comedy

12. We have already said that it is not in the negation of the finite by the Infinite, understood in its abstraction and logical formalism, that the idea of the Infinite, or the Infinite in thought, is to be interpreted. On the contrary, the idea of the Infinite, or the Infinite in thought, is the proper and irreducible figure for the

negation of the finite. The *in* of infinity is not a *not* like any other; its negation is the subjectivity of the subject, which is behind intentionality. The difference between the Infinite and finite is behind intentionality. The difference between the Infinite and the finite is a nonindifference of the Infinite to the finite, and is the secret of subjectivity. The figure of the Infinite-put-in-me, and, according to Descartes, contemporaneous with my creation,[13] would mean that the not-being-able-to-comprehend-the-Infinite-by-thought is somehow a positive relationship with this thought - but with this thought as passive, as a *cogitatio* as though dumbfounded and no longer, or not yet, commanding the *cogitatum*, not yet hastening toward adequation between the term of the spontaneous teleology of consciousness and this term given in being. Such an adequation is the destiny of the essential teleology of consciousness, which proceeds to its intentional term, and conjures up the presence of re-presentation. Better yet, the not-being-able-to-comprehend-the-Infinite-by-thought would signify the condition - or the unconditionality - of thought, as though to speak of the noncomprehension of the Infinite by the finite did not amount to simply saying that the Infinite is not finite, and as though the affirmation of the difference between the Infinite and the finite had to remain a verbal abstraction, without consideration of the fact that through the noncomprehension of the Infinite by thought, thought is posited as thought,[14] as a posited subjectivity, that is, is posited as self-positing. The Infinite has nothing to add on to itself so as to affect subjectivity; its very in-finity, its difference from the finite, is already its nonindifference to the finite. This amounts to a *cogitatio not comprehending* the *cogitatum* which affects it utterly. The Infinite affects thought by devastating it and at the same time calls upon it; in a "putting it back in its place" it puts thought in place. It awakens it. The awakening of thought is not a welcoming of the Infinite, is not a recollecting, not an assuming, which are necessary and sufficient for *experience*. The idea of the Infinite puts these in question. The idea of the Infinite is not even taken up as love, which is awakened when the arrow strikes, but then the subject stunned by the trauma finds himself forthwith in the immanence of a state of soul. The Infinite signifies precisely prior to its manifestation; here the meaning is not reducible to manifestation, the representation of presence, or teleology. Here meaning is not measured by the possibility or impossibility of the truth of being, even if this antecedent signification should, in one way or another - and if only through its trace - show itself in the enigmas involved in saying.

13. What then is the plot of meaning, other than that of re-presentation and of empirical experience, which is hatched in the idea of the Infinite - in the monstrosity of the Infinite *put* in me - an idea which in its passivity over and beyond all receptivity is no longer an idea? What is the meaning of the trauma

of awakening, in which the Infinite can neither be posited as a correlate of the subject, nor enter into a structure with it, nor become its contemporary in a co-presence - but in which it is transcended? How is transcendence as a relationship thinkable if it must exclude the ultimate and the most formal co-presence which a relationship guarantees to its terms?

The *in* of the Infinite designates the depth of the affecting by which subjectivity is affected through this "putting" of the Infinite into it, without prehension or comprehension. It designates the depth of an undergoing that no capacity comprehends, that no foundation any longer supports, where every process of investing fails and where the screws that fix the stern of inwardness burst. This putting in without a corresponding recollecting devastates its site like a devouring fire, catastrophying its site, in the etymological sense of the word.[15] It is a dazzling, where the eye takes more than it can hold, an igniting of the skin which touches and does not touch what is beyond the graspable, and burns. It is a passivity or a passion in which desire can be recognized, in which the *"more in the less"* awakens by its most ardent, noblest and most ancient flame a thought given over to thinking more than it thinks.[16] But this desire is of another order than the desires involved in hedonist or eudaemonist affectivity and activity, where the desirable is invested, reached, and identified as an object of need, and where the immanence of representation and of the exterior world is restored. The negativity of the *in* of the Infinite - otherwise than being, divine comedy - hollows out a desire which cannot be filled, nourishes itself with its very augmentation, and is exalted as a desire, withdraws from its satisfaction in the measure that it approaches the desirable. It is a desire that is beyond satisfaction, and, unlike a need, does not identify a term or an end. This endless desire for what is beyond being is dis-inter*estedness*, transcendence - desire for the Good.

But if the Infinite in me means a desire for the Infinite, is one certain of the transcendence which *passes* there? Does not desire restore the contemporaneousness of desiring and the desirable? Or, in other words, does not the desiring being derive from the desirable a complacency in desiring, as though it had already grasped it by its intention? Is not the disinter*estedness* of the desire for the Infinite an inter*estedness*? We have spoken of a desire for the Good beyond being, a transcendence, without giving our attention to the way interestedness is excluded from the desire for the Infinite, and without showing how the transcendent Infinite deserves the name Good, when its very transcendence can, it seems, only mean indifference.

14. Love is possible only through the idea of the Infinite - through the Infinite put in me, through the "more" which devastates and awakens the "less," turning away from teleology, destroying the moment and the happiness of the end. Plato forces out of Aristophanes an admission which, coming from

the lips of the master of comedy, is striking indeed: "These are the people who pass their whole lives together; yet they could not explain what they desire of one another."[17] Hephaestus will say that they want to become "one instead of two,"[18] and he thus assigns an end to love and reduces it to a nostalgia for what was in the past. But why can the lovers themselves not say what they ask from one another beyond pleasure? Diotima will put love's intention beyond this unity but will find love to be indigent, needy, and subject to vulgarity. The celestial and the vulgar Venus are sisters. Love is complacent in waiting for the lovable, that is, it enjoys the lovable through the representation which fills up the waiting. Perhaps pornography is that, arising in all eroticism, as eroticism arises in all love. Losing in this enjoyment the inordinateness of desire, love is concupiscence, in Pascal's sense of the term,[19] an assuming and an investing by the *I*. The *I think* reconstitutes presence and being, inter*estedness* and imma-nence, in love.

Is a transcendence of the Desirable beyond the inter*estedness* and eroticism in which the Beyond abides possible? Affected by the Infinite, Desire cannot proceed to an end which it would be equal to; in Desire the approach distances, and enjoyment is but the increase of hunger. Transcendence or the disinterest-*edness* of Desire "passes" in this reversal of terms. How? And in the transcen-dence of the Infinite what dictates to us the word Good? For disinter*estedness* to be possible in the Desire for the Infinite, for the desire beyond being, or transcendence, not to be an absorption in immanence, which would thus make its return, it is necessary that the Desirable or God remain separated in the Desire; as desirable it is near but different: Holy. This can only be if the Desirable orders me to what is the nondesirable, the undesirable par excellence - the other (*autrui*). The reference to the other (*autrui*) is an awakening, an awakening to proximity, and this is a responsibility for the neighbor, to the point of substitut-ing for him. Elsewhere[20] we have shown that substitution for the other (*autrui*) lies in the heart of responsibility, an undoing of the nucleus of the transcenden-tal subject, the transcendence of goodness, the nobility of a pure *supporting*, an ipseity of pure election. Such is Love without Eros. Transcendence is ethics, and subjectivity, which is not, in the last analysis, the "I think" (which it is at first) or the unity of "transcendental apperception," is, as a responsibility for the Other (*Autrui*), a subjection to the other (*autrui*). The I is a passivity more passive still than any passivity because it is from the first in the accusative - oneself [*soi*] - and never was in the nominative; it is under the accusation of the other (*autrui*), even though it be faultless. It is a hostage for the other (*autrui*), obeying a command before having heard it, faithful to a commitment that it never made, to a past that has never been present. This wakefulness or openness to oneself is completely exposed, and sobered up from the ecstasy of intention-ality. We have designated this way for the Infinite, or for God, to refer, from the heart of its very desirability, to the nondesirable proximity of others, by the term "illeity"; it is the extraordinary reversal of the desirability of the Desirable, the supreme desirability, calling to itself the rectilinear straightforwardness of Desire. Through this reversal the Desirable escapes desire. The goodness of the Good - the Good which never sleeps or nods - inclines the movement it calls forth, to turn it from the Good and orient it toward the other (*autrui*), and only thus toward the Good. Here is an obliqueness that goes higher than straightforwardness. The desirable is intangible and separates itself from the relationship with desire which it calls for; through this separation or holiness it remains a third person, the *he* in the depth of the You. He is Good in just this eminent sense; He does not fill me up with goods but compels me to goodness, which is better than goods received.[21]

To be good is a deficit, waste and foolishness in a being; to be good is excellence and elevation beyond being. Ethics is not a moment of being; it is otherwise and better than being, the very possibility of the beyond.[22] In this ethical reversal, in this reference of the Desirable to the Nondesirable, in this strange mission that orders the approach to the other (*autrui*), God is drawn out of objectivity, presence, and being. He is neither an object nor an interlocutor. His absolute remoteness, his transcendence, turns into my responsibility - nonerotic par excellence - for the other (*autrui*). And this analysis implies that God is not simply the "first other (*autrui*)," the other (*autrui*) par excellence, or the "absolutely other (*autrui*)," but other than the other (*autre qu'autrui*), other otherwise, other with an alterity prior to the alterity of the other (*autrui*), prior to the ethical bond with the other (*autrui*) and different from every neighbor, transcendent to the point of absence, to the point of a possible confusion with the stirring of the *there is*.[23] In this confusion the substitution for the neighbor gains in dis-inter*est*edness, that is, in nobility, and the transcendence of the Infinite arises in glory. Such transcendence is true with a dia-chronic truth and without any synthesis, higher than the truths that are without enigma.[24] For this formula "transcendence to the point of absence" not to mean the simple explicitation of an ex-ceptional word, this word itself has to be put back into the significance of the whole plot of the ethical or back into the divine comedy without which it could not have arisen. That comedy is enacted equivocally between temple and theater, but in it the laughter sticks to one's throat when the neighbor approaches - that is, when his face, or his forsakenness, draws near.

Phenomenology and Transcendence

15. The exposition of the ethical signification of transcendence and of the Infinite beyond being can be worked out beginning with the proximity of the neighbor and my responsibility for the other (*autrui*).

Until then a passive subjectivity might seem something constructed and abstract. The receptivity of finite knowledge is an assembling of a dispersed given in the simultaneity of presence, in immanence. The passivity "more passive still than any passivity" consisted in undergoing - or more exactly in having already undergone, in a nonrepresentable past which was never present - a trauma that could not be assumed; it consisted in being struck by the "*in*" of infinity which devastates presence and awakens subjectivity to the proximity of the other (*autrui*). The noncontained, which breaks the container or the forms of consciousness, thus *transcends* the essence or the "move" of knowable being which carries on its being in presence; it transcends the inter*estedness* and simultaneity of a representable or historically reconstitutable temporality; it transcends immanence.

This trauma, which cannot be assumed, inflicted by the Infinite on presence, or this affecting of presence by the Infinite - this affectivity - takes shape as a subjection to the neighbor. It is thought thinking more than it thinks, desire, the reference to the neighbor, the responsibility for another.

This abstraction is nevertheless familiar to us in the empirical event of obligation to the other (*autrui*), as the impossibility of indifference - impossible without fail - before the misfortunes and faults of a neighbor, the unexceptionable responsibility for him. It is impossible to fix limits or measure the extreme urgency of this responsibility. Upon reflection it is something completely astonishing, a responsibility that even extends to the obligation to answer for another's freedom, to be responsible for his responsibility, whereas the freedom which would demand an eventual commitment or even the assuming of an imposed necessity cannot find a present that includes the possibilities which belong to the other (*autrui*). The Other's freedom can neither constitute a structure along with my freedom, nor enter into a synthesis with it. Responsibility for the neighbor is precisely what goes beyond the legal and obliges beyond contracts; it comes to me from what is prior to my freedom, from a nonpresent, an immemorial. A difference gapes open between me and the other that no unity of transcendental apperception can undo. My responsibility for the other (*autrui*) is precisely the nonindifference of this difference - the proximity of the other. An absolutely extra-ordinary relation, it does not reestablish the order of representation in which every past returns. The proximity of a neighbor remains a dia-chronic break, a resistance of time to the synthesis of simultaneity.

The biological human brotherhood - conceived with the sober coldness of Cain - is not a sufficient reason for me to be responsible for a separated being. The sober coldness of Cain consists in conceiving responsibility as proceeding from freedom or in terms of a contract. But responsibility for the other comes from what is prior to my freedom. It does not come from the time made up of presences, nor presences that have sunk into the past and are representable, the time of beginnings or assumings. It does not allow me to constitute myself into an *I think*, substantial like a stone, or, like a heart of stone, existing in and for oneself. It ends up in substitution for the other, in the condition - or the unconditionality - of being a hostage. Such responsibility does not give one time, a present for recollection or coming back to oneself; it makes one always late. Before the neighbor I am summoned and do not just appear; from the first I am answering to an assignation. Already the stony core of my substance is dislodged. But the responsibility to which I am exposed in such a passivity does not apprehend me as an interchangeable thing, for here no one can be substituted for me; in calling upon me as someone accused who cannot reject the accusation, it obliges me as someone unreplaceable and unique, someone chosen. Inasmuch as it calls upon my responsibility it forbids me any replacement. Unreplaceable in responsibility, I cannot, without defaulting, incurring fault, or being caught up in some complex, escape the face of a neighbor; here I am pledged to the other without being able to take back my pledge.[25] I cannot evade the face of the other (*autrui*), naked and without resources. The nakedness of someone forsaken shows in the cracks in the mask of the personage, or in his wrinkled skin;[26] his being "without resources" has to be heard like cries not voiced or thematized, already addressed to God. There the resonance of silence - *Geläut der Stille*[27] - certainly sounds. We here have come upon an imbroglio that has to be taken seriously: a relationship to . . . that is not represented, without intentionality, not repressed; it is the latent birth of religion in the other (*autrui*), prior to emotions or voices, prior to "religious experience," which speaks of revelation in terms of the disclosure of being, when it is a question of an unwonted access, in the heart of my responsibility, to an unwonted disturbance of being. Even if one says right away, "It was nothing." "It was nothing" - it was not being, but otherwise than being. My responsibility in spite of myself - which is the way the other's (*autrui*) charge falls upon me or disturbs me, that is, is close to me - is the hearing or understanding of this cry. It is awakening. The proximity of a neighbor is my responsibility for him; to approach is to be one's brother's keeper; to be one's brother's keeper is to be his hostage. Immediacy is this. Responsibility does not come from fraternity, but fraternity denotes responsibility for the other (*autrui*), antecedent to my freedom.

16. To posit subjectivity in this responsibility is to catch sight of a passivity in it, is never passive enough, that of being consumed for the other (*autrui*). The very light of subjectivity shines and illuminates out of this ardor, although the ashes of this consummation are not able to fashion the kernel of a being existing in and for itself, and the I does not oppose to the other any form that protects itself or provides it with a measure. Such is the consuming of a holocaust. "I am

dust and ashes," says Abraham in interceding for Sodom.[28] "What are we?" says Moses more humbly still.[29]

What is the meaning of this assignation in which the nucleus of the subject is uprooted, undone, and does not receive any form capable of assuming this? What do these atomic metaphors mean, if not an I torn from the concept of the ego and from the content of obligations for which the concept rigorously supplies measure and rule, and thus left to an unmeasured responsibility, because it increases in the measure - or in the immeasurableness - that a response is made, increasing gloriously. This is the I that is not designated but which says "here I am." "Each of us is guilty before everyone, for everyone and for every thing, and I more than the others," writes Dostoyevsky in *The Brothers Karamazov*.[30] The I which says I is not that which singularizes or individuates a concept or a genus. It is I, unique in its genus, who speaks to you in the first person. That is, unless one could maintain that it is in the individuation of the genus or the concept of the ego that I myself awaken and expose myself to others, that is, begin to speak. This exposedness is not like self-consciousness, the recurrence of the subject to himself, confirming the ego by itself. The recurrence in awakening is something one can describe as a shudder of incarnation through which *giving* takes on meaning, as the primordial dative of the *for another*, in which a subject becomes a heart, a sensibility, and hands which give. But it is thus a position already deposed of its kingdom of identity and substance, already in debt, "for the other" to the point of substitution for the other, altering the immanence of the subject in the depths of its identity. This subject unreplaceable for the responsibility assigned to him finds in that very fact a new identity. But in extracting me from the concept of the ego, the fission of the subject is a growth of obligation in proportion as obedience grows, the augmentation of guilt that comes with the augmentation of holiness, the increase of distance proportionate to the approach. Here there is no rest for the self sheltered in its form, in its ego-concept! There are no "conditions," not even those of servitude. There is an incessant solicitude for solicitude, the extreme of passivity in responsibility for the responsibility of the other. Thus proximity is never close enough; as responsible, I am never finished with emptying myself of myself. There is infinite increase in this exhausting of oneself, in which the subject is not simply an awareness of this expenditure, but is its locus and event and, so to speak its goodness. The *glory of a long desire*! The subject as a hostage has been neither the experience nor the proof of the Infinite, but a witness borne of the Infinite, a modality of this glory, a testimony that no disclosure has preceded.

17. This growing surplus of the infinite that we have ventured to call *glory* is not an abstract quintessence. It has a signification in the response to the

summons which comes to me from the face of a neighbor, and which could not be evaded; it is the hyperbolic demand which at once exceeds that response. This comes as a surprise for the respondent himself by which, ousted from his inwardness as an ego and a "being with two sides," he is awakened, that is, exposed to the other without restraint or reserve. The passivity of such an exposure to the other (*autrui*) is not exhausted in some sort of being open to the other's (*autrui*) look or objectifying judgment. The openness of the ego exposed to the other is the breakup or turning inside out of inwardness. Sincerity is the name of this extraversion.[31] But what else can this inversion or extra-version mean but a responsibility for others such that I keep nothing for myself? A responsibility such that everything in me is debt and donation and such that my being-there is the ultimate *being-there*[32] where the creditors find the debtor? It is a responsibility such that my position as a subject in its *as for itself* is already my substitution or expiation for others. Responsibility for the other (*autrui*) - for his distress and his freedom - does not derive from any commitment, project or antecedent disclosure, in which the subject would be posited for itself before being-in-debt. Here passivity is extreme in the measure (or in-ordinate-ness) that the devotion for the other is not shut up in itself like a state of soul, but is itself from the start given over to the other.

This excess is *saying*. Sincerity is not an attribute which eventually receives the saying; it is by saying that sincerity - exposedness without reserve - is first possible. Saying makes signs to the other (*autrui*), but in this sign signifies the very giving of signs. Saying opens me to the other (*autrui*) before saying what is said, before the said uttered in this sincerity forms a screen between me and the other. A saying without words, but not with empty hands. If silence speaks, it is not through some inward mystery or some sort of ecstasy of intentionality, but through the hyperbolic passivity of giving, which is prior to all willing and thematization. Saying bears witness to the other (*autrui*) of the Infinite which rends me, which in the Saying awakens me.

Language understood in this way loses its superfluous and strange function of doubling up thought and being. Saying as testimony precedes all the said. Saying, before setting forth a said, is already the testimony of this responsibility - and even the saying of a said, as an approach to the other, is a responsibility for him. Saying is therefore a way of signifying prior to all experience. A pure testimony, it is a martyr's truth which does not depend on any disclosure or any "religious" experience; it is an obedience that precedes the hearing of any order. A pure testimony, it does not testify to a prior experience, but to the Infinite which is not accessible to the unity of apperception, nonappearing and dispro-portionate to the present. Saying could neither include nor comprehend the Infinite; the Infinite concerns and closes in on me while speaking through my mouth. And the only pure testimony is that of the Infinite. This is not a psychological wonder, but the modality in which the Infinite *comes to pass*, signifying through him to whom it signifies, understood inasmuch as, before any commitment, I answer for the other (*autrui*).

Like someone put under leaden skies that suppress every shadowy corner in me, every residue of mystery, every mental reservation, every "as for me . . . ," hardening or relaxing of the plot of things by which escape would be possible, I am a testimony, or a trace, or the glory of the Infinite, breaking the bad silence which harbors Gyges's secrecy.[33] There is extra-verting of subject's inwardness; the subject becomes visible before becoming a seer! The Infinite is not "in front of" me; I express it, but precisely by giving a sign of the giving of signs, of the "for-the-other" in which I am dis-interested: here I am (*me voici*)! The accusative here is remarkable: here I am, under your eyes, at your service, your obedient servant.[34] In the name of God. But this is without thematization; the sentence in which God gets mixed in with words is not "I believe in God." The religious discourse that precedes all religious discourse is not dialogue. It is the "here I am" said to a neighbor to whom I am given over, by which I announce peace, that is, my responsibility for the other. "Creating language on their lips. . . . Peace, peace to him who is far and to him who is near, says the Eternal."[35]

Prophetic Signification

18. In the description which has been elaborated up to now there has been no question of the transcendental condition for some sort of ethical experience. Ethics as substitution for the other (*autrui*), giving without reserve, breaks up the unity of transcendental apperception, that condition for all being and all experience. Dis-inter*estedness* in the radical sense of the term, ethics designates the improbable field where the Infinite is in relationship with the finite without contradicting itself by this relationship, where on the contrary it alone *comes to pass* as Infinity and as awakening. The Infinite transcends itself in the finite, it *passes* the finite, in that it directs the neighbor to me without exposing itself to me. This order steals into me like a thief, despite the outstretched nets of consciousness, a trauma which surprises me absolutely, always already *passed* in a past which was never present and remains unrepresentable.

One can call this intrigue of infinity, where I make myself the author of what I understand, *inspiration*. It constitutes, prior to the unity of apperception, the very psyche in the soul. In this inspiration, or prophesying, I am the go-between for what I set forth. "God has spoken that you shall not prophesy," says Amos,[36] comparing the prophetic reaction to the passivity of the fear which takes hold of him who hears the roaring of wild beasts. Prophesying is pure testimony, pure because prior to all disclosure; it is subjection to an order before understanding the order. In the recoverable time of reminiscence, this anachronism is no less paradoxical than a prediction of the future. It is in prophesying that the Infinite passes - and awakens. As a transcendence, refusing objectification and dialogue, it signifies in an ethical way. It *signifies* in the sense in which one says *to mean an order*, it *orders*.

19. In sketching out, behind philosophy where transcendence is always reduced, the outlines of prophetic testimony, we have not entered into the shifting sands of religious experience. To say that subjectivity is the temple or the theater of transcendence and that the understanding of transcendence takes on an ethical meaning does indeed not contradict the idea of the Good beyond being. This idea guarantees the philosophical dignity of an undertaking in which the signifyingness of meaning is separated from the manifestation or the presence of being. But one can only wonder if Western philosophy has been faithful to this Platonism. It discovered intelligibility in terms in conjunction, posited by relation with one another, signifying one another; for Western philosophy, being, thematized in its presence, is illuminated in this way. The clarity of the visible signifies. The appropriate trope for the signifyingness of signification is: the-one-for-the-other. But signifyingness becomes visibility, immanence, and ontology, inasmuch as the terms unite into a whole, and even their history is systematized, so as to be clarified.

On the pages of this study, transcendence as the ethical structure, the-one-for-the-other, has been formulated in terms of signifyingness and intelligibility.[37] The trope of intelligibility takes form in the ethical one-for-the-other, a signifyingness prior to that which terms in conjunction in a system acquire. But does this signifyingness more ancient than all patterns really *take form*? We have shown elsewhere the latent birth of systems and philosophy out of this august intelligibility; we shall not return to that here.[38]

The intelligibility of transcendence is not something ontological. The transcendence of God cannot be stated or conceived in terms of being, the element of philosophy, behind which philosophy sees only night. But the break between philosophical intelligibility and the beyond being, or the contradiction there would be in com-prehending infinity, does not exclude God from signifyingness, which, if it is not ontological, does not simply amount to thoughts bearing on being in decline, to views lacking necessity and wordplays.

In our times - is this its very modernity? - a presumption of being an ideology weighs on philosophy. This presumption cannot claim to be a part of philosophy, where the critical spirit cannot content itself with suspicions, but owes it to itself that it bring forth proofs. This presumption, which is irrecusable, draws its force from elsewhere. It begins in a cry of ethical revolt, bearing witness to responsibility; it begins in prophecy. Philosophy does not become suspect at just any moment in the spiritual history of the West. To recognize with philosophy - or to recognize philosophically - that the real is rational and that the rational is alone real, and not to be able to smother or cover over the cry of those who, the morrow after this recognition, mean to transform the world, is already to move in a domain of meaning which the inclusion cannot comprehend and among reasons that "reason" does not know, and which have not begun in philosophy.[39] A meaning thus seems to bear witness to a beyond which would not be the no-man's-land of non-sense where opinions accumulate. *Not to philosophize would not be "to philosophize still,"* nor to succumb to opinions. There is meaning testified to in interjections and outcries, before being disclosed in propositions, a meaning that signifies as a command, like an order that one signifies. Its manifestation in a theme already devolves from its signifying as ordering; ethical signification signifies not *for* a consciousness which thematizes but *to* a subjectivity, wholly an obedience, obeying with an obedience that precedes understanding. Here is a passivity still more passive than that of receptivity in knowing, the receptivity that assumes what affects it. In this signification the ethical moment is not founded on any preliminary structure of theoretical thought, on language or on any particular language. Language then has over signification only the hold a form has, clothing matter. This recalls the distinction between form and signification, which shows itself in that distinction and through its references to a linguistic system. The distinction holds even if this *said* has to be *unsaid* - and it will have to so as to lose its linguistic alternation. The signification will indeed have to be reduced and lose the "stains" to which it owed its exposition to the light or its sojourn in shadow. An alternating rhythm of the said and the unsaid, and the unsaid being unsaid in its turn, will have to be substituted for the unity of discourse. There is here a breakup of the omnipotence of the logos, that of system and simultaneity. The logos breaks up into a signifier and a signified which is not *only* a signifier. This negates the attempt to amalgamate signifier and signified and to drive transcendence from its first or last refuge, in consigning all thought to language as a system of signs. Such an attempt was elaborated in the shadow of a philosophy for which meaning is equivalent to the manifestation of being, and manifestation equivalent to being's *esse.*

Transcendence as signification and signification as the signification of an order given to subjectivity before any statement are the pure one-for-the-other. Poor ethical subjectivity deprived of freedom! - unless this would be the trauma of a fission of the self that occurs in an adventure undergone with God or through God. But in fact this ambiguity also is necessary to transcendence. Transcendence owes it to itself to interrupt its own demonstration and monstration, its phenomenality. It requires the blinking and dia-chrony of enigma, which is not simply a precarious certainty but breaks up the unity of transcendental apperception, in which immanence always triumphs over transcendence.

NINE

Transcendence and Intelligibility
(1984)

This essay, originally presented as a lecture at the University of Geneva on June 1, 1983, was published in 1984 as a small book together with a transcription of conversations with Levinas, led by Jean Halpérin, that took place the day after Levinas's presentation.[1] It represents the latest restatement of the basic argument that Levinas has developed and refined in his work since the 1950s. As such, this essay resembles the structure of Levinas's earlier attempts to give an overview and entry point to his thinking in "Philosophy and the Idea of Infinity" and "Transcendence and Height." The innovation of this essay is that Levinas's opposition to the dominant tendencies in modern European philosophy, whether they are identified as dialectical, phenomenological, or ontological, is specifically couched in terms of the privilege of presence. Also, his interpretation of the Cartesian idea of the infinite is given a much more overtly theological orientation than in earlier texts, which doubtless reflected his increasing propensity to introduce theological language into his philosophical writings.

Levinas begins by sketching the defining characteristic of the modern European philosophical tradition in terms of the primacy given to knowledge. According to Levinas, what Hegelian dialectics, Husserlian phenomenology, and Heideggerian fundamental ontology share is a privilege given to the temporal mode of presence. All objects must show themselves upon the horizon of presence if they are to be accessible to philosophical analysis or description. Thus the primacy of knowledge and presence in modern European philosophy entails that everything that is other (an object, thing, or being), is, in principle, reducible or accessible to thought, specifically theoretical contemplation. As Levinas puts it, knowledge is a relation of the Same with the Other, in which the Other is reduced to the Same and where thinking relates itself to the Other as something that is already its own, already proper to it. The melting pot for this transmutation of otherness into sameness goes by various names: the ego, the self, consciousness, self-consciousness, mind, or *Dasein*. Thus it is Levinas's contention that the central tradition in modern European philosophy has no place for, or interest in, the Other qua Other, that is, as that which resists or refuses the ego's powers of conceptualization and thematization. With a gesture that has remained constant in his work, however, Levinas's diagnosis of the limitations of the philosophical tradition does not lead him to reject philosophy as a mode of discourse capable of addressing the Other qua Other but rather leads him to seek "another phenomenology," an alternative conception of philosophy centered in what one might call a post-Kantian conception of metaphysical transcendence, that is, a conception of transcendence that is cognizant of the Kantian critique of the transcendental illusion of traditional metaphysics. Before going on to outline this phenomenology, Levinas offers some intriguing suggestions as to how the primacy of knowledge and presence has been challenged from within the modern European tradition, giving the examples of the Kantian primacy of practical reason and Bergson's concept of duration - *la durée* - a mode of temporality, Levinas claims, that announces the possibility of novel conceptions of intelligibility and transcendence.

According to Levinas, what is required for this new concept of transcendence is a model of thinking which cannot be reduced to a relation of adequation between thought and the object or matter of thought, that is, which is irreducible to phenomenological correlation, i.e., Husserl's noesis/noema structure. The Cartesian idea of the infinite provides Levinas with the *formal* structure of such a conception of transcendence. By definition, the idea of the infinite contains more than it is capable of containing; it somehow thinks more than it is able to think; it is not the noesis of a noema. Levinas's most celebrated and audacious claim is that the formal structure of transcendence found in the idea of the infinite is accomplished *concretely* in the ethical relation to the other human (*autrui*). This claim, however, is not explored at length in "Transcendence and Intelligibility," and Levinas focuses rather on the theological dimension to transcendence, which is a central point of the third of Descartes's *Meditations*. The essay closes with some illuminating and rich remarks on the affectivity of transcendence - love or adoration - which, once again, is claimed to be accomplished socially in the relation to the other human.

Thus if traditional philosophy, which culminates, for Levinas, in phenomenology, is premised upon the reduction of transcendence to an intelligibility rooted in immanence, then Levinas is here proposing an alternative phenomenology faithful to what he here calls the "unthought" of the philosophical tradition, namely, "the search for the human or interhuman intrigue as the fabric of ultimate intelligibility." This intrigue is the intelligibility of the transcendent as transcendent.

The Mind as Knowledge

It is in the human psychism understood as *knowledge* - going as far as self-consciousness - that the philosophy transmitted to us situates the natural place of the sensible and the origin of philosophy; it is in terms of knowledge and consciousness that philosophy looks into the mind.

The philosopher's attention is directed to human lived experience which is recognized and acknowledged as experience, that is, which lets itself legitimately be converted into teaching, into object lessons of dis-covery or presence. But even beneath our relations with other men and the social group and even beneath what is called the "relation to God" or revelation of God, one would like to perceive or suppose experiences which are termed collective or religious. That all intelligibility - and even the "sense" of God - lays claim to knowledge, that intelligibility seeks in knowledge the support of a presence, indeed that it seeks a foundation for itself; all this, according to philosophy, goes without saying. In the *Meditations*, Descartes extends to the entire soul the term *cogito*, a term borrowed from the intellectual activity of doubt - that is, from a process concerned with the true. One recalls the formula of the Second Meditation: "What is a thing which thinks, that is a thing which doubts, conceives, affirms, denies, wills, does not will, which also imagines and feels?"[2] I presume that to feel signifies here both sensation and emotion. I presume as well that the diverse forms of thought evoked do not simply designate the species of a genre but also the different moments, the articulations, of a structure or the multiple dimensions of the same act of consciousness, which is the act of knowing.

Science and Presence

As knowledge, thinking is the way in which an exteriority is found within a consciousness which does not cease to identify itself, without recourse to any distinct sign, and is called the Ego or the Same. Knowledge is a relation of the *Same* with the *Other* in which the Other is reduced to the Same and divested of its strangeness, in which thinking relates itself to the other but the other is no longer other as such; the other is already appropriated (*le propre*), already *mine.* Henceforth, knowledge is without secrets or open to investigation, that is to say, it is a *world.* It is immanence. An immanence which is also a temporal mode, where knowledge imposes itself as privileged: a presence which is also the fact-of-being. Presence as an exposition in the absolute frankness of *being,* which also signifies gathering and synchrony without flaw, evasion, or shadow. An *appearance* and a *being-given.* Behind the dia-chrony, the becoming of experiences and the dissimulations of the *before* and the *after,* of the past and the future (which are the temporal failures of presence but are nevertheless susceptible to the recuperation of this presence in the guise of the thinkable, indeed, susceptible to re-presentation, in all senses of the term), the procedures of knowledge reestablish presence in the eternity of an ideal presence. Reminiscence and imagination assure the synchrony of the ideal presence to comprehension and together maintain that which, in the *experience* of the entity "submitted to time," is already lost or is only to come. It is perhaps this adequation of knowledge to the entity which permits it to be said that one only learns what one already knows, that nothing absolutely new, nothing other, nothing strange, nothing transcendent, could either affect or truly enlarge a mind committed to contemplating everything, or that, like the *Timaeus,* the "circle of the Same surrounds that of the Other."[3] By way of "objective spirit,"[4] discourse is capable of putting together contradictory thoughts despite dispersions and exclusions. And the first-person present verb of the *cogito* already signifies - and perhaps signifies above all - the *transcendental apperception,* which includes the thinkable in its totality and thus constitutes the autonomy of knowledge, which is self-supporting and gathers itself in the systematic unity to which the consciousness of an "I" lends itself. From whence the integration into the system: the simultaneity of that which succeeds itself, of all that can seem *other* in succession.[5]

Being and Being Given

But presence in its exposition, in its frankness of being, is ipso facto a being-given, a letting-be-taken, and therefore, in its concreteness, it is the offering of itself to the hand which takes and, consequently, through the muscular contraction of the grasp - through what Husserl calls kinesthesis[6] - it refers to a solid which the hand encompasses or which the finger of the hand indicates; and already it *refers itself* - through a perception which had been an aim and intention and therefore a finality, a wish or a desire - presence already refers itself to *something*, to a term, to a being (*étant*). Indeed, we think that the being (*étant*) thereby belongs to the concreteness of the understanding of *being*.[7] It is perception, grasped through presence, through the being-given and thus *acquisition*, a deposit in the home, and consequently it is the promise of *satisfaction* made to a greedy and hegemonic ego. Satisfaction is the emphasis of immanence, a plenitude of adequation in the *satis* which thus implies the unintelligibility of that which surpasses its measure, the ceaseless temptation of atheism.[8]

Presence as a letting-itself-be-taken, as the chance of understanding; knowledge remains linked to perception and to apprehension and to the grasp even in the con*cept* or the Be*griff*,[9] which retains or recalls the concreteness of the grasp and, in its syntheses, imitates them, whatever the degree of idealization of which knowledge as the gaze is capable; synthesis as seizure and assemblage. *These metaphors are to be taken seriously and literally.* They belong to the phenomenology of immanence.[10]

The Phenomenology of Immanence

Even before the technical ascendancy over things which the knowledge of the industrial era has made possible and before the technological development of modernity, knowledge, by itself, is the project of an incarnate practice of seizure, appropriation, and satisfaction. The most abstract lessons of the science of the future will rest upon this familiarity with the world that we inhabit in the midst of things which are held out to the grasp of the hand. *Presence*, of *itself*, becomes the now.[11]

Knowledge rests on things given in a world that is given, which Husserl will call the life-world, the famous *Lebenswelt*, where, for all that, Husserl will not find a pretext for critique, and where he will not denounce any deviation from a society seemingly delivered over to technological domination.[12] Husserl perceives at the base of our human and physical-mathematical exact sciences a given world which thus lends itself to the grasp and to manipulation. Husserl will complain that the overabstract reflection upon science conducted by epistemology *underestimates* this. In this underestimation, he would certainly see a threat to the truth to which man's scientific enterprise is devoted, which in itself does not proceed from any perversion of the mind.

But thus is also affirmed, across European philosophy, *knowledge* esteemed as the very business of the human to which nothing remains absolutely other. The doctrine of absolute knowledge, of the freedom of the satisfied man, Hegelianism - in which the many different attempts of Western thinking result, as they also result in Husserlian phenomenology - promotes a thinking which, in the plenitude of its ambitions, takes no interest in the other qua other. The other qua other cannot be accommodated in the noema of a noesis and could nevertheless be important to the human. The labor of thinking gets the better of the alterity of things and men, and it is in this that rationality itself resides. The conceptual synopsis is stronger than all the diversity and incompatibility of unassemblable terms, stronger than any diachrony which would want to be radical and irreducible. In the same way, consciousness is intentionality in Husserlian phenomenology: cogitation comes out of itself, but the cogitatum is present to cogitation, the *noema* equals the *noesis* and corresponds to its intention. It suffices for Husserlian phenomenology to interrogate the intentions of thinking in order to know where thought wants to get to ("worauf sie eigentlich hinaus will").[13] Nothing ever comes to unseat this intentional will of thought or fails to measure up to it.

The Notion of Transcendence and the End of Metaphysics

But do the notions of transcendence, alterity, and absolute novelty - the notion of the absolute - still allow themselves to be named as intelligible if, precisely, the notions of the other, the transcendent, and the absolute break with the knowledge which would have invested and assimilated them and with the world where they could appear but already make up immanence? Is it sufficient to maintain this intelligibility in a purely negative fashion in relation to knowledge, appearance, and presence? Unless the intelligibility of the alterity of the other, of transcendence, calls for another phenomenology, even if it were the destruction of the phenomenology of appearance and of knowledge.

Within the context of the history of reason, *The Critique of Pure Reason* was largely motivated by the formal contradictions which stalemated the philosophical use of reason. These terminated the long journey in *search of absolute truth* beyond the given, exceeding the scope set by the critique of transcendental apperception. Nevertheless, the very meaning of the *meta* of metaphysics has not been condemned as nonsense by the *Critique*. It sounded the knell of metaphysics understood as searching beyond the experience of identities which could be grasped in an eternal presence, which, from then on, could only appear to be beyond as according to the illusion of worlds behind the scenes.[14] This Kantian critique of metaphysics is no doubt akin to the nevertheless anti-Kantian message of a very great philosopher who remains in purgatory - Bergson - for whom the march of Western philosophy in search of an absolute - or transcendent - order of the Eternal would have been only the deformation of the technological mind turned toward action on matter and space. (This is an anticipation unappreciated by the Heideggerian critiques of metaphysics which proceed from the will to power.)[15] This is an essential point of this critique, which also resembles, at least in spirit, Heidegger's famous proclamation of the end of metaphysics insofar as he denounces it as a misunderstanding of the ontological difference between *being* and *being* (*étant*) and in which he prohibits speculation which would think being starting from beings.[16] Does not the true signification of the end of metaphysics, from Kant to Heidegger, consist in affirming that thinking beyond the given no longer amounts to bringing to light the *presence* or the *eternity* of a universe of beings or of secret or sacred principles, hidden in the prolongation of that which is given and which would be the task of metaphysical speculation to dis-cover? Is this sufficient in order to denounce transcendence as non-sense, the very *meta* of metaphysics? And what if its alterity or its beyond was not a simple dissimulation to be unveiled by the gaze but a non-in-difference, intelligible according to a *spiritual intrigue wholly other than* gnosis.

Otherwise than According to Knowledge

I would like to suggest that in modern philosophy this new intrigue manifests itself - despite the reversions of philosophy to ontology and knowledge, despite the relapses - in the entire history of our philosophy: beginning with Kant himself, notably in the doctrine of the primacy of practical reason.[17] A few words as well about Bergson, whom I would not want to have disturbed in the depths of purgatory for nothing: Bergson is an essential step in the movement which puts in question the framework of a spirituality borrowed from knowledge and therefore from the privileged and primary signification of presence, being, and ontology. Is it still necessary today to introduce an educated audience, but one which manages to forget the unforgettable, to the Bergsonian distinction between the time of everyday life and the time of interior life or duration?[18] On the one hand, the time of common sense - which, essentially, remains that of science - the measurable time of our watches, the time of Aristotle understood as a number representing movement, that is, a time which can be approached through its expression and through its spatial measurement by chronometers, whether they be watches or water clocks. And on the other hand, the duration which is pure change and which does not need to search beneath this change for any identical substratum. This is the bursting forth of incessant novelty. The absolute novelty of the new. This is the spirituality of transcendence, which does not amount to an assimilating act of consciousness. The uninterrupted bursting forth of novelties would make sense, precisely beyond knowledge, through its absolute and unforeseeable novelty. "Most philosophers," Bergson writes, "treat the succession of time as a missed coexistence and duration as privation," as the mobile image of immobile eternity. "Because of this they do not manage, whatever they do, to represent to themselves the radical novelty of unforeseeability."[19] Against the consciousness which englobes and organizes the system through knowledge and against the tendency to equate and reduce, this is a new mode of intelligibility. Prior to logic, the bursting forth of duration would sketch the horizons of intelligibility. Does not temporality itself announce itself here as a transcendence, as a thinking under which, independently of any experience, the alterity of absolute novelty, the absolute in the etymological sense of the term, would burst forth?

Does Bergson go that far? Does he not introduce knowledge behind duration? Does he not speak, in expressing the "intuition of duration," of a duration which is experienced rather than of a duration substituting itself for the act of experience? That is possible.

Thought as Religion

But what can one seek beneath thinking other than consciousness? Finally, what is this thinking we are seeking, which is neither assimilation of the Other to the Same nor integration of the Other into the Same, a thinking which does not bring all transcendence back to immanence and does not compromise transcendence in understanding it? What is needed is a thought which is no longer constructed as a relation of thinking to what is thought about, in the domination of thinking over what is thought about; what is needed is a thought which is not restricted to the rigorous correspondence between noesis and noema and not restricted to the adequation where the visible must be equal to the intentional aim (*la visée*), to which the visible would have to respond in the intuition of truth; what is needed is a thought for which the very metaphor of vision and aim (*visée*) is no longer legitimate.[20]

An impossible demand! Unless these demands are an echo of what Descartes called the idea of the infinite in us - thinking beyond what is capable of being contained in the finitude of the *cogito*.[21]

The idea of the Infinite - even if it is only named, recognized and in some way operative through its mathematical signification and usage - conserves for reflection the paradoxical knot which is already tied to religious revelation. Revelation, which is from the start linked in its *concreteness* to obligations toward humans - the idea of God as love of the neighbor - is "knowledge" of a God who, offering himself in this "opening," would also remain absolutely other or transcendent.

Would not religion be the original combination of circumstances - which nevertheless need not be judged contingent - in which the infinite in its ambiguity, both truth and mystery, comes to the idea? But is it then definite that the coming of the infinite to the idea is a feat of *knowledge*, the manifestation whose essence consists in establishing - or in reestablishing - the order of *immanence*? Above all, is it definite, as a certain consensus and perhaps a venerable tradition tend to admit, that immanence is *the supreme grace of spiritual energy*, that the revelation of a God is a *disclosure* and is achieved in the *adequation of truth*, in the grasp which that which thinks exercises on that which is thought, and thus that meaning or intelligibility would be an economy, in the etymological sense of the term, the economy of a house, of a home, of a certain investment, of a grasping, a possessing, a self-satisfaction and an enjoyment?[22]

The Idea of the Infinite in Us

The idea of the infinite - an exceptional and unique idea which, according to Descartes, is the thought addressed to God. It is a thought which, in its phenomenology, does not allow itself to be reduced, without remainder, to the act of consciousness of a subject, to pure thematizing intentionality. Contrary to the ideas according to which thinking progressively seizes the world, which are always on the level of the "intentional object," the *ideatum* and the *grasp*, the idea of the Infinite would contain more than it is capable of containing, more than its capacity as a *cogito*. The idea of the Infinite would somehow think beyond what it thinks. In its relation to what should be its "intentional correlate," it would be thrown off course, not resulting in anything or arriving at an end, and precisely not arriving at the finite, at a term or close. Certainly it is necessary to distinguish between, on the one hand, the pure failure of the nonachievement of an intentional aim which would still be ruled by a finality and, on the other hand, the deportation or the transcendence beyond any end and any finality: the thinking of the absolute without this absolute being reached as an end, which again would have signified finality and finitude. The idea of the Infinite is a thought released from consciousness, not according to the negative concept of the unconscious but according to the thought, perhaps the most profoundly considered thought, of the release with regard to being, of dis-inter-est: a relation without a hold on being and without subservience to the *conatus essendi*, contrary to knowledge and to perception.[23] *Concretely*, this does not become some sort of modification of vision as a pure negative abstraction but is accomplished ethically as a relation to the other man.

According to Descartes, who identifies the idea of the perfect with the idea of God, the finite thought of man could never derive the Infinite from itself. It would be necessary for God himself to have put it in us. And Descartes's entire interest is concentrated on this problem of the existence of God. The incessant return of metaphysics! But how could this idea of the Infinite be held in a finite thought? The arrival, descent, or contraction of the infinite in a finite thought names in any case an event which describes the sense of what we designate by God, rather than the immediately given, of an object which is adequate to - or equatable with - the intention of an act of knowledge in the heart of the world.

The Logos of the Infinite

But the exception of the idea of the infinite implies the awakening of a psychism which is reduced to neither pure correlation nor noetico-noematic parallelism, which the least biased analysis finds in human thinking if it is approached through knowledge. This is an exception which upsets the Aristotelian thesis of a theology reserved for a God who would be his own and only theologian, the only one capable of thinking himself, as Pierre Aubenque emphasized.[24] An exception showing human thought thinking precisely as theology! But the logos of this theology would differ from the theoretical intentionality and from the adequation of thinking with that which is thought, which, through the unity of transcendental apperception, assures itself of a sovereign ego in its exclusive isolation as a *cogito* and its gathering and synthesizing reign. This is an exception to the commonly accepted phenomenology of thought, which, in an essential sense, is precisely atheist insofar as it is a thinking which equals the thought that fills it and satis-fies it, apprehending the given in the inevitable reversal of any passivity of experience into an activity of consciousness which accepts that which strikes it, which is never violated. The exception is a thinking which is no longer *aim, vision, will,* or *intention.*

In the idea of the Infinite, which is also the idea of God, the affection of the finite by the infinite precisely produces itself, beyond the simple negation of one by the other, beyond the pure contradiction which would oppose them and separate them or which would expose the other to the hegemony of the one understood as an "I think." An affection which must be described otherwise than as an appearance, otherwise than as a participation in a content, or a comprehension. An irreversible affection of the finite by the infinite. A passivity and a patience which are not recuperated in a thematization but in which, as love and fear of God - or the adoration and dazzling of which Descartes speaks in the last paragraph of the Third Meditation[25] - the idea of God is affectivity from top to bottom. An affectivity which does not amount to the *Befindlichkeit* of *Sein und Zeit* or the anxiety of *Jemeinigkeit* for its finitude of being-toward-death, which always comes to increase the intentionality of sentiment felt by a being belonging to the world.[26] An affection of the finite by the infinite which it is not a question of reducing! An exit in the idea of the infinite, in theological affection, outside the *Jemeinigkeit* of the Cogito and of its immanence taken for authenticity, toward a thinking which thinks more than it thinks - or which does *better* than think. It goes toward the Good. This is a dis-inter-ested Affectivity - or Desire - in which plurality as social proximity does not need to be gathered under the unity of the One, which no longer signifies a simple lack of coincidence, a pure and simple absence of unity. The excellence of love and sociality, of "fear for the others" and responsibility for the others, which is not my anxiety for my death, *mine*.[27] Transcendence would no longer be a failed immanence. In sociality - which is no longer a simple aim but responsibility for the neighbor - it would have the excellence proper to the mind, which is precisely perfection or the Good. A sociality which, in opposition to all knowledge and all immanence, is a *relation with the other as such* and not with the other as a pure part of the world.

Doing Phenomenology

That this affectivity of adoration and this passivity of dazzling permit a further developed phenomenological interpretation or that they can be joined through an analysis which, from the beginning, places itself before the interpersonal order of the alterity of the other man, my neighbor and my responsibility for the other (*autrui*) - all this is obviously beyond the framework of the Cartesian texts and we will not develop it here.

But to do phenomenology is not only, against the surreptitiousness, sliding, and substitution of sense, to guarantee the signifyingness of a language threatened in its abstraction or in its isolation. It is not only to control language by interrogating the thoughts which offend it and make it forget. It is above all to search for and recall, in the horizons which open around the first "intentions" of the abstractly given, the human or interhuman intrigue which is the concreteness of its unthought (it is not purely negative!), which is the necessary "staging" ("*mise en scène*") from which the abstractions are detached in the *said* of words and propositions. It is to search for the human or interhuman intrigue as the fabric of ultimate intelligibility. And perhaps it is also the way for the wisdom of heaven to return to earth.[28]

The Intelligibility of the Transcendent

That the idea of the infinite, in its passivity, can be understood as the domain of the uncertainty of a self-preoccupied humanity incapable of embracing the infinite and for whom the fact of being struck by God could only be a last resort of finitude, is probably the misrecognition of the irreducible originality of alterity and transcendence and a purely negative interpretation of ethical proximity and love, an obstinate insistence on expressing them in terms of immanence, as if possession or fusion - the ideal of an intentional conscious-ness - exhausted spiritual energy.[29] That the proximity of the Infinite and the sociality that it founds and commands can be better than the *coincidence of unity*; that sociality is an irreducible excellence through its very plurality, even if one cannot say it exuberantly without falling back into the poverty of a proposition; that the relation to or non-indifference toward the other does not consist, for the Other, in being converted into the Same; that religion is not a moment in the "economy" of being; that love is not a demi-god[30] - that is certainly also signified by the idea of the infinite in us or by the humanity of man understood as the theology or the intelligibility of the transcendent.

But perhaps this theology already announces itself in the very wakefulness of insomnia,[31] in the vigil and troubled vigilance of the psyche before the moment when the finitude of being, wounded by the infinite, is prompted to gather itself into the hegemonic and atheist Ego of knowledge.

Peace and Proximity

(1984)

The dominant trend in the reception of Levinas's work hitherto can perhaps be summarized in a single phrase: ethics is first philosophy. That is to say, the most primordial datum in human experience is the face-to-face relation with the other human (*autrui*), which is described in "Paix et proximité" in terms of peace and love.[1] A question that is often rightly raised - and more often intended as a criticism - with regard to this conception of ethics is the following: what is the relation between the experience of the face-to-face and the spheres of reason, law, justice, and universality, spheres which, in the Western liberal tradition at least, are at the basis of the political organization of society, ensuring the legitimacy of institutions and underwriting the rights and duties of citizens? In brief, what is the relation between ethics and politics?

Far from a blind spot in Levinas's work, one finds - and with an increasing insistence - an attempt to traverse the passage from ethics to politics. In each of his two major works, *Totality and Infinity* and *Otherwise than Being or Beyond Essence*, Levinas endeavors to build a bridge from ethics, conceived as the nontotalizable relation with the other human, to politics, understood as the relation with the third party (*le tiers*), that is, to all the others that make up society (TeI 187–90/TaI 212–14, AE 199–207/OB 156–62). Levinas begins his analysis with the statement of the domination of a totalizing politics linked to the fact of war, that is to say, the Hobbesian claim that the peaceful order of society is constituted in opposition to the threat of the war of all against all. For Levinas, the domination of the category of totality in Western philosophy is linked to the domination of totalizing forms of politics - ultimately, National Socialism and Stalinism - and the complete reduction of the ethical to the political. As Levinas writes in *Totality and Infinity*, "Politics left to itself bears a tyranny within itself" (TeI 276/TaI 300).

Thus, one might conclude, Levinas's ethical thinking is a critique of politics, which would indeed justify the critical question raised above. As becomes clear in the final part of the following essay, however, Levinas does not want to reject the order of political rationality and its consequent claims to universality and justice; rather, he wants to criticize the belief that *only* political rationality can answer political problems and to show how the order of the state rests upon the irreducible ethical responsibility of the face-to-face relation. Levinas's disruption of totalizing politics permits the deduction of an ethical structure irreducible to totality: the face-to-face, proximity, peace, or love. Thus Levinas's thinking does not result in an apoliticism or ethical quietism - which, incidentally, is the substance of his critique of Martin Buber's I-Thou relation; rather, ethics leads back to politics, to the demand for a just polity. Indeed, one might go further and claim that the ethical is ethical for the sake of politics, that is, for the sake of a transformed conception of politics and society.

In "Peace and Proximity," the question of the passage from ethics to politics is articulated around the theme of Europe and more specifically what Levinas refers to as "the ethical moment in the crisis of Europe." This crisis is the result of an ambiguity at the heart of the European liberal tradition, where the attempt to found a political order of peace on the "Greek wisdom" of autonomy, solidarity, and reciprocity becomes a guilty conscience that recognizes how this political order has turned into - and indeed often legitimized - the violence of imperialism, colonialism, and genocide. With the rise of antiethnocentric disciplines, such as cultural anthropology, in European universities, we see Europe turned against Europe and forced to recognize a deficiency in its ethical resources. Responding to this crisis, Levinas wonders whether one might not ask if the ambiguous Hellenic peace of the European political order presupposes another order of peace, located not in the unity or totality of the state or nation but rather in fellowship with the other human, an order of sociality and love. If the ethical crisis of Europe is based in its unique attachment to a Greek heritage, then Levinas is suggesting that this heritage needs to be supplemented by a Biblical tradition which would be rooted in the acknowledgment of peace as a responsibility to the other. It is in no way a question of moving from the paradigm of Athens to that of Jerusalem but rather of recognizing that both are simultaneously necessary for the constitution of a just polity. As Levinas states in the discussion that follows "Transcendence and Height," "Both the hierarchy taught by Athens and the *abstract* and slightly *anarchical* ethical individualism taught by Jerusalem are *simultaneously necessary* in order to suppress violence."

I

The problem of Europe and peace is precisely the problem posed by the contradiction in our consciousness (*conscience*)[2] as Europeans. It is the problem of the humanity within us, of the centrality of Europe whose "vital forces" - those where the brutal perseverance of beings in their being still remains active - are already seduced by peace, by peace in preference to violence, and, more precisely still, by the peace of a humanity which, European within us, has already decided in favor of Greek wisdom such that human peace is awaited on the basis of the True. Peace on the basis of the Truth - on the basis of the truth of a knowledge where, instead of opposing itself, the diverse agrees with itself and unites; where the stranger is assimilated; where the other is reconciled with the identity of the identical in everyone. Peace as the return of the multiple to unity, in conformity with the Platonic or Neoplatonic idea of the One.[3] Peace on the basis of the truth, which - marvel of marvels - commands humans without forcing them or combating them, which governs them or gathers them together without enslaving them, which, through discourse, can convince rather than vanquish, and which masters the hostile elements of nature through calculation and the know-how of technology. Peace on the basis of the state, which would be a gathering of humans participating in the same ideal truths. Peace which is savored as tranquillity that guarantees a solidarity - the exact measure of reciprocity in services rendered among fellows: the unity of a Whole wherein everyone finds their repose, their place, their seat. Peace as tranquillity and repose! Peace as repose among beings well-placed or reposing on the underlying solidity of their substance, self-sufficient in their identity or capable of being satisfied and seeking satisfaction.

But the conscience of the European is henceforth guilty because of the contradiction that rends it at the very hour of its modernity, which is probably that of the balance sheets drawn up in lucidity, that of full consciousness. This history of peace, freedom, and well-being promised on the basis of a light projected by a universal knowledge on the world and human society - and even on religious teachings that seek justification in the truths of knowledge - this history does not recognize itself in its millennia of fratricidal, political, and bloody struggles, of imperialism, of human hatred and exploitation, up to our century of world wars, genocides, the Holocaust, and terrorism; of unemployment, the continuing poverty of the Third World; of the pitiless doctrines and cruelties of fascism and National Socialism, up to the supreme paradox where the defense of the human and its rights is inverted into Stalinism.

Hence the contestation of the centrality of Europe and its culture. A weariness of Europe! A break in the universality of theoretical reason, which arose early in the "Know thyself" in order to seek the entire universe in self-consciousness. Hence the affirmation and valorization of particular cultures at all corners of the world. An affirmation finding an echo and recognition - and often an origin - and always a sympathetic intelligence at the summits of the European University itself. An interest directed, in our old world in the name of Europe's ancient universalism itself, at the innumerable particularisms which have pretensions to be its equal. An interest that no longer derives from some taste for "barbarous exoticism" but from the exaltation of a logic *other* than the logic of Aristotle, a thought other than civilized. An exaltation which is perhaps explained by a remorse nourished by the memory of colonial wars and of a long oppression of those who were once called savages, of a long indifference to the sorrows of an entire world. And thus, the contestation of the centrality of Europe from Europe itself. But perhaps, precisely in this way, a testimony to a Europe that is not simply Hellenic! And also in this way, the problem of knowing what is the right contribution of the latter in a Europe that one would like to think faithful to all of its promises.

Europe against Europe, under yet another aspect and with regard to the most dramatic possibilities. The great empires which, to such a large extent, decide the destiny of our planet, issue from a European politics, economy, science, and technology and from their power of expansion. Universalism or imperialism! European empires extending beyond geographical Europe, rivaling one another in power, to the point of preparing - if necessary - to destroy the very earth that bears humanity. Explosion of the earth itself by an energy that the search for truth - become modern science - released from being. It is here that truth threatens being itself, it is here that truth threatens, we might say, being as being, and disqualifies the Europe that discovered these forces, and left them uncovered. But, doubtless, this way of disqualifying and accusing already proceeds from a spiritual vocation in which the love of wisdom does not translate or dry up the powers of love.

II

This guilty conscience does not only express a contradiction between a specific cultural project and its effects. It is not uniquely made up of the seductions of a peace guaranteeing everyone the tranquillity of their happiness and the freedom to possess the world and, doubtless also, the possibility of possession that nothing should spoil. It is not the failure of a speculative or dialectical project in the Hegelian style - a project indifferent to wars, murders, and suffering, insofar as these are necessary for the unfolding of rational thought, which is also a politics - insofar as these are necessary in the formation of concepts of which the logic and the rational accomplishment alone would count. It is not the intellectual deception of a system belied by the incoherences of the real that is the drama of Europe. Nor is it even just the danger of dying that frightens everyone. There is anxiety in committing the crimes even when the concepts are in agreement with each other. There is an anxiety of responsibility that is incumbent on everyone in the death or suffering of the other (*autrui*). The fear of everyone for themselves in the mortality of everyone does not succeed in *absorbing* the gravity of murder committed and the scandal of indifference to the suffering of the other (*autrui*). Behind the danger that everyone runs for themselves in an insecure world, there dawns the consciousness of the immediate immorality of a culture and a history. Will we not have heard, then, in the vocation of Europe - prior to the message of truth it bears - the "You shall not kill" of the Ten Commandments and the Bible? In chapter 32 of Genesis, Jacob is troubled by the news that his brother Esau - friend or foe - is marching to meet him "at the head of four hundred men." Verse 8 tells us: "Jacob was greatly afraid and anxious."[4] What is the difference between fright and anxiety? The rabbinic commentator, the celebrated Rashi,[5] makes it clear: he was frightened of his own death but was anxious he might have to kill.

In thinking about this ethical moment in our European crisis - in thinking about our anxiety - or the anxiety of Jacob - troubled at the prospect of committing violence - albeit necessary for the logical unfolding of history - albeit necessary in its unfolding commanded by the march of truth, advancing in absolute thought and promising at the end of the journey the peace of the "identity of the identical and the nonidentical,"[6] in thinking about this ethical moment in our European crisis (notably testified to in the philosophical work of Franz Rosenzweig, schooled in Hegelian thought but also acquainted with the First World War, though only the First),[7] one can ask oneself if peace has not to respond to a call more urgent than that of truth and initially distinct from the call of truth. One can ask oneself if one should not understand the very ideal of truth - which no European could refuse - already in terms of an ideal of peace which, more ancient than that of knowledge, only comes to open itself to the call of truth. One can ask oneself if knowledge itself and the politics ruling history do not come into their high office when they already respond to the demand of peace and let themselves be guided by this demand. But in this case, peace would no longer amount to a simple confirmation of human identity in its substantiality, to its freedom made up of tranquillity, to the repose of a being found founded in itself, in its identity as an ego. Henceforth it would no longer be a matter of the bourgeois peace of the man who is at home with himself behind closed doors, rejecting the outside that negates him; it would no longer be a matter of peace conforming to the ideal of the *unity of the One* which every alterity disturbs. In a sensibility where the scandal of murder does not find itself suffocated even when violence is rationally necessary - peace could not mean the serene calm of the identical; nor could alterity be justified uniquely as the logical distinction of *parts belonging to a divided whole*, which rigorously reciprocal relations unite into a whole.

One must precisely place in question the conception according to which, in human multiplicity, the ego would be reduced to a part of a Whole, which reconstitutes itself in the image of an organism - or a concept - whose unity is the coherence of its members, or a comprehensive structure. It is necessary to ask oneself - and this would be the other side of the alternative - with regard to the identity of the ego, if the alterity of the other (*autrui*) has not - *straightaway* - an absolute character, in the etymological sense of the term[8] - as if the other (*autrui*) were not merely other in a logical sense, other of an alterity logically surmountable in a common *genus* - or transcendentally surmountable in lending itself to the synthesis operated by a Kantian "I think."[9] It is necessary to ask oneself if peace, instead of being the result of an absorption or disappearance of alterity, would not on the contrary be the *fraternal* mode of a proximity to the other (*autrui*), which would not simply be the failure to coincide with the other but would signify precisely the *surplus* of sociality over every solitude - the *surplus* of sociality and of love. We do not use this word, so often abused, lightly.[10]

Peace as a relation with an alterity, irreducible to a common genus where, already in a logical community, it would only have a relative alterity. Peace independent, then, of any belonging to a system, irreducible to a totality and refractory to synthesis. A project of peace different from the political peace spoken of above. An ethical relation which, thus, would not be a simple deficiency or privation of the unity of the One reduced to the multiplicity of individuals in the extension of a genus! Here, on the contrary, in ethical peace, the relation is with the inassimilable other, the irreducible other, the other, unique. The unique alone is irreducible and absolutely other!

But the unicity of the unique is the unicity of the beloved. The unicity of the unique signifies in love. Hence peace as love. Not that the unicity of alterity is henceforth thought of as some subjective illusion of the lover. Quite the contrary, the *subjective* as such would be precisely the breakthrough - across the impassive essence of being, and across the rigor of its logical forms and genera, and across the violence of its perseverance in being - toward the unique, toward the absolutely other, through love, human proximity, and peace. A proximity different from some "short distance" measured in geometrical space separating the one from the others. Peace different from the simple unity of the diverse integrated by synthesis. Peace as a relation with the other in its logically indiscernible alterity, in its alterity irreducible to the logical identity of a final difference attaching to a genus. Peace as an incessant watch over this alterity and this unicity. Proximity as the impossible assumption of difference, impossible definition, impossible integration. Proximity as impossible appearing. But proximity! Husserl's famous "appresentation,"[11] not as an impoverished representation but as the mysterious surplus of the beloved. The proper excellence of transcendence without reference to the immanence of the true, which in the West passes for the supreme grace of the spiritual. Indeed, it is evident that it is in the knowledge of the other (*autrui*) as a simple individual - individual of a genus, a class, or a race - that peace with the other (*autrui*) turns into hatred; it is the approach of the other as "such and such a type."

III

We have not conducted this formal analysis of peace - as the *relation* with the unique and the other - a relation designated by the general term *love* - without attempting to deformalize these structures and rediscover them in their concreteness, that is, without a phenomenology. We have thought that the unicity and alterity of the unique is concretely the face of the other human, of which the original epiphany lies not in the visibility of a plastic form, but in "appresentation." The thought that is awake to the face of the other human is not a thought of . . . , a representation, but straightaway a thought for . . . , a nonindifference for the other, upsetting the equilibrium of the steady and impassive soul of pure knowledge, a watching over the other human in his or her unicity which is indiscernible to knowledge, an approach of the first comer in his or her proximity as neighbor and unique. Face - before any particular expression and beneath any expression, which is already a countenance given to the self, hiding the nudity of the face. Face which is not dis-closure,[12] but the pure denuding of exposure without defense. Exposure as such, extreme exposure to death, to mortality itself. Extreme precariousness of the unique, precariousness of the stranger. The nudity of pure exposure, which is not simply the emphaticalness of the known, of the disclosed in truth: exposure which is expression, first language, call and assignation.

The face is thus not exclusively a human face. In Vassili Grossman's *Life and Fate* the story is of the families, wives, and parents of political detainees traveling to the Lubyanka in Moscow for the latest news. A line is formed at the counter, a line where one can see only the backs of others. A woman awaits her turn: "[She] had never thought that the human back could be so expressive, and could convey states of mind in such a penetrating way. Persons approaching the counter had a particular way of craning their neck and their back, their raised shoulders with shoulder blades tense like springs, which seemed to cry, sob, and scream."[13] The face as the extreme precariousness of the other. Peace as awakeness to the precariousness of the other.

For, in this extreme straightforwardness of the face and its expression, assignation and demand that concern the ego, that concern *me*. In this extreme straightforwardness - its right over me. The demand that concerns me as an ego is the concrete circumstance where this right signifies. As if the invisible death which the face of the other (*autrui*) faces were *my* affair, as if this death regarded me. In this call to responsibility of the ego by the face which summons it, which demands it and claims it, the other (*autrui*) is the neighbor.

By starting with this extreme straightforwardness of the face of the other (*autrui*), we have previously been able to write that the face of the other in its precariousness and defenselessness, is for me at once the temptation to kill and the call to peace, the "You shall not kill."[14] The face which already accuses me makes me suspicious but already claims me and demands me. The right of the human is here, in this straightforwardness of exposition, of commandment and of assignation, a right more ancient than all conferment of dignity and every merit. The proximity of the neighbor - the peace of proximity - is the responsibility of the ego for an other, the impossibility of letting the other alone faced with the mystery of death. Concretely, this is the susception of dying for the other. Peace with the other (*autrui*) goes that far. It is the whole gravity of love of the neighbor, of love without concupiscence.

Peace as love of the neighbor, where it is not a matter of peace as pure rest that confirms one's identity but of always placing in question this very identity, its limitless freedom and its power.

IV

But the order of truth and knowledge has a role to play in this peace of proximity and in the ethical order it signifies. To a great extent, it is the ethical order of human proximity that gives rise to or calls for the order of objectivity, truth, and knowledge. Which is extremely important for the very sense of Europe: its Biblical heritage implies the necessity of the Greek heritage. Europe is not a simple confluence of two cultural currents. It is the concreteness where theoretical and Biblical wisdom do better than converge. The relation with the other and the unique that is peace comes to demand a reason that thematizes, synchronizes and synthesizes, that thinks a world and reflects on being, concepts necessary for the peace of humanity.

Doubtless, responsibility for the other human being is, in its immediacy, anterior to every question. But how does responsibility obligate if a third party troubles this exteriority of two where my subjection of the subject is subjection to the neighbor? The third party is other than the neighbor but also another neighbor, and also a neighbor of the other, and not simply their fellow. What am I to do? What have they already done to one another? Who passes before the other in my responsibility? What, then, are the other and the third party with respect to one another? Birth of the question.

The first question in the interhuman is the question of justice. Henceforth it is necessary to know, to become consciousness. Comparison is superimposed onto my relation with the *unique* and the incomparable, and, in view of equity and equality, a weighing, a thinking, a calculation, the comparison of incomparables, and, consequently, the neutrality - presence or representation - of being, the thematization and the visibility of the face in some way de-faced as the simple individuation of an individual; the burden of ownership and exchange; the necessity of thinking together under a synthetic theme the multiplicity and the unity of the world; and, through this, the promotion in thought of intentionality, of the intelligibility of the relation, and of the final signifyingness of being; and, through this, finally, the extreme importance in human multiplicity of the political structure of society, subject to laws and thereby to institutions where the *for-the-other* of subjectivity - or the ego - enters with the dignity of a citizen into the perfect reciprocity of political laws which are essentially egalitarian or held to become so.

But the forms of spirit which are thus promoted and the notions such as being or rational truth which thus assume an original character in every sense and the political unity with the institutions and relations that are established on this basis are, at every moment, on the point of carrying within themselves their center of gravity and of weighing on their own account the destiny of humanity, as the source of conflicts and violence. Consequently, it seemed to us important to recall peace and justice as their origin, justification, and measure; to recall that this justice, which can legitimate them ethically -that is, preserve for the human its proper sense of dis-inter-estedness[15] under the weight of being - is not a natural and anonymous legality governing the human masses, from which is derived a technique of social equilibrium, placing in harmony the antagonistic and blind forces through transitory cruelties and violence, a State delivered over to its own necessities that it is impossible to justify. Nothing would be able to withdraw itself from the control of the responsibility of the "one for the other," which delineates the limit of the State and does not cease to appeal to the vigilance of persons who would not be satisfied with the simple subsumption of cases under a general rule, of which a computer is capable.

It is not without importance to know - and this is perhaps the European experience of the twentieth century - if the egalitarian and just State in which the European is accomplished - and which it is a matter of founding and, above all, preserving - proceeds from a war of all against all - or from the irreducible responsibility of the one for the other, and if it can ignore the unicity of the face and love. It is not without importance to know this so that war does not become the institution of a war with a good conscience in the name of historical necessities. Consciousness is born as the presence of the third party in the proximity of the one for the other and, consequently, it is to the extent that it proceeds from this that it can become dis-inter-estedness. The foundation of consciousness is justice and not the reverse. Objectivity reposing on justice. To the extravagant generosity of the for-the-other is superimposed a reasonable order, ancillary or angelic, of justice through knowledge, and philosophy here is a *measure* brought to the infinity of the being-for-the-other of peace and proximity, and is like the wisdom of love.[16]

NOTES

1. Is Ontology Fundamental?

1. This essay, "L'ontologie est-elle fondamentale?" was first published in the *Revue de Métaphysique et de Morale* 56 (1951), pp. 88–98. It was reprinted in EN 13–24. An English translation by Peter Atterton appeared in *Philosophy Today*, Summer 1989, pp. 121–29. The text published here, based on Atterton's translation, was extensively revised by Simon Critchley and Adriaan Peperzak. Notes were prepared by Adriaan Peperzak.

2. When Levinas published this essay (in 1951), *authentique* was the standard translation of Heidegger's *eigentlich* into French.

3. In his first essay on Heidegger, "Martin Heidegger et l'ontologie" (1932), Levinas translated *Dasein* as *être ici-bas* (being here-below); see EDE 58 and 65. In other places Levinas uses *être-là* (being there; see EDE 52). In a later paper, "L'ontologie dans le temporel" (presented in 1940, then published in 1948 in a Spanish translation), Levinas writes: "All translations of this word [*Dasein*] would mask the amphibological character of the substantive verb [*Sein*], to which the addition of the prefix *Da* is essential. . . . We therefore transcribe it without further ado" (EDE 81).

4. Plato's orientation toward an "up there" and Hegel's philosophy of historical progress are here contrasted with Heidegger's understanding of Being; see *Being and Time* § 31.

5. See Husserl, *Logische Untersuchungen* II, §9, on *Bedeutungsintention* and Levinas, TIP 101 ff.; TIH 65 ff.

6. See *Being and Time* § 44.

7. *Being and Time* §§ 9, 15–22, 29, and 31–32.

8. Levinas uses the word *embarqué*, which is probably an allusion to Pascal's famous sentence on the "wager," "Yes, but one must wager; this is not voluntary, you are embarked" (*Pensées*, edition Brunschvicg, n. 233), a sentence to which Levinas refers explicitly in a similar context in "Martin Heidegger et l'ontologie" (EDE 72).

9. Levinas adds the following note: "Cf. our remarks on this subject in Jean Wahl's 'Esquisse pour une histoire de l'existentialisme,' (1947), pp. 95–96"; trans. F. Williams and S. Maron, *A Short History of Existentialism* (New York: Philosophical Library, 1979), pp. 47–53.

10. *Nicomachean Ethics* 1177 a 12-1179 a 32.

11. *Offenheit* is used often by Heidegger in his later work, but the "openness of being" is already indicated in *Being and Time* § 44, where Heidegger explains "truth" (*Wahrheit*) as unconcealedness, *alētheia*, *Lichtung*, and *Erschlossenheit*.

12. This is an allusion to the circle of comprehension characteristic for the explication of being, as is shown in *Being and Time* §§ 32 and 63.

13. This translation of the *Da* in *Dasein* by the French version (*ecceité*) of the late medieval category *haecceitas* could be justified on the basis of the meaning of the Latin *ecce: da*, "there it (the here and now) is."

14. Here and in the following sections Levinas reflects on Heidegger's "ontological difference" between *Sein* (*être*, being) and *Seiendes* (*l'étant*, which we translate either as "a being" or as "beings").

15. See *Being and Time* § 26.

16. This is an allusion to Heidegger's *Sein-lassen*, for example in *Letter on Humanism* (1946); "Denn sie läßt das Sein - sein." See "Brief über den Humanismus," *Wegmarken*, Gesamtausgabe 9 (Frankfurt: Klostermann, 1976), p. 358; trans. Frank Capuzzi,

"Letter on Humanism," in *Martin Heidegger: Basic Writings*, expanded edition, ed. D. F. Krell (New York: Harper & Row, 1993), p. 259.

17. See *Being and Time* §§ 15–22.

18. See, for example, Plato, *Theaetetus* 150a–151d, *Meno* 80d–82e.

19. "L'essence du discours est prière." The translation does not express the ambiguity of the French *prière* (politely or insistently asking, imploring), which is also used between human interlocutors.

20. See Auguste Comte, *Système de politique positive* or *Traité de sociologie, instituant la religion de l'humanité*, 4 vol. (Paris, 1951–54). Although Comte mentions "the Religion of Humankind" in his preface to the first volume (pp. 18–20), its description is not given before the *conclusion générale* of the "Discours préliminaire" (pp. 321–99 of vol. 1). See *System of Positive Polity* (New York: Franklin, 1968?), vol. 1, pp. xxiv–xxv and 257–321.

21. "Je peux vouloir." For a full understanding of this passage in which the word *pouvoir* ("power," but also "can" and "being able") is repeated many times, one must grasp the allusions to Husserl's "I can" (*Ich kann, je peux*), passim in *Cartesian Meditations*, and Heidegger's *Seinkönnen* (*Being and Time* §§ 54–60). See Levinas's explanation of the latter in EDE 66–68.

2. Transcendence and Height

1. "Transcendance et hauteur," followed by a discussion and an exchange of letters, first appeared in *Bulletin de la Société Française de Philosophie* 56 (1962). It was reprinted in Catherine Chalier and Miguel Abensour, eds., *Levinas* (Paris: Herne, 1991), pp. 97–112. This translation was prepared by Tina Chanter, Simon Critchley, and Nicholas Walker and revised by Adriaan Peperzak. Notes were prepared by Adriaan Peperzak.

2. In Hegel's *Encyclopedia of the Philosophical Sciences*, "soul," "consciousness," and "spirit" are the topics of the three chapters that form his "philosophy of subjective spirit," but this is an integral part of the universe of beings, which Hegel interprets as the self-realization of the (original and absolute) Spirit. Under the influence of Kojève's interpretation of Hegel's *Phenomenology of Spirit*, Levinas calls the whole of Hegel's philosophy (of absolute Spirit) a "History." Since Hegel, in his *Logic*, sees "Being" as the original category in which all the elements of Spirit are contained, implicitly, Levinas can equate this "History" with the History of Being and thus see in it one of the varieties of Western ontology.

3. See Martin Heidegger, "Brief über den Humanismus," *Wegmarken*, Gesamtausgabe 9 (Frankfurt: Klostermann, 1976), p. 331; trans. Frank Capuzzi, "Letter on Humanism," in *Martin Heidegger: Basic Writings*, expanded edition, ed. D. F. Krell (New York: Harper & Row, 1993), p. 234.

4. See André Lalande, *Vocabulaire technique et critique de la philosophie* (Paris: Alcan, 1926–32), p. 454. Lalande argues for "the privilege of identity in writing that difference is always imposed on the mind as a problem that must be solved. The movement of understanding goes from the other to the same; therefore one can say that the latter expresses the nature of spirit in a more essential way."

5. See M. Heidegger, *Nietzsche* (Pfullingen: Neske, 1961), vol. 1, pp. 56–59; trans. D. F. Krell, *Nietzsche: The Will to Power as Art* (New York: Harper & Row, 1976), pp. 46–48.

6. This is a play on the French expression "laisser la proie pour l'ombre" (to give up what one already has for an uncertain alternative).

7. See Descartes's Third Meditation in *Oeuvres de Descartes*, ed. C. Adam and P.

Tannery (Paris: Vrin, 1973), vol. 7, p. 43; trans. J. Cottingham et al., *The Philosophical Writings of Descartes* (Cambridge: Cambridge University Press, 1984), vol. 2, p. 29.

8. See S. Kierkegaard, *Philosophical Fragments by Johannes Climacus*, trans. Howard V. and Edna H. Hong (Princeton: Princeton University Press, 1985), p. 45, and Vladimir Jankélévitch, *Philosophie première: Introduction à une philosophie du presque* (Paris: PUF 1954), pp. 120–22.

9. In Homer's *Odyssey*, Penelope told her suitors that she would choose one of them to be her husband when she had finished weaving Laertes's shroud, but each night she unraveled the work she had done during the day. Book II, l. 93ff.; Book XIX, l. 139ff.; and Book XXIV, l. 128ff.

10. "Le Moi [. . .] ne peut plus pouvoir." See the discussion of *pouvoir* in n. 21 to chap. 1 in this volume. It carries overtones of "power." *Peut* does not restrict human existence to a capability but indicates the *moral* "impossibility" of treating the Other as subordinate to the I. I am not allowed to posit myself as a power who reduces all otherness to being an element of my self-realization.

11. For Heidegger's analysis of *Geworfenheit* and *Schuld*, see *Being and Time* §§ 38 and §§ 54–60; see also §§ 29 and 31.

12. *Scrupulus* (Latin) means a small pebble. Levinas refers here to Paul Ricoeur's interpretation of the scrupulous conscience, typical for the Phariseans' way of life, in Ricoeur, *Finitude et culpabilité II* (Paris: Aubier, 1960), pp. 115–34; trans. Emerson Buchanan, *The Symbolism of Evil* (Boston: Beacon Press, 1969), pp. 118–39.

13. This remark, and in a sense the entire text of "Transcendence and Height," are part of Levinas's ongoing discussion with Heidegger's conception of truth as "A-lētheia" and disclosure. See *Sein und Zeit* § 44 and many of Heidegger's later publications.

14. In *Republic* 509b Socrates says that "the good" is not *ousia* (essence, being) but rises "above and beyond the *ousia* in dignity and power." Plotinus quotes and interprets this, for example, in *Enneads* VI, 7 (esp. 33–41).

15. Tel xii; Tal 24.

16. "Homo sum: humani nihil a me alienum puto." Terence, "The Self Tormentor," in *Terence*, trans. John Sargeant, Loeb Classical Library, vol. 1 (London: Heinemann, 1920), p. 124, ll. 77–78.

17. Jean-Paul Sartre, *Situations IV*, (Paris: Gallimard, 1964), pp. 275–76; trans. Benita Eisler, *Situations* (London: Hamish Hamilton, 1965), p. 314.

3. Meaning and Sense

1. "La signification et le sens" appeared first in *Revue de Métaphysique et de Morale* 69 (1964), pp. 125–56 and was reprinted in *Humanisme de l'autre homme* (Montpellier: Fata Morgana, 1972), pp. 17–63 and 105. A translation by Alphonso Lingis appeared in CP 75-107. In HAH (p. 105) Levinas wrote the following note: "The ideas developed in this study were presented at the Collège Philosophique in 1961, 1962, and 1963, and in January 1963 at the Faculté Universitaire Saint Louis in Brussels. The last part of this text was presented, in another context, on May 12, 1963, during the colloquium of the Philosophical Society of Leuven and published as 'La trace de l'autre' in the September 1963 issue of *Tijdschrift voor Filosofie*" (pp. 605–23). This translation has been revised by Simon Critchley and Adriaan Peperzak, who also prepared the notes.

2. There is an play here on the word *metaphor* - literally, "what carries something away."

3. A metaphor, which gives meaning to a reality, can thus be explained in two ways: (1) by a fault in perception - this is discussed in the third through sixth paragraphs of this chapter; or (2) by the excellence of perception - this is discussed in the seventh

through twelfth paragraphs. The first way is followed from Plato to Husserl; the second has its greatest defender in Heidegger.

4. The quotation is from the Gospel of Saint John 3:8. See the discussion in Anatole France, "Ariste et Polyphile ou le langage métaphysique," *Le jardin d'Epicure* (Paris: Calmann-Lévy, 1924), pp. 179–223; trans. Alfred Allinson, "Aristos and Polyphilos on the Language of Metaphysics," *The Garden of Epicurus* (London: Bodley Head, 1926), pp. 207–28.

5. See E. Husserl, *Logische Untersuchungen*; trans. J. N. Findlay, *Logical Investigations* (New York: Humanities Press, 1970), VI, §§ 45 and 46, and Levinas's commentary in TIPH 121–24, TIH 80–82, and EDE 26–29. The text is teeming with Husserlian expressions, such as *hyletische Data, Sinngebung* (meaning bestowal), *unerfüllt* (unfulfilled), *bedeutende Intention* (signitive intention), *Ausdruck* (expression), *Konstitution* (constitution).

6. We are translating *signification* by "meaning"; *sens* by "sense." *Sens* can designate both "meaning" and "direction"; this duality is felt throughout this essay. Hence the relationship with *droiture* - "straightforwardness" of a conscious movement. But *droiture* also conveys a sense of "uprightness."

7. "Pure receptivity" is a concept found in Kant and French idealists such as Alain. The second possible explanation for metaphors, which Levinas here begins to consider, is linked to Husserl's analysis of "horizons" and "world" and the phenomenology of Heidegger and Merleau-Ponty.

8. See the first quatrain of Rimbaud's *Voyelles*: "A noir, E blanc, I rouge, U vert, O bleu: voyelles, Je dirai quelque jour vos naissances latentes" (A black, E white, I red, U green, O blue. Vowels, one day I will tell your hidden births), *Oeuvres complètes* (Paris: Gallimard, 1963), pp. 103–4; trans. Paul Schmidt, *Arthur Rimbaud: Complete Works* (New York: Harper & Row, 1967), p. 123.

9. Plato, *Seventh Letter* 341b–344d; cf. *Phaedrus* 275b–278b.

10. Plato, *Cratylus* 396c–397d, 400d–408c.

11. In the fourth poem of *Les fleurs du mal*, Baudelaire stresses the "correspondence" between sounds, perfumes, and colors, and of the senses with the spirit. See "Correspondances," *Les fleurs du mal*, critical edition (Paris: José Corti, 1968), p. 34; trans. Georg Dillon, "Correspondences," *Flowers of Evil* (New York: Harper & Bros., 1936), p. 196.

12. M. Dufrenne, *La notion d'a priori* (Paris: Presses Universitaires de France, 1959), p. 99; trans. E. Casey, *The Notion of the A Priori* (Evanston: Northwestern University Press, 1966), p. 82. Cf. Levinas's article "A priori et subjectivité. A propos de *La notion de l'a priori* de M. Mikel Dufrenne" in EDE, pp. 179–86.

13. According to information supplied by M. Levinas, the reference here is to a lecture by M. Henri Birault.

14. See K. Löwith, *Gesammelte Abhandlungen. Zur Kritik der geschichtlichen Existenz* (Stuttgart: Kohlhammer, 1960), p. 222, who refers here to B. Snell, *Die Entdeckung des Geistes* (1955), pp. 258 ff.; trans. T.G. Rosenmeyer, *The Discovery of Mind* (New York: Harper & Row, 1960), pp. 200–201.

15. See Heidegger, "Brief über den Humanismus," *Wegmarken*, GA 9, pp. 313 and 333; trans. *Martin Heidegger: Basic Writings*, expanded edition, pp. 217 and 237.

16. This description of *das Seiende im Ganzen* (Beings as a whole) as a totality and a creative assembling or arranging refers to Heidegger's *Lichtung, Sammlung*, and *Geschick*.

17. In this and in what follows Levinas is concerned not only with Heidegger but also with Merleau-Ponty. According to information supplied by Levinas, this study was written after he read Maurice Merleau-Ponty, *Signes* (Paris: Gallimard, 1960); trans. Richard C. McCleary, *Signs* (Evanston: Northwestern University Press, 1964).

18. See Maurice Merleau-Ponty, *L'oeil et l'esprit* (Paris: Gallimard, 1964); trans.

Carleton Dallery, "Eye and Mind," in James M. Edie, ed., *The Primacy of Perception* (Evanston: Northwestern University Press, 1964).

19. The transcendental philosophy of Kant and his successors also seeks the conditions of possibility which precede our experiential knowledge. See Immanuel Kant, *Kritik der reinen Vernunft*; trans. Norman Kemp Smith, *Critique of Pure Reason* (London: Macmillan, 1964), on the difference between *Erfahrung* and *Anschauung*, B 202 ff. and 218 ff.

20. See Merleau-Ponty, *Signes*, pp. 115–122; *Signs*, pp. 92–97.

21. See Maurice Merleau-Ponty, *Phénoménologie de la perception*, pp. 106–13; trans. Colin Smith, *Phenomenology of Perception* (London: Routledge & Kegan Paul, 1962), pp. 90–97.

22. This evolution is evident in Merleau-Ponty's posthumously published *Le visible et l'invisible* (Paris: Gallimard, 1964); trans. Alphonso Lingis, *The Visible and the Invisible* (Evanston: Northwestern University Press, 1968).

23. Heidegger, "Brief über den Humanismus," *Wegmarken*, GA 9, p. 342; trans. *Martin Heidegger: Basic Writings*, expanded edition, p. 245.

24. See Kant, *Kritik der reinen Vernunft* (*Critique of Pure Reason*), B 68–72.

25. According to Plato, the intelligible (as the true reality which can only be reached through thought) is indeed present in the sensible world, which is characterized by change and becoming, but thought must pass beyond it to the truth. The ideas are not submerged in sensibility but remain intrinsically independent of it. The contemporary movements of thought which Levinas discusses here contest this intrinsic transcendence of the ideas. The truth itself has become historical. For the three varieties of this anti-Platonism summarized here, compare Hegel's *Phänomenologie des Geistes*, Bergson's *Essai sur les données immédiates* (1889), and Merleau-Ponty's *Signes*, esp. pp. 105–42 (*Signs*, pp. 84–113).

26. Greece. Cf. E. Husserl, *Die Krisis der Europäischen Wissenschaften und die Transzendentale Phänomenologie* (Husserliana VI) (The Hague: Martinus Nijhoff 1976, 2nd ed.), pp. 321–23; trans. David Carr, *The Crisis of European Sciences and Transcendental Phenomenology* (Evanston: Northwestern University Press, 1970), pp. 277–79. Concerning colonialism, see sec. 8 of this essay.

27. *Republic* 394 b: "a simple story without mimesis."

28. See Plato, *Philebus* 25b–27c, concerning the third sort of being, which is "mixed together" from infinity and finitude. One should perhaps also think of Plato's analysis in the *Republic* of *thumos*, which shares in rationality (*logistikon*) as well as in the lower faculty of desire (*epithymētikon*).

29. As this is to be found in Henri Bergson, *L'évolution créatrice*; trans. Arthur Mitchell, *Creative Evolution* (New York: Henry Holt, 1937).

30. See Henri Bergson, *Les données immédiates de la conscience*; trans. F. L. Pogson, *Time and Free Will* (New York: Harper & Row, 1960), and *Matière et mémoire*; trans. Nancy Margaret Paul and W. Scott Palmer, *Matter and Memory* (London: George Allen & Unwin, 1919).

31. *Empyreum* or *empyrean* is not a term used in Plato but in another Greek tradition; it was taken up by medieval theology and by Dante. It refers to the highest or furthest removed heaven, realm of fire. Levinas uses the term here to remind the reader of Plato's myths about the abode of the blessed. See Plato, *Gorgias* 523a–527d, *Phaedo* 107c–115d, *Republic* 614c ff., *Phaedrus* 246d ff.

32. Plato, *Meno* 82b.

33. Levinas refers here to Claude Lévi-Strauss, who dedicated his book *La pensée sauvage* (1962) (*The Savage Mind*) to Merleau-Ponty. See also Merleau-Ponty, "From Mauss to Claude Lévi-Strauss," in *Signes*, pp. 142–57; *Signs*, pp. 114–24.

34. The Hegelian translation of Aristotle's *energeia*, in which *ergon* (work) is heard, by

Wirklichkeit, in which *Werk* and *wirken* ("work" and "to work") can be heard, was used by Marx in the economic sense evoked in this section.

35. *Republic* 471c–541b.

36. Essence is used here in the active and "transitive" sense of the word, as Heidegger takes it in using the word *Wesen*. See also Merleau-Ponty, *Signes*, pp. 20–31, 84–104; *Signs*, pp. 14–22, 67–83.

37. Parmenides, fragment VIII, 43–44.

38. *Sens unique* carries the meaning of both "the only meaning" and "one-way direction," as in the traffic code.

39. F. Nietzsche, *Die fröhliche Wissenschaft* (*The Gay Science*), § 343.

40. Here *economy* (from Greek *oikos*, "home") refers to the ego that cares about itself and turns the world into a home within which it can enjoy itself. See TIH, sec. 3.

41. See Aristotle's *Physics* 267b 6–9, and *Metaphysics* 1072a 18–1073a 13, 1074b 15–1075a 11, cf. 1064a 37.

42. An epicycle is a circle which is described by a star, whose midpoint again turns in a circle around the earth. Whenever Ptolemaic astronomy came across facts that did not fit into its model, it brought in new epicycles, thus saving its theory at the cost of higher complication.

43. Heidegger, *Being and Time* § 4.

44. Cf. J.-P. Sartre's "Existence precedes essence." See *L'existentialisme est un humanisme*, p. 12; trans. Bernard Frechtman, *Existentialism Is a Humanism* (New York: Philosophical Library, 1947), p. 15.

45. *Gratitude* and *obéissance* allude to Heidegger's *Danken* (to thank); see his *Was heißt Denken* (Tübingen: Niemeyer, 1971), pp. 93–95; trans. Fred D. Wieck and J. Glenn Gray, *What Is Called Thinking?* (New York: Harper & Row, 1968), pp. 145–47, and his interpretation of *hören* (to hear, to listen) as related to *Gehorsamkeit*, p. 84; trans., p. 119.

46. This is an allusion to Heidegger's *Warten*; see his *Gelassenheit* (Pfullingen: Neske, 1959), pp. 44–46, 49–54; trans. John M. Anderson and E. Hans Freund, *Discourse on Thinking* (New York: Harper & Row, 1966), pp. 67–69, 71–76.

47. The word *sens* in *sens de l'histoire* is as ambiguous as *sens* in *sens unique*.

48. Cf. Aristotle, *Metaphysics* 1074b 34, and G. W. F. Hegel's *Enzyklopädie der philosophischen Wissenschaften*, which ends with a quotation from Aristotle, *Metaphysics* 1072b 18–30.

49. See Eric Weil, *Logique de la philosophie* (Paris: Vrin, 1950), pp. 70–86.

50. Deuteronomy 3:23–28, 32:48–52.

51. *L'être pour-au-delà-de-ma-mort*, in opposition to Heidegger's *Sein zum Tode*, *être-pour-la-mort* (being toward death, cf. *Being and Time* §§ 46 ff.).

52. The Greek word *leitourgia* means public service performed by private citizens at their own expense.

53. Léon Blum, *A l'échelle humaine* (Paris: Gallimard, 1945), pp. 213–14, trans. W. Pickles, *For All Mankind* (New York, 1946), p. 185.

54. Paul Valéry, "Cantique des colonnes," *Oeuvres I* (Paris: Gallimard, 1957), p. 116: trans. David Paul, *Poems* (Princeton: Princeton University Press, 1971), p. 123:

> Que portez-vous si haut
> Egales Radieuses?
> - Au désir sans défaut
> Vos grâces studieuses!
>
> - What is it you hear so high,
> Equals in Radiance?
> - To the faultless desire
> Our studious graces.

55. Plato, *Philebus* 51e–52d, and *Republic* 584b ff.

56. Martin Heidegger, *Sein und Zeit* (Frankfurt: Klostermann, 1977), GA 2, p. 254: "Das Dasein ist Seiendes, dem es in seinem Sein um dieses selbst geht"; trans. John Macquarrie and Edward Robinson, *Being and Time*, p. 236: "Dasein is an entity for which, in its Being, that Being is an issue."

57. *Republic* 369e–372c.

58. Levinas often uses the word *absolu* in the double sense of "absolute" and "absolved or separated from." In the latter sense the face can be called a (concrete) "abstraction."

59. Cf. Levinas's critique of representational thinking in EDE 23–26.

60. This chapter describes the persecution and suffering of the "servant of the Lord."

61. Cf. Levinas's "Philosophy and the Idea of the Infinite," in CP 47–59; revised translation with notes in A. Peperzak, *To the Other: An Introduction to the Philosophy of Emmanuel Levinas* (West Lafayette: Purdue University Press, 1993), pp. 88–119.

62. Cf. Levinas's commentary on Husserl's conception of truth as the "fulfilling of 'empty' intentions" in TIPH 101 ff.; TIH 65 ff.

63. *Phaedo* 62b.

64. Levinas refers to the third Colloque Philosophique de Royaumont, devoted to Husserl's philosophy. The proceedings were published under the title *Husserl* (Paris: Editions de Minuit, 1959). The quoted words from Merleau-Ponty are to be found on p. 158.

65. *Phaedo* 65a–67b.

66. *Le Moi* suggests an ego in the accusative, me who discovers myself responsible for the Other without having chosen this responsibility. In his later work Levinas insists on the passivity of this me.

67. Esp. in Léon Brunschvicg, *Les âges de l'intelligence* (Paris: Vrin, 1934); oral communication from the author.

68. See F. Nietzsche on the *Hinterweltler*, in *Also sprach Zarathustra* (*Thus Spoke Zarathustra*), I, 3.

69. Plato, *Parmenides* 137e–142a.

70. See J.-P. Sartre, *L'être et le néant* (Paris: Gallimard, 1943), p. 313; trans. Hazel E. Barnes, *Being and Nothingness* (New York: Washington Square Press, 1956), pp. 343–44.

71. Valéry, "Cantique des Colonnes," p. 118: "C'est un profond jadis, Jadis jamais assez!"; trans. *Poems*, p. 127: "A deep long since it is, Never long since enough!"

72. From *il* (French for "he" or "it") or from the Latin *ille* (that one there, at a distance).

73. Levinas refers here to "Roger Laporte's remarkable work *La Veille* [Paris: Gallimard, 1963], which also contains the notion *Il*."

74. Cf. H. Bergson, *Essais sur les données immédiates de la conscience* (*Time and Free Will*), chap. 2.

75. *Enneads* V, 5, 5. This English quote translates Emile Bréhier's French translation in Plotinus, *Ennéades* (Paris: Les Belles Lettres, 1931), pp. 96–98, which Levinas quotes here.

76. Cf. Exodus 33:18–23.

77. Genesis 1:27.

4. Enigma and Phenomenon

1. "Enigma et phénomène" was published in *Esprit* 33, no. 6 (June 1965), pp. 1128–42, and reprinted in Emmanuel Levinas, *En découvrant l'existence avec Husserl et Heidegger*, 2d ed. (Paris: Vrin, 1967), pp. 203-17. Alphonso Lingis's translation into English was published, with notes by Adriaan Peperzak, in CP 61–74. For this

collection, the translation was revised by Robert Bernasconi and Simon Critchley. The notes were augmented by Bernasconi.

2. Eugène Ionesco, "La cantatrice chauve," *Théâtre* (Paris: Gallimard, 1954), p. 28; trans. Donald M. Allen, "The Bald Soprano," *Four Plays* (New York: Grove Press, 1958), p. 23.

3. Levinas alludes to de Saussure's distinction between a diachronic study of language and other systems of cultural expression and a synchronic study. The latter makes a cross section across time in order to expose a structure within which the elements are simultaneous. A diachronic study follows down the transformation of structural elements in the course of time.

4. On the Good, see Plato, *Republic* 505a, 507a3, 508e, 509b, 577b; on the One, see Plato, *Parmenides* 135ff., and Plotinus, *Enneads*, V, 1 and VI, 9.

5. Michel Foucault's *L'histoire de la folie* (Paris: Plon, 1961), allows us to use such terms without simply referring to a disordered reason committing errors. (EL)

6. Levinas adds here a note: This approach is made in *feeling*, whose fundamental tonality is *Desire* in the sense we have given this term in *Totality and Infinity*. Desire, distinguished from tendency and from need, does not belong to activity but constitutes the intentionality of the affective order. One can ask if the remarkable and demystifying criticisms Michel Henry draws up against the intentionality of affectivity, which, despite Scheler's and Heidegger's analyses, would remain of intellectual origin (see *L'essence de la manifestation* [Paris: Presses Universitaires de France, 1963], pp. 707–57; trans. Girard Etzkorn, *The Essence of Manifestation* [The Hague: Martinus Nijhoff, 1973], §§63–65, pp. 565–604), succeed in driving every moment of transcendence from feeling. It has to be said that this transcendence consists in going beyond being, which here means that the aim aims at what refuses the correlation which every aim as such established and which consequently is nowise represented, not even conceptually. The primordial feeling, precisely in its ambiguity, is this desire for Infinity, the relationship with the Absolute which does not become correlative with it, and consequently in a sense leaves the subject in immanence. Is not this the immanence which Jean Wahl once called "the greatest transcendence . . . , that which consists in transcending transcendence, that is, relapsing into immanence" (see Wahl's *Existence humaine et transcendance* [Neuchâtel: Editions de la Baconnière, 1944], p. 38).

7. Vladimir Jankélévitch seeks, however, to penetrate into order with the *glimpse* (*l'entrevision*), even if the regularity of phenomena is to invade this breakthrough, as the waves of the Red Sea invaded the passage which had, for one night, broke through them. All his recent work, and in particular *Philosophie première: Introduction à une philosophie du "presque"* (Paris: Presses Universitaires de France, 1954), speaks of this with inimitable precision and subtlety. Our own project owes a great deal to his work. Bergson's analysis of the idea of order is to be found in *L'évolution créatrice* (Paris: Félix Alcan, 1910), pp. 227–37; trans. Arthur Mitchell, *Creative Evolution* (New York: Henry Holt, 1926), pp. 220–36. His analysis of the idea of nothingness is given in the same work, pp. 301–22; trans., pp. 278–98. (EL)

8. Spinoza, *Ethics*, Pt. 2, prop. 2.

9. A note by Levinas refers here to Jean Hyppolite, *Leçon inaugurale au Collège de France* (Paris: Nogent-le-Rotrou, 1964), and to Jacques Derrida, *Introduction à l'Origine de la géométrie de Husserl* (Paris: Presses Universitaires de France, 1962); trans. John P. Leavey, Jr., *Edmund Husserl's "Origin of Geometry": An Introduction*, 2d ed. (Lincoln: University of Nebraska Press, 1989). On p. 33 of his *Leçon inaugurale* Hyppolite cites Derrida's *Introduction*, p. 166 (trans., p. 149), confirming the close relation of these two thinkers.

10. Levinas adds here in a note: Formerly we refused this term [*prochain*], which seemed to us to suggest community by neighboring. Now we retain in it the abruptness

of the disturbance, which characterizes a neighbor inasmuch as he is the first one to come along. Cf. *Bulletin de la Société Française de Philosophie*, July–September, 1962, pp. 107–8 (session of January 17, 1962) (EL). The text Levinas refers to is "Transcendence and Height" (chap. 2 in this volume).

11. *Défaitisme* (defeatism) continues the end of the prior sentence: ". . . *le visage est défait* (decomposed, undone) *et nu* (naked)."

12. In Greek, *ainigma* means an obscure or equivocal word, a riddle.

13. Levinas had used the phrase "persecuted truth" as part of an exposition of Kierkegaard's thought in "Existenz und Ethik," an essay published in German in 1963 and reprinted in French in NP 102–3.

14. Jeanne Delhomme's *La pensée interrogative* [Paris, Presses Universitaires de France, 1954] renews the problem of modality, and, further, that of dogmatism and criticism, by refusing to the categorical judgment, and even to the certainty of the *Cogito*, the right to measure modality. Certainty itself must be measured by interrogation, which is a beginning of consciousness as such. What one calls the "first light" is from the first, and, vertiginously, an "I wonder" or "I ask myself" (*"je me demande"*), and not an "I understand being." The "I-myself" of the asking would be the first reflection. On many points, our own endeavor to grasp the trace as an emptiness that is not reducible to nothingness (which is contemporaneous with being!) nor to the sign of an absent plenitude recuperable by re-presentation rejoins Mme. Delhomme's interrogation, despite the wholly different orientation of our efforts (note by Levinas). Cf. also Levinas's article on this book, "Pénélope ou la pensée modale," in NP 69–77.

15. Cf. Levinas's descriptions of the erotic in TeI 233–44; TaI 256–66.

16. Cf. Treatise *Berakhot* 7a, a passage referring to Exodus 3:6. (EL's note)

17. Exodus 33:18–23.

18. Cf. I. Kant, *Critique of Pure Reason*, A 22–26, B 37–42.

19. Banquo, referring to the witches, says, "The earth hath bubbles, as the water has, and these are of them" *Macbeth* I.iii.79–80.

20. 1 Kings 19:12.

21. "The philosophy of history and the history of philosophy aim beyond the individual and the event, which, insofar as they commingle identity with duration, dissociate temporality and historicity for the profit of a sort of intemporal time. . . . The time that is recovered is not the time past, but the time that is surpassed." H. Gouhier, *L'histoire et sa philosophie* (Paris: Vrin, 1952), [p. 144]. (EL)

22. The French *fin* means end, goal, and is associated with *fini* - finite.

23. Cf. Levinas's account of the invocation of God in the You (*Tu*) which becomes He in the name. "Le Nom de Dieu d'après quelques textes talmudiques," ADV 151; BV 122.

24. Cf. Heidegger's use of the term *Lichtung* (clearing) in "Brief über den Humanismus," *Wegmarken*, GA 9, pp. 325, 331–32, and 361; trans., *Martin Heidegger: Basic Writings*, expanded edition, pp. 231, 235, and 262.

25. "Beyond being" (*epekeina tes ousias*) is an expression in Plato's *Republic* 509b (cf. also 517bc and 518d), where it characterizes the Good. Plotinus uses the same expression with regard to the One in *Enneads* V, 1, 8 and V, 6, title.

5. Substitution

1. "La substitution" was part of a public lecture given at the Faculté Universitaire Saint-Louis, Brussels, November 30, 1967. It was a continuation of the discussion held the day before entitled "Proximité," which was based on the study "Langage et proximité" and subsequently appeared in the second edition of *En découvrant l'existence avec Husserl et Heidegger* (Paris: Vrin, 1967), pp. 217–36 ["Language and Proximity," in

Collected Philosophical Papers, trans. A. Lingis (The Hague: Martinus Nijhoff, 1987), pp. 109–26]. The two lectures "Proximity" and "Substitution" were given under the general title "Beyond Essence." The present text [as published in the *Revue Philosophique de Louvain* 66 (1968), pp. 487–508] represents the final version of the discussion. Certain themes have been formulated in a more strenuous manner for the reader, who can "withstand" more than the listener. Some notes have been added in an attempt to clarify the perspectives opened by the particular subject matter. (EL) Translated by Peter Atterton, Simon Critchley, and Graham Noctor. Notes prepared by Robert Bernasconi. Notes by Emmanuel Levinas are identified by (EL) at the end of the note.

2. "Adumbrations" in English, like "silhouettes" in French, is the standard translation for Husserl's *Abschattungen*.

3. See Edmund Husserl, *Zur Phänomenologie des Inneren Zeitbewusstseins (1893–1917)*, ed. R. Boehm, Gesammelte Werke X (The Hague: Martinus Nijhoff, 1966), esp. §§ 35–36 and 52, pp. 73–75 and 368–82; trans. John Barnett Brough, *On the Phenomenology of the Consciousness of Internal Time (1893–1917)*, Collected Works, vol. 4 (Dordrecht: Kluwer, 1991), pp. 77–79 and 379–94.

4. Here there can be no question of analyzing this "mystery," which is realized in "narration." (EL)

5. See "Language and Proximity" in EDE 218 [CP 109–10]. (EL)

6. If the anarchical were not signaled *within* consciousness, it would *reign* in its own way. The anarchical is possible only when contested by the discourse which betrays, and yet translates, without annulling, its an-archy. The notion of an *abuse of language* demands stringent thought. (EL)

7. Husserl's *Sinngebung*. See, for example, *Ideen zu einer reinen Phänomenologie und Phänomenologischen Philosophie*, Erstes Buch. Gesammelte Werke III (The Hague: Martinus Nijhoff, 1950), § 55, pp. 134–36; trans. F. Kersten, *Ideas Pertaining to a Pure Phenomenology and to a Phenomenological Philosophy*, Collected Works, vol. 2 (The Hague: Martinus Nijhoff, 1982), pp. 128–30.

8. The phrase *fields of consciousness* was coined by William James in *Talks to Teachers on Psychology* (London: Longmans, Green, 1908), pp. 17-18. It was taken up into phenomenology by Aron Gurwitsch in *Théorie du champ de la conscience* (1957); trans., *The Field of Consciousness* (Pittsburgh: Duquesne University Press, 1964).

9. See Bergson's *Creative Evolution* [see chap. 4, n. 7] regarding the notion of disorder, which warrants close attention. Subversion and revolution are still within order. To recall Hegel, that which appears to consciousness in the experience of a "new object" as the "nothingness of the first" shows itself to the philosopher, who is in a position to see "behind the back of consciousness," as the result of a genesis, born in the midst of the same dialectical order (cf. Hegel, *Phénoménologie de l'Esprit*, trans. Jean Hyppolite, pp. 75–77) [*Phänomenologie des Geistes*, Gesammelte Werke 9 (Hamburg: Felix Meiner, 1980), pp. 60–61, trans. A. V. Miller, *Phenomenology of Spirit* (Oxford: Oxford University Press, 1977), pp. 55–56]. This movement of genesis, traversing the State, ends in absolute knowledge as the accomplishment of consciousness. The notion of anarchy introduced here precedes the political (or antipolitical) meaning popularly ascribed to it. It cannot, under pain of contradiction, be set up as a principle (in the sense the anarchists intend when, for example, they maintain that anarchy is the mother of order). Anarchy, unlike *arche*, cannot be sovereign. It can only disturb, albeit in a radical way, the State, prompting isolated moments of negation *without any* affirmation. The State, then, cannot set itself up as a Whole. But, in return, anarchy is allowed a say. (EL)

10. An inability which is *said* all the same. An-archy does not *reign*, and so remains ambiguous and enigmatic. It leaves a trace which discourse, in the pain of expression, tries to say. Yet it leaves only a trace. (EL)

11. *Mé-ontologique*. Levinas changed it to *méta-ontologique* when the essay was revised for inclusion in AE 125; OB 102.

12. Such is a relation without any a priori deriving from spontaneity, be it that spontaneity which ontology asks of finite thought, and which, as pure receptivity and in order to welcome a being, must operate as a transcendental imagination, formative of the imaginary, cavity of nothingness. (EL)

13. Consciousness is the game par excellence, a "transcendental imagination." (EL).

14. ". . . everything turns on grasping and expressing the true, not as *substance*, but equally as *subject*." G. W. F. Hegel, *Phänomenologie des Geistes*, p. 18; trans., *Phenomenology of Spirit*, p. 10. Translation modified.

15. We do not go so far as to write *essance*, like Jacques Derrida (whose remarkable work must be given the highest praise) writes *différance*. (EL)

16. The Parcae, or Fates, were the three Roman goddesses of Destiny, who presided over birth, marriage, and death. They corresponded to the Greek Moirai and were commonly depicted as spinning thread in an act that measured out the life span of human beings. See Pierre Grimal, *The Dictionary of Classical Mythology*, trans. A. R. Maxwell-Hyslop (Oxford: Basil Blackwell, 1986), p. 344.

17. Cf. *En découvrant l'existence . . .*, 2d ed., pp. 217–233 ["Language and Proximity," CP 109-15]. (EL)

18. J.-P. Sartre, *L'être et le néant*, pp. 37–84; trans. *Being and Nothingness*, pp. 119-158. G. W. F. Hegel, *Wissenschaft der Logik*, Gesammelte Werke 21 (Hamburg: Felix Meiner, 1985), pp. 144–51; trans. A. V. Miller, *Science of Logic* (London: George Allen & Unwin, 1969), pp. 157–64.

19. *Unicum* is from the Latin adjective *unicus*, which means "one and no more" or "unique." *Hapax* is a Greek word which means "once only."

20. For "immanent time," as well as for the time-constituting flux or flow that Husserl refers to as "absolute subjectivity" and which Levinas alludes to in the second sentence of the next paragraph, see Husserl, *On the Phenomenology of the Consciousness of Internal Time*, esp. secs. 36 and 37.

21. "We are, so to speak, innate to ourselves." G. W. Leibniz, *Nouveaux Essais sur l'entendement*, Philosophische Schriften 5, ed. C. Gerhardt (Hildesheim: Georg Olms, 1978), p. 93; trans. Peter Remnant and Jonathan Bennett, *New Essays on Human Understanding* (Cambridge: Cambridge University Press, 1981), Book I, chap. 3, p. 102.

22. Within the amphibology, that is, of being and beings - verb and noun - "temporalized" in time. (EL)

23. Anguish - in French, *angoisse* - derives from the Latin *angustia*, which has the sense of "narrowness" or "constriction."

24. Heidegger's analysis describes the anguish arising from the limitation of being. To the extent that the analysis is not to be read merely as psychological or anthropological, it teaches us that form (which according to our philosophical tradition *defines* being) is always too small for being. Definition in terms of form, "formness," beauty, luster, and appearing, is also a strangulation, that is, anguish itself. The disproportion between being and its phenomenality, the fact that being is cramped in its manifestation, would be produced under the anthropological modes of finite being, as a being-existing-toward-death. The measure of determination would thus be the ill-fitting measure of a Nessus tunic. Yet anguish as being-toward-death is also the hope of reaching the space of nonbeing. This possibility of deliverance (and the temptation of suicide) arises in the anxiety of death. As nothingness, death is an opening in which along with being the anguish arising from being's definition is engulfed. By contrast, anxiety, as the narrowness of a "passage into fullness," is the recurrence of the Oneself, a recurrence without evasion or defection. Such is a responsibility stronger than death, affirmed by Plato in his own fashion in the *Phaedo* when condemning suicide (62b). (EL)

25. The very notion of the *hither side* is without doubt justified by this extract from the *Parmenides*. It is a question of a retreat, a reclusion which remains a presence in the world and in history, and which does not go outside the World so as to become, in

chimerical fashion, a force liberated from the world, endowed with spiritual powers capable of triumphs or failures. Triumphs and failures presuppose personal freedom and, consequently, an Ego endowed with a political and religious sovereignty and principality. On this side, the Ego is a self, no longer part of being or history, neither an effect at rest nor a cause in movement. (EL)

26. Mal-heur. Le malheur means "misfortune," "bad luck." (EL)

27. The body is neither an obstacle opposed to the soul nor a tomb that imprisons it. It is the very susceptibility of the Self, a susceptibility to wounding and sacrifice. (EL)

28. See Plato, Timaeus 52–53, and Aristotle, Physics Bk. II. 3, esp. 194b 23–26.

29. This freedom enveloped in a responsibility that it cannot shoulder is the way of a creature, the unlimited passivity of the self, the noncondition of the self. (EL)

30. Respectively, Husserl's Ego-pole from Ideas, Second Book, secs. 22 and 23, and Heidegger's care (Sorge) from Being and Time, sec. 64.

31. Hegel, Phänomenologie des Geistes, pp. 430–31; trans., Phenomenology of Spirit, pp. 489–90.

32. Jean Nabert, Eléments pour une éthique (Paris: Aubier, 1962), p. 72; trans. William J. Petrek, Elements for an Ethic (Evanston: Northwestern University Press, 1969), pp. 51–52.

33. Eugen Fink, Spiel als Weltsymbol (Stuttgart: Kohlhammer, 1960), and Jeanne Delhomme, La pensée interrogative (Paris: Presses Universitaires de France, 1954). On the latter, see also Levinas's essay "Pénélope ou la pensée modale" in NP 69–77.

34. In the final three studies of the second edition of our book En découvrant l'existence avec Husserl et Heidegger, all the descriptions of the face which refer to the ambiguity or the very enigma of anarchy: the Illeity of the infinite in the face, as the trace of the withdrawal of the Infinite as Infinite, accomplished before arrival, whereby the Other (Autrui) commands my responsibility - remain descriptions of the nonthematizable, of the anarchic, and consequently do not lead to any theological thesis. Language is nevertheless able to speak of it, thereby confirming the impossibility of the an-archic constituting itself as a sovereignty, whence the very noncondition of anarchy. Yet the hold of language over the anarchic is not a mastery, for otherwise anarchy would be subordinated to the arche of consciousness. This hold is the struggle and pain of expression, giving rise to discourse along with the necessity of the State and the arche of sovereignty. (We allude to this in the final paragraph of the present study, and hope to speak of it further at a later date.) It is also clear that in our interpretation of signifyingness, the practical order (and the religious which is inseparable from the practical) is defined in terms of the an-archic. Theology is possible only as a contestation of the religious, which is nevertheless confirmed through the struggles or failures of theology. (EL) [The last three essays in En découvrant l'existence avec Husserl et Heidegger are "The Trace of the Other," "Enigma and Phenomenon," and "Language and Proximity." In the 1974 version of "Substitution" Levinas indicated that the topic that in 1968 he had said would be taken up at a later date had been addressed in the second half of the third section of chap. 5 of Otherwise than Being, pp. 156 ff.]

35. The suffering of the other, my pity for this suffering, the other's sorrow over my pity, my sorrow over this sorrow, and so on - this vortex stops with me. Throughout this sequence it is I who admit of one movement more. My suffering is the focus of all sufferings - and all faults. Even the faults of my persecutors, which amounts to suffering the ultimate persecution, that is, suffering absolutely. (EL)

36. For example, Thomas Hobbes, Leviathan, ed. Michael Oakshott (Oxford: Basil Blackwell, 1957), chap. 13–15, pp. 80–105.

37. "Je est un autre": Arthur Rimbaud, letter to George Izambard, May 13, 1871, in Oeuvres Complètes, ed. Rolland de Renéville and Jules Mouquet (Paris: Gallimard, 1963), p. 268 [trans. Louise Varèse, Illuminations and Other Prose Poems (New York: New Directions, 1957), p. xxvii]. (EL)

38. *Excidence* means "extirpation, destruction." It is an unusual word, deriving from the Latin *excido* (whose root is *caedo*), which means "to cut out" or "to cut off."

39. The phrase "a fine risk" is Plato's *kalos gar ho kindunos*, *Phaedo* 114d.

40. Alphonse de Waehlens, *La philosophie et les expériences naturelles* (The Hague: Martinus Nijhoff, 1961), p. 13.

41. In this way theological language destroys the religious situation of transcendence. The infinite presents itself an-archaically, and thematization is deprived of "the experience" which alone could lend it credence. Language *about* God rings false or turns into myth. (EL)

42. We have said that proximity, obsession, and subjectivity do not lead back to consciousness. But, rather than attesting to a preconscious stage or to a repression which would suppress them, their nonconsciousness confirms their exception from the totality, that is to say, their refusal of manifestation. To the extent that essence is inseparable from exhibition and thus from the ideality of the logos and the kerygmatic principality, this exception is nonbeing or anarchy, this side of the, still ontological, alternative of being and nothingness, this side of *essence*. To be sure, nonconsciousness is the distinguishing feature of mechanical phenomena or the repression of psychic structures, whence the pretension of mechanism or psychologism to universality. But the nonconscious may be read otherwise, in terms of its traces, undoing the categories of mechanism. The nonconscious is understood as the nonvoluntariness of persecution, which, as persecution, interrupts every justification, every apology, and every logos. This reduction to silence is a passivity this side of all material passivity. This side of the neutrality of things, absolute passivity becomes incarnation, corporeality, that is to say, susceptibility to pain, outrage, and unhappiness. In its susceptibility, it bears the trace of this *hither side* of things as a responsibility for what the persecuted, in her or his ipseity, did not will, that is, a responsibility for the very persecution she or he undergoes. (EL)

43. Perhaps the notion of anarchy accounts for the notion of valuing, whose dimension is so difficult to distinguish from the being of beings. To value is indeed "to weigh" on the subject, although otherwise than in terms of a cause weighing on an effect, a being weighing on the thought to which it presents itself, an end weighing on the tendency or will it solicits. What does this *otherwise* mean? We think that in valuing there arises a susceptibility which is incapable of thematizing or assuming what it receives, a susceptibility that makes itself responsible *in spite of itself*. In its original influence, prior to any intentional movement, without the possibility of a free attitude towards it, value renders things "pure" or "impure." The death of the Other makes me impure owing to its proximity and explains the "Noli me tangere." There is not here a phenomenon of mystical mentality, but an indelible moment, which the notion of value recalls. (EL)

44. If obsession is suffering and "contrariness," it is because the altruism of the hostage-subjectivity is not an inclination, is not the *natural* benevolence associated with the moral philosophers of sentiment. It is contrary to nature, a nonvoluntary election, inseparable from the persecution to which no consent is thinkable - anarchic. Persecution reduces the ego to the self, to the absolute accusative whereby the Ego is accused of a fault which it neither willed nor committed, and which disturbs its freedom. Persecution is a traumatism, violence par excellence, without warning, without a priori, without the possibility of apology, without logos. Persecution leads back to a resignation without consent and as a result traverses a night of the unconscious. This is the meaning of the unconscious, the night where the ego comes back to itself in the traumatism of persecution, a passivity more passive still than all passivity, on this side of identity, becoming the responsibility of substitution. (EL)

45. The Ego is not universalizable: I remain *here*, despite every ecstasis (except the ecstasis of death) and despite every "concept of the Ego." I cannot absolve myself, that

is to say, detach myself from myself (a matter of suspending the original responsibility of the hither side, outside of the free dialogical exchange of questions and answers that persecution paralyses by placing in question), although I am in a position to pardon others in their alterity or in their subsumption under the concept of the Ego. Such is the priority of the Self prior to all freedom, or nonfreedom. (EL)

46. Levinas has in mind primarily Heidegger's "Letter on Humanism"; see also Levinas's "Humanism and An-archy" in HAH 65–82; CP 127–139.

47. "Death is the possibility of the absolute impossibility of Dasein." M. Heidegger, *Sein und Zeit*, Tübingen, Niemeyer, 1953, p. 250; trans. J. Macquarrie and E. Robinson, *Being and Time*, Oxford, Basil Blackwell, 1967, p. 294.

6. Truth of Disclosure and Truth of Testimony

1. "Verité du dévoilement et vérité du témoignage" was first published in *Le témoignage*, ed. E. Castelli (Paris: Aubier-Montaigne, 1972). The text was elaborated and extended in *Otherwise than Being* (AE 179–94; OB 140–52). The text was translated by Iain MacDonald and revised by Simon Critchley. Notes were prepared by Adriaan Peperzak.

2. Cf. M. Heidegger, *Being and Time* § 65 (*Endlichkeit*), §38 (*Geworfenheit*), § 44 (*Wahrheit*), §§ 46ff. (*Sein zum Tode*).

3. *Ideas* §§ 104, 113–15. Husserl refers to Brentano in §85. Cf. Brentano's *Psychologie von empirischen Standpunkt* (Hamburg: Meiner, 1874); trans. A. C. Rancurello et al., *Psychology from an Empirical Standpoint* (London: Routledge, 1973). Cf. also Levinas TIP 91–97; TIH 57–61.

4. Levinas probably intends a double entendre in using *la question* for an interrogation under torture. Has the philosophical critique of testimonial truth in its various (for instance, religious) forms not suppressed the most important question (the question of the Good)?

5. With the expression *le dire*, which can be read as a synonym for "to testify" or "to give testimony," Levinas makes a transition to his technical use of the expression *le Dire*, as explained in chap. 1 of *Otherwise than Being* (chap. 2 in this volume).

6. See Plato, *Republic* 508e; Plotinus, Enneads VI, 9.

7. See the essay "Substitution," chap. 5 in this volume.

8. Levinas refers here to p. 279 of "Au-delà de l'essence," published in *Revue de Métaphysique et de Morale* 75 (1970), pp. 265–83. The quote does not appear on p. 279, however, but a somewhat different version is found on p. 273. This version, again slightly changed, appears also in chap. 1 of *Otherwise than Being*, AE 12; OB 10.

9. F. Dostoyevsky, *The Brothers Karamazov*, trans. D. Magarshack (Harmondsworth: Penguin, 1984), vol. 1, p. 339. [Translation modified to reflect the French translation given by Levinas. The English translation reads: "every one of us is responsible for everyone else in every way, and I most of all."]

10. The "glory" of Jahweh indicates the epiphany of God's majesty and sanctity. Cf., for example, Exodus 14:18; 16:7–10; 24:15ff.; 33:18; 39:21–29; Isaiah 6:1ff.; 35:1–4; 44:23.

11. Genesis 3:8. The translation reflects that of Levinas in the French. The King James translation reads: "walking in the garden in the cool of the day."

12. Levinas adds here the following note: After or before the lies that the Saying undergoes in the Said - in the words and verbal indifference in which information is exchanged - pious vows issue forth - and responsibilities are avoided.

13. Cf. Plato, *Republic* 359c–360d.

14. *Me voici*; see chap. 8, n. 34.

15. Isaiah 65:24. Levinas's translation insists on "me": "Avant qu'ils appellent, moi, je repondrai."

16. The "salut" in "le salut qu'il rend à autrui" means at the same time "greeting" and "salvation".

7. Essence and Disinterestedness

1. "Au-delà de l'essence" (Beyond being), *Revue de Métaphysique et de Morale* 75 (1970), pp. 265–83 . The translation presented here, chap. 1 of *Otherwise than Being*, trans. Alphonso Lingis (1981), has been revised by Simon Critchley and Adriaan Peperzak. Notes were prepared by Adriaan Peperzak.

2. Levinas adds here the following note: "The term *essence*, which we do not dare spell *essance*, designates the *esse*, the process or event of being, distinguished from the *ens*, the *Sein* differentiated from the *Seiendes*." In later publications Levinas does use the term *essance* in order to express the active and transitive meaning of being, which he extensively describes in the second chapter of *Otherwise than Being*. He does not deny the importance of the ontological difference between being (*Sein*) and beings (*ens*, *Seiendes*) but denies its ultimacy or absoluteness.

3. See Plato, *Republic* 509b9, where "the good" is characterized as *epekeina tès ousias* (beyond essence). In the *Sophist* the five "genera" studied are *being*, *change* and *rest*, *sameness* and *otherness*. *Nonbeing* is problematic; it does not have the same status as those "highest genera" (258c ff.).

4. The terminology ("speculative dialectic," "negativity," etc.) shows that Levinas thinks here more of Hegel than of Plato.

5. Levinas refers in a note to his description of the "there is" (*il y a*) in *De l'existence à l'existant* (1947), pp. 93 ff.; trans. Alphonso Lingis, *Existence and Existents* (The Hague: Martinus Nijhoff, 1978), pp. 52–54.

6. *Arrière-monde* translates Nietzsche's *Hinterwelt*: a "world" (or heaven) behind the real world of human history.

7. Aristotle's insight that *being* cannot be an all-encompassing genus but instead "is said in many modes," combined with several hints in his work (*Metaphysics* 1003a33–b19, 1028b1–7, 1060b37–1061a7; *Nicomachean Ethics* 1096b25–29), was developed into the theory of the "analogy," or "analogical unity of being," by the great thinkers of the thirteenth century. See, for example, Aquinas, *Summa Theologica* I, qu. 13, a.5–6.

8. The word *intéressement* can be used for the attempt to heighten interest of employees in their business through profit-sharing schemes. Levinas hears the verb *intéresser* (French heir of the Latin *interesse*) as the active business of being (*esse*) which weaves all beings together in one big business or economy inspiring them with a common desire to pursue their own interest. If the terms *essence* and *essance* stress the active and transitive meaning of being, this universal interestedness could also be rendered by "inter-essence." The word *désintéressement*, as opposed to *essence* in the title of this chapter, must, consequently, be read as a movement away from the interested business of being, a movement of nonparticipation, ex-ception, or transcendence.

9. This sentence presents Hegel's theory of Spirit, which integrates all its negations (see the preface of the *Phenomenology of Spirit*) and Heidegger's analysis of death (*Sein und Zeit* §§ 46–53) as two integrative forms of coping with negativity. Instead of respecting the irreducibility of certain negations, these are understood as elements within the Spirit's or human beings' lives.

10. Spinoza identified the actual essence of each being with its *conatus essendi*, i.e., its striving to persevere in (or to maintain) its being (*Ethica* III, *propositiones* 6 and 7). Levinas often uses the abridged expression *conatus* (in Latin) to evoke the essence of beings as ongoing self-maintenance and expansion.

11. Levinas finds the *essoufflement* (getting out of breath) and *retenue* (reserve, reticence), which seem to belong to any thematization of that which transcends essence, in Plato's *Republic* 506e, where Socrates dismisses the question of "what the good itself is" because it seems "to surpass his assault."

12. The allusion is easier heard in French, since *prochain* (in *amour du prochain*) is closer to *proximus* and *proximity*, which indicate the closeness of someone or something who is next to or beside the speaker.

13. Since *origin* (*archē*, fundament, principle) and *original* belong to the ontological tradition, Levinas prefers the term *preoriginal* to indicate what precedes the order of being (with its principles and origin).

14. "Foreword" translates "le propos" (the point, issue, purpose) "de l'avant-propos" (pre-face or fore-word of the saying which "precedes" the said).

15. This statement is an allusion to the saying that to translate (*traduire*) is to betray (*trahir*).

16. This is possibly an allusion to the scholastic conception of philosophy as *ancilla theologiae* (maid of theology). If the thematizing language of philosophy constitutes a said, it can neither replace nor engulf the saying but rather must always refer to it as the prephilosophical language to which it owes its own existence and meaning, although it is also indispensable for the saying.

17. *Apophantic* and *apophansis*, extensively thematized by Heidegger, come from the Greek verb *apophaino*: "to show, to unveil, to reveal." *Angelic* (*angélique*) hints at the meaning of the Greek *angelos*: "messenger."

18. Levinas refers here in a note to chap. 5, sec. 3, of *Otherwise than Being*.

19. *An-archic* means not having an (ontological) ground or origin or beginning (*archē*) (see n. 13). It is therefore a synonym for the nonoriginal in the sense of the "preoriginal."

20. Levinas attached here the following note: "The significations that go beyond formal logic show themselves in formal logic, if only by the precise indication of the sense in which they break with formal logic. The indication is the more precise in the measure that this reference is conceived with a more rigorous logic. The myth of the subordination of all thought to the comprehension of being is probably due to this revealing function of coherence, whose lawlike character formal logic sets forth, and in which the divergency between signification and being is *measured*, in which the metaphysical *hither side* itself, contradictorily enough, appears. But logic interrupted by the structures of what is *beyond being* which show themselves in it does not confer a dialectical structure to philosophical propositions. It is the superlative, more than the negation of categories, which interrupts the system, as though the logical order and the being it succeeds in espousing retained the superlative which exceeds them. In subjectivity the superlative is the exorbitance of a non-place, in the caress and in sexuality - the 'excess' of tangency, as though tangency admitted a gradation, up to contact with the entrails, a skin going under another skin."

21. Levinas often borrows the conceptual pair *diachrony-synchrony* from Saussurean linguistics, where they are used to contrast the diachronic evolution of linguistic elements and the synchronic aspect of their state at a certain moment or period of time.

22. This is a very succinct summary of *Otherwise than Being*, chap. 5, sec. 5: "Skepticism and Reason." The classical refutation of skepticism claims that the skeptical thesis (e.g., "truth is impossible") *at the same time* affirms that truth is impossible and claims that this thesis is true. The skeptical position is therefore self-contradictory, if its thesis and its affirmation are articulated synchronically.

23. *Epos* (Greek for "word") is here a synonym for "the said."

24. "Il s'agit de penser la possibilité d'un arrachement à l'essence." Is it possible to "think," i.e., to acquire a concept, a structure, or a representation of this nonessence? Levinas insists on the word *penser* by adding the following note to it: "We will of course have to show that the necessity of thinking is inscribed in the meaning of transcendence."

25. "Il signifie le non-lieu." *Non-lieu* means the dismissal of a legal case. Here it also means the impossibility of "placing" transcendence as an element *within* an encompass-

ing horizon or structure of constellation, i.e., transcendence is without place in the world. Levinas is probably polemicizing here against Heidegger, who sometimes explained the task of thinking as an *Er-ört-erung*: a dis-covering of the place (*Ort*) of its topic. See Heidegger's *Unterwegs zur Sprache* (Pfullingen: Neske 1965), pp. 37–39; trans. Peter D. Hertz, *On the Way to Language* (New York: Harper & Row, 1971), pp. 159–61; and *Der Satz vom Grund* (Pfullingen: Neske 1957), p. 106; trans. Reginald Lilly, *The Principle of Reason* (Bloomington: Indiana University Press, 1991), p. 60.

26. Plato, *Sophist* 240 bc, 241d, 256d ff.

27. "Les choses se montrent, les bagages se plient et les idées se comprennent." Human subjectivity is characterized by a passivity which is not preceded or caused by any activity. It is a self (*soi*), not primarily an *ego* but "me".

28. *Kerygma* (proclamation) is close to *epos* (see n. 23).

29. Levinas uses here and elsewhere the verb *se passer*, which we often render "to take place." However, *se passer* indicates also a movement of passing; "to happen" or "to come to pass" are also possible translations. In using *se passer* Levinas possibly thinks of Heidegger's *Ereignis* and the *sich ereignen* of being.

30. See Kant's *Critique of Pure Reason*, B 481 and 483.

31. Cf. Paul Valéry's "Cantique des Colonnes."

32. Levinas refers here to his essay "Enigme et phénomène" (chap. 4 of this volume).

33. "La subjectivité est précisément le noeud et le dénouement . . ."

34. Levinas attached here the following note: "The Good invests freedom - it loves me before I love it. Love is love through this antecedence. The Good would not be the term of a need susceptible of being satisfied; it is not the term of an erotic need, a relationship with the Seductive which resembles the Good to the point of being indistinguishable from it, but which is not its other but its imitator. The Good as the Infinite has no other, not because it would be the whole but because it is Good and nothing escapes its goodness."

35. *Sollen* (ought) recalls Kant's and Fichte's conceptions of morality as an endless tangential approximation to the ideal of human perfection.

36. *Glory* is an allusion to the Biblical expression "the glory of Jahweh"; see, for example, Numbers 14:22 and Exodus 14:18, 16:7–10, 24:15–17, 33:18.

37. In a note Levinas refers here again to "Enigme et phénomène," (chap. 4 in this volume).

38. The concepts "trace" and "illeity" were analyzed in the essay "La trace de l'autre" (EDE 187–202) which was integrated into "La signification et le sens," the translation of which constitutes chap. 3 of this volume; see esp. sec. 9.

39. See Martin Buber, *Ich und Du* (Leipzig: Insel, 1923); trans. Walter Kaufmann; *I and Thou* (New York: Macmillan, 1988).

40. Plato, *Timaeus* 48a ff.

41. "Où il n'est plus question du Moi, mais de moi."

42. A note by Levinas adds here: "The ego is not the specification of the more general concept of the Soul. Kant has seen this in certain passages of the Transcendental Dialectic, when he insists on the fact that to pass from one subject to another subject is the positive act of putting oneself in his place (B 405, A 354)."

43. Concerning the notions involved in this paragraph, Levinas refers to his book *L'humanisme de l'autre homme*, translated in CP 75–152.

44. Kant, *Critique of Pure Reason* B 518 (A 490) ff.

45. Martin Heidegger, *Nietzsche* (Pfullingen: Neske 1961), vol. 2, p. 451; trans. Joan Stambaugh, *The End of Philosophy* (New York: Harper & Row, 1973), p. 46.

46. Levinas adds here the following precision in a footnote: "in the sense of dissimulation and suspension of being behind the beings it illuminates."

47. Cf. Heidegger's use of *ousia* and *parousia* for the "presence" (*Anwesenheit*) of being, for example in *Being and Time* § 26.

48. Using several Hegelian expressions, such as *die Arbeit des Begriffs* and *die schöne Seele*, Levinas summarizes here his rather Kojèvean understanding of Hegel's *Phenomenology of Spirit*.

49. "Un profond jadis."

50. Although "the argument" of *Otherwise than Being* finishes here, we have decided to present also the tenth and last section of the first chapter because it gives some invaluable indications about Levinas's "method."

51. *Otherwise than Being* is divided into "The Argument" (chap. 1), "The Exposition" (chaps. 2–5), and an epilogue, "In Other Words" ("Autrement dit," chap. 6).

52. "A fine risk" (*le beau risque*) alludes to Socrates's phrase "Kalos gar ho kindunos" in Plato's *Phaedo* 114d. In the *Sophist* 263e Plato defines thinking (*dianoia*) as "the inner dialogue of the soul with itself without voice." That the justification of the beginning in philosophy presupposes the entire system (and thus its completion) is affirmed repeatedly by Hegel, for example in the preface of his *Phänomenologie des Geistes*, pp. 21–22; trans., *Phenomenology of Spirit*, pp. 13–14.

8. God and Philosophy

1. Many notes in this chapter are by the author; they are indicated by "(EL)" at the end of the note. Notes added by Robert Bernasconi are identified by "(RB)." "God and Philosophy" was first published in French as "Dieu et la Philosophie" in *Le Nouveau Commerce* 30–31 (1975), pp. 97–128, preceded by the following "Preliminary Note" written by the author:

> The ideas put forth here have already been presented in different forms in lectures given at the University of Lille on March 13, 1973; at the annual congress of the Association des Professeurs de Philosophie des Facultés Catholiques de France on May 1, 1973; at the symposium organized by the Académie des Sciences et des Humanités d'Israël and the Philosophy Department of the University of Jerusalem, in honor of the ninetieth birthday of Professor Hugo Bergman on December 23, 1973, (delivered in Hebrew); at the Facultés Universitaires Saint-Louis at Brussels on February 20–21, 1974; at the meeting organized by the Centre Protestant d'Études on March 3, 1974; and at the Faculté de Théologie Protestante at Geneva on March 4, 1974. The text we are publishing here is based on the core content of each of these lectures. This itinerary of lectures has given it an ecumenical character. We mention this especially in order to render homage to the life and work of Professor Hugo Bergman, who, having very early settled in Jerusalem, was always faithful to Israel's universal vocation which the state of Zion ought to serve only, to make possible a discourse addressed to all men in their human dignity, so as then to be able to answer for all men, our neighbors.

"Dieu et la philosophie" was reprinted with only minor corrections, such as correcting the numbering of some of the paragraphs, in DVI 93–127. The translation by Alphonso Lingis and Richard Cohen, published in CP 153–174, was revised for this edition by Robert Bernasconi and Simon Critchley. Robert Bernasconi prepared additional notes.

2. Traditionally attributed to the *Protrepticus* of Aristotle, although his authorship is now disputed. See Anton-Hermann Chroust, *Aristotle: Protrepticus, a Reconstruction* (Notre Dame: University of Notre Dame Press, 1964), pp. 48–49. Jacques Derrida quoted it at the end of "Violence et métaphysique," *L'écriture et la différence* (Paris: Seuil, 1967), p. 226; trans. Alan Bass, "Violence and Metaphysics," *Writing and Difference* (Chicago: University of Chicago Press, 1978), p. 152. (RB)

3. Jeanne Delhomme, *L'impossible interrogation* (Paris: Desclée, 1971), p. 218. (RB)

4. Judah Halevi, *The Kuzari* (New York: Schocken Books, 1964); Blaise Pascal, "Le

mémorial," *Pensées*, ed. Louis Lafuma (Paris: Seuil, 1962), no. 913, p. 361; trans. A. J. Krailsheimer, "The Memorial," *Pensées* (Harmondsworth: Penguin, 1966), p. 309. (RB)
   5. Cf. Emmanuel Levinas, *Autrement qu'être ou au-delà de l'essence*, pp. 195–207 [OB 153–62. See also DE 109–113; EE 65–67]. (EL)
   6. Which is required by justice, itself required by vigilance, and thus by the Infinite in me, by the idea of infinity. (EL)
   7. The notion of experience is inseparable from the unity of presence, or simultaneity. It thus refers to the unity of apperception which does not come from the outside and "become conscious" of simultaneity. It belongs to the very "way" of presence; for presence, being, is only possible as a thematization or gathering of the transitory, and thus as a phenomenon, which is thematic exhibition itself. But all signification does not derive from experience, does not resolve into a manifestation. The formal structure of signifyingness, the-one-for-the-other, does not from the first amount to a "showing oneself." Suffering for another, for example, has a meaning in which knowing is adventitious. The adventure of knowledge which is characteristic of being, ontological from the first, is not the only mode, nor the preliminary mode, of intelligibility or meaning. Experience as the source of meaning qua knowing has its motivation in a meaning that at the start is not a knowing at all. This is not to deny that philosophy is itself knowledge. But the possibility for knowing to take in all meaning does not reduce all meaning to the structures that its exhibition imposes. This then suggests the idea of a dia-chrony of truth in which the said has to be unsaid, and the unsaid, unsaid in its turn. In this sense the skeptical essence of philosophy can be taken seriously: skepticism is not an arbitrary contestation; it is a doctrine of inspection and testing, although not reducible to testing of the scientific sort. (EL)
   8. Edmund Husserl, *Ideen zu einer reinen Phänomenologie und Phänomenologischen Philosophie, Zweites Buch* (The Hague: Martinus Nijhoff, 1952), §§ 4 and 11, pp. 4–12 and 24–27; trans. R. Rojcewicz and A. Schuwer, *Ideas Pertaining to a Pure Phenomenology and to a Phenomenological Philosophy*, Book II (Dordrecht: Kluwer, 1989), pp. 6–13 and 27–29. (RB)
   9. This possibility of conjuring away or missing the division of truth into two times - that of the *immediate* and that of the *reflected* - deserves consideration and prudence. It does not necessarily lead to the subordination of one to the other. Truth as *dia-chrony*, as refusal of synchronization and synthesis, is perhaps proper to transcendence. (EL)
   10. N. Malebranche, *Entretiens sur la métaphysique et sur la religion, Oeuvres complètes*, vols. 12 and 13 (Paris: Vrin, 1984), p. 53; trans. Willis Doney, *Dialogues on Metaphysics* (New York: Abaris Books, 1980), p. 47. (RB)
   11. The latent birth of negation occurs not in subjectivity but in the idea of the Infinite. Or, if one prefers, it is in subjectivity qua idea of the Infinite. It is in this sense that the idea of the Infinite, as Descartes affirms, is a "genuine idea" and not merely what I conceive "by the negation of what is finite." (EL)
   12. Inquiring after the "manner in which I have acquired this idea," the sense of this receptivity, Descartes says in the Third Meditation: "For I have not received it through the senses, and it is never presented to me unexpectedly, as are the ideas of sensible things when these things present themselves, or seem to present themselves, to the external organs." In the ideas of sensible things, the surprise of the experience is taken up by the understanding, which extracts from the senses the clearly and distinct intelligible, and this allows one to say that the sensible things "seem to present themselves to the external organs of my senses." This is the very process of receptivity! "It [the idea of infinity]," Descartes continues, "is also not a pure production or fiction of my mind; for it is not in my power to take from or add anything to it. And consequently there is nothing more to say than that, like the idea of myself, it was born and produced with me ever since I was created." (EL) Levinas quotes the French

translation of 1647 by Louis-Charles d'Albert. *Oeuvres de Descartes*, ed. C. Adam and P. Tannery, vol. 9, pp. 40-41. The translation given here is from the French. For a translation of the original Latin, which employs the phrase "innate in me" where the French text employs the locution "ever since I was created," see *The Philosophical Writings of Descartes*, vol. 2, p. 35. (RB)

13. See preceding note. (EL)

14. Or, as Descartes says, "which is *created*." (EL)

15. "For lo the LORD is coming forth from his place, and he will descend and tread upon the heights of the earth; and the mountains shall melt under him, and the valleys be split asunder, like wax before the fire, like waters poured down a precipice" (Micah 1:3-4). "What sustains yields to what is sustained," is overwhelmed or gives way. This "structure" (which is, so to speak, de-structure itself) is what is announced and expressed in this text, which we cite independently of considerations of its authority and "rhetoric" as Holy Scripture. (EL)

16. Cf. Emmanuel Levinas, *Totalité et infini*, sec. 1, pp. 1-78 [trans., TaI 33-104]. (EL)

17. Plato, *Symposium*, 192c. (EL)

18. Ibid., 192e. (EL)

19. Pascal's *Pensées* is filled with negative remarks about the concupiscence of the flesh. For example, "There are some who see clearly that man has no other enemy but concupiscence, which turns him away from God"; *Pensées*, Fragment 269, pp. 127-28; trans., p. 110. (RB)

20. See *Otherwise than Being, or Beyond Essence*, chap. 4. (EL)

21. Franz Rosenzweig interprets the *response* given by man to the love with which God loves him as the movement unto the neighbor. See *Der Stern der Erlösung*, Part II, Book II [Gesammelte Schriften II, The Hague: Martinus Nijhoff, 1976, pp. 174-228; trans. William W. Hallo, *The Star of Redemption*, New York, Holt, Rinehart and Winston, 1971, pp. 156-204]. This takes up the structure which commands a homiletic theme in Jewish thought. The "fringes" on the corners of their garments, whose sight should remind the faithful of "all the commandments of the Eternal" (Numbers 15:38-40), are in Hebrew called *tsitsith*. The ancient rabbinical commentary *Siphri* connects this word with the verb *tsouts* of which one form, in the Song of Songs 2:9, means "to observe" or "to look at" as in "My beloved . . . peereth through the lattice." The faithful looking at the "fringes" which remind him of his obligations, thus returns the gaze of the beloved who observes him. This would be the vis-à-vis or the face-to-face with God! (EL)

22. It is the meaning of the beyond, of transcendence, and not ethics, that our study is pursuing. It finds this meaning in ethics. There is *signification*, for ethics is structured as the-one-for-the-other; there is signification of the beyond being, for one finds oneself outside of all finality in a responsibility which ever increases, in a dis-interestedness where a being undoes itself of its being. (EL)

23. Trace of a past which was never present, but this absence still disturbs. (EL)

24. Dia-chronic truth; that is, the dia-chrony of truth that is without any possible synthesis. Contrary to what Bergson teaches us, there would be "a disorder" which is not another order, there where the elements cannot be made contemporary, in a way, for example (but is this an example or the ex-ception?), in which God contrasts with the presence of re-presentation. (EL) For Bergson on disorder, see "Substitution," n. 9. (RB)

25. A devotedness as strong as death, and in a sense stronger than death. In *finitude* death outlines a destiny which it interrupts, but nothing can dispense me from the response which I am *passively* held to. The tomb is not a refuge; it is not a pardon. The debt remains. (EL)

26. Cf. AE 115; OB 90. (RB)

27. The phrase is Heidegger's from *Unterwegs zur Sprache* (Pfullingen: Neske, 1959), pp. 215 and 230; trans. Peter D. Hertz, *On the Way to Language* (New York: Harper &

Row, 1971), p. 108, and "Language," trans. Albert Hofstadter, in *Poetry, Language, Thought* (New York: Harper & Row, 1971), p. 207. (RB)

28. Genesis 18:27. (EL)

29. Exodus 16:7. (EL)

30. Fyodor Dostoyevsky, *The Brothers Karamazov*, vol. 1, p. 339. See also chap. 6, n. 9 above. (RB)

31. The-one-for-the-other, the formal structure of signification, the signifyingness or rationality of signification, here does not begin by being exposed in a theme. It is my openness to the other, my sincerity or *veracity*. (EL)

32. *Être-là*, a literal translation of Heidegger's *Dasein*. (RB)

33. Levinas refers to the legend of Gyges frequently in *Totality and Infinity* to describe a being for whom the world is a spectacle (TeI 32, 62, 144, 148, and 197; TaI 61, 90, 170, 173 and 222). Gyges is also a figure in Rosenzweig's *Der Stern der Erlösung*, p. 231; trans. *Star of Redemption*, p. 207. The story was told by Herodotus (I. 8 ff.), but Levinas takes it up in the form presented by Plato, where Gyges found a ring which rendered him invisible when he turned its bezel toward him (*Republic*, 359d–360b). (RB)

34. *Me voici* is, of course, in the accusative in French but not in English. The Hebrew *hineni* is found in the context of many important moments in the Bible, including Genesis 22:7 and 11, Exodus 3:4, 1 Samuel 3:8, and Isaiah 6:8. See also the "Hier bin ich" of Rosenzweig's *Der Stern der Erlösung*, p. 196; trans. *Star of Redemption*, p. 176. (RB)

35. Isaiah 57:18. (EL)

36. Amos 2:12. (EL)

37. It is quite remarkable that the word signifyingness [*signifiance*] has empirically the meaning of a mark of attention given to someone. (EL)

38. See *Autrement qu'être*, pp. 59 and 195. (EL) OB 46 and 153. (RB)

39. "Was vernünftig ist, das ist wirklich; und was wirklich ist, das ist vernünftig"; G. W. F. Hegel, *Grundlinien der Philosophie des Rechts*, Theorie Werkausgabe 7 (Frankfurt: Suhrkamp, 1970), p. 24; trans. H. B. Nisbet, *Elements of the Philosophy of Right* (Cambridge: Cambridge University Press, 1991), p. 20. In an interview with Richard Kearney, Levinas stated, "When I spoke of the overcoming of Western ontology as an 'ethical and prophetic cry' in 'God and Philosophy,' I was in fact thinking of Marx's critique of Western idealism of a project to understand the world rather than to transform it"; *Dialogues with Contemporary Continental Thinkers* (Manchester: Manchester University Press, 1984), p. 69. (RB)

9. Transcendence and Intelligibility

1. This translation of *Transcendance et intelligibilité* (Genève: Labor et Fides, Centre Protestant d'Etudes, 1984) is by Simon Critchley and Tamra Wright. Notes were prepared by Simon Critchley.

2. *Oeuvres de Descartes*, ed. C. Adam and P. Tannery, vol. 7, p. 28; Descartes, *Meditations on First Philosophy*, in *The Philosophical Writings of Descartes*, vol. 2, p. 19.

3. Plato, *Timaeus* 35–37. The reference is to Timaeus's account of cosmogony and to Plato's doctrine of anamnesis, expounded in the *Meno*, both of which are viewed by Levinas as refusals of any form of otherness irreducible to the Same or ego.

4. The reference is to Hegel, for whom objective spirit is the common spirit of a social group embodied in customs, law, and institutions.

5. The reference is to Kant's *Critique of Pure Reason*. On transcendental apperception, see A 107–30 passim and B 129–43. On succession, see the "Second Analogy," B 232–56.

6. On kinesthesis in Husserl, see *Ideen zu einer reinen Phänomenologie und phänomenologischen Philosophie*, Zweites Buch; trans. *Ideas Pertaining to a Pure Phenomenology and to a Phenomenological Philosophy*, Second Book, "The Aestheta in Their Relation to the Aesthetic Body," § 18. On the relation of kinesthesis to the hand, see "The Constitution of Psychic Reality through the Body," §§ 35–38.

7. The reference is to Heidegger's notion of *Seinsverständnis*, where any understanding of entities - however vague and average - is claimed to presuppose some understanding of being. See *Sein und Zeit*, pp. 5–8; trans. *Being and Time*, pp. 24–28.

8. *Satisfaction* derives from the Latin *satisfacere*, literally meaning "to make enough," where the *satis* connotes sufficiency and plenitude, also conveyed by the English term *satiety*.

9. Levinas is playing on the analogous Latin and Germanic etymology of these terms where the activity of knowledge is linked to seizing, grasping, and gathering.

10. For example, in the *Ideen zu einer reinen Phänomenologie*, Husserl describes the basic field of phenomenology as the investigation of the immanent being of pure consciousness revealed after the transcendental reduction of the natural attitude.

11. "La *présence*, de soi, se fait main-tenant." Levinas is alluding to the relation between the presence of the now (*maintenant*), as the privileged temporal mode in the activity of knowing, and its connection to the hand (*la main*), as that which seizes, grasps, and reduces the objects that are presently available, transforming them into items of knowledge.

12. On the *Lebenswelt* in Husserl, see Part IIIa of *Die Krisis der europäischen Wissenschaften und die transzendentale Phänomenologie* (The Hague: Martinus Nijhoff, 1976); trans. D. Carr, *The Crisis of European Sciences and Transcendental Phenomenology* (Evanston: Northwestern University Press, 1970): "The way back into phenomenological transcendental philosophy by inquiring back from the pregiven lifeworld," §§ 28–55.

13. As one possible example of such a formulation in Husserl, see the following passage from the *Krisis*, p. 321, trans., p. 275: ". . . das besondere Telos . . . ist eine unendliche Idee, auf die im Verborgenen das gesamte geistige Werden sozusagen hinaus will (. . . the particular telos . . . is an infinite idea toward which in concealment, the whole spiritual becoming aims, so to speak)."

14. The reference is to Kant's exposure of the claims of traditional, dogmatic metaphysics as a transcendental illusion in the "Dialectic" to the *Critique of Pure Reason*, B 85–88, B 352 ff.

15. On Bergson as an unacknowledged precursor for Heidegger's thinking of metaphysics and technology, see Levinas's remarks in a 1988 interview, "L'autre, utopie et justice." Levinas remarks, "Can one not find . . . in Bergson's last works, the critique of technological rationalism so important to Heidegger's work?" *Entre nous: Essais sur le penser-à-l'autre* (Paris: Grasset, 1991), pp. 253-54. The text of Bergson's that Levinas has in mind here is *Creative Evolution*. For the most succinct statement of Heidegger's account of metaphysics and technology, see "Überwindung der Metaphysik" in *Vorträge und Aufsätze* (Pfullingen: Neske, 1961); trans. Joan Stambaugh, "Overcoming Metaphysics," in *The End of Philosophy* (New York: Harper & Row, 1973).

16. As one place among many where Heidegger makes this claim, see, "Das Ende der Philosophie und die Aufgabe das Denkens" in *Zeit und Sein* (Tübingen: Niemeyer, 1988); trans. J. Stambaugh, "The End of Philosophy and the Task of Thinking," in *On Time and Being* (New York: Harper & Row, 1972).

17. See Kant, "On the Primacy of Pure Practical Reason in Its Association with Speculative Reason," *Kritik der praktischen Vernunft* (Hamburg: Meiner, 1985), pp. 138–40; trans. L. White Beck, *Critique of Practical Reason* (Indianapolis: Bobbs-Merrill, 1956), pp. 124–26.

18. The reference here is to Bergson's *Essai sur les données immédiates de la conscience*, *Oeuvres*, ed. A. Robinet (Paris: Presses Universitaires de France, 1963); trans. F. L. Pogson, *Time and Free Will* (London: MacMillan, 1950). In *Ethique et infini*, Levinas lists the latter as one of the five great books in the history of philosophy (EeI 34; EaI 37–38). What is most important for Levinas in Bergson is his theory of *la durée*, namely that the dominant conception of time in physics and philosophy - time as linear, homogeneous, measurable, and representable - is derived from a more primordial experience of time as duration that describes our lived experience of temporality. Indeed, Levinas claims that Bergson prepares the way for Heidegger's analysis of the finite temporality of *Dasein* in *Being and Time*.

19. On time as duration and its relation to foresight, see Bergson, *Oeuvres*, pp. 120–30; *Time and Free Will*, pp. 183–98.

20. *Visée* is the usual French translation of Husserl's *Meinung*, meaning as meant or intended. For an explanation of *Meinung* see the First Book of *Ideas*, § 95.

21. The reference here is to Descartes's Third Meditation, in *Oeuvres de Descartes*, pp. 34–52; *The Philosophical Writings of Descartes*, pp. 24–36, see esp. pp. 31–32. See also in this regard Levinas's discussion of the idea of the infinite in "Transcendence and Height," chap. 2 in this volume.

22. On economy in Levinas, see Part II of *Totality and Infinity*. See also sec. 4 of "Meaning and Sense," chap. 3 in this volume.

23. On dis-inter-est (*dés-inter-essement*) and the *conatus essendi*, see "Essence and Disinterestedness," chap. 7 in this volume.

24. Pierre Aubenque, *Le problème de l'être chez Aristote: Essai sur la problématique aristotélicienne* (Paris: Presses Universitaires de France, 1962), pp. 380 and 388, commenting on Aristotle *Metaphysics* A, 2, 983 a 5–6.

25. *Oeuvres de Descartes*, p. 52; *The Philosophical Writings of Descartes*, pp. 35–36. In this regard, see the discussion that follows "Transcendence and Height," chap. 2.

26. On *Befindlichkeit* (state-of-mind, attunement, situatedness), *Angst* (anxiety) and *Jemeinigkeit* (mineness), see *Sein und Zeit* (*Being and Time*), §§ 28, 9 and 40, respectively. Levinas is here opposing Heidegger's treatment of affectivity (*affectio, pathos*) in terms of mood (*Stimmung*) or the basic mood (*Grund-Stimmung*) of anxiety, which Levinas sees as returning to mineness and thereby closing off an encounter with an alterity that resists thematization.

27. Levinas is here alluding to the celebrated death-analysis in *Being and Time* (§§ 46–53), where authentic being-toward-death is posited as a possibility of *Dasein*, albeit the possibility of impossibility. In this regard, see Levinas's "Mourir pour . . . ," in EN 219–30.

28. For an analogous account of phenomenology as the method of intentional analysis, see the introductory note to "Meaning and Sense," chap. 3.

29. Title of a book by Henri Bergson: *L'énergie spirituelle* (Paris: Felix Alcan, 1919); trans. H. Wildon Carr, *Mind-Energy* (New York: Henry Holt, 1920).

30. The allusion here is to Plato's *Symposium*, where Diotima, through the person of Socrates, personifies love as "half-way between mortal and immortal" (203b), as an intermediary between the gods and humans.

31. Insomnia is an oblique presence in much of Levinas's writing, but the main reference is to *Existence and Existents* (DE 109–13, EE 65–67).

10. Peace and Proximity

1. "Paix et proximité" was first presented as a paper at the January 29, 1984, conference "The Cultural Identity of Europe: The Ways of Peace" held in Turin. It was

published in *Les Cahiers de la Nuit Surveillée*, no. 3: *Emmanuel Levinas*, ed. J. Rolland (Lagrasse: Verdier, 1984), pp. 339–46. The essay was translated by Peter Atterton and Simon Critchley. Notes were prepared by Simon Critchley.

2. It should be noted that in French *conscience* means both "consciousness" and "conscience," an ambiguity Levinas is keen to exploit in the present context.

3. The problem of the one (*hen*) in Platonism and Neoplatonism is that of how the multiplicity of the world order can proceed from the ultimate absolute unity.

4. The corresponding passage in the King James version of the Bible (verse 7) reads, "Then Jacob was greatly afraid and distressed."

5. Rashi is the acronym of Rabbi Shelomoh ben Yitshaq of Troyes (1040–1105), the most influential Jewish commentator on the Bible and Babylonian Talmud.

6. The reference here is to Hegel's notion of the Absolute understood as the goal of logic, history, and philosophy. This specific formulation appears in Hegel's 1801 *Differenzschrift*: ". . . the Absolute itself is the identity of identity and nonidentity . . ." *Gesammelte Werke*, vol. 4 (Hamburg: Meiner, 1968), p. 64; trans. H. S. Harris and W. Cerf, *The Difference between Fichte's and Schelling's Systems of Philosophy* (Albany: State University of New York Press, 1977), p. 156.

7. Franz Rosenzweig, whose *Star of Redemption* was such a decisive influence on Levinas's *Totality and Infinity* (he writes in the preface that the book was "too often present . . . to be cited" [TeI XVI; TaI 28]), wrote his doctoral thesis on Hegel; it was subsequently published in two volumes as *Hegel und der Staat* (Aalen: Scientia Verlag, 1962).

8. *Absolute* derives from the Latin *absolutus* and *absolvere*, which means absolved, apart, freed, detached from, or disengaged.

9. In the *Critique of Pure Reason* (B 131–36), Kant claims that the "I think" must accompany all my representations. That is, I can only synthesize the plurality of representations - and hence be said to know at all - insofar as these representations are *mine*. This is what Kant calls the principle of apperception, which is "the highest principle in the whole sphere of human knowledge."

10. It should be noted that Levinas's evaluation of the word *love* has changed. In *Totality and Infinity* there is virtually an opposition between the terms *love* and *ethics*, which echoes the distinction between need and desire, and symmetry and asymmetry: "The metaphysical event of transcendence - the welcome of the other (*autrui*), hospitality, desire, and language - is not accomplished as love" (TeI 232; TaI 254).

11. For Husserl, *Appräsentation* is that process whereby something else is made present through what is immediately or directly given. This is "famously" (as Levinas puts it) discussed in the constitution of intersubjectivity in the Fifth of the *Cartesianische Meditationen* (The Hague: Martinus Nijhoff, 1978), trans. D. Cairns, *Cartesian Meditations* (The Hague: Martinus Nijhoff, 1973); where Husserl argues that along with or through my direct presentation or perception of a person's body or behavior, I can have an appresentation of that person's states of mind.

12. On the distinction between the exposure of the face and the disclosure of entities, which is one of Levinas's differences with Heidegger, see chap. 6, "Truth of Disclosure and Truth of Testimony."

13. Levinas's translation; cf. Vassili Grossman, *Life and Fate*, trans. R. Chandler (London: Collins Harvill, 1985), p. 683.

14. Cf. TeI 173; TaI 199.

15. On *dés-inter-essement*, see chap. 7, "Essence and Disinterestedness."

16. The final paragraph of this essay repeats formulations from *Otherwise than Being* (AE 203–5; OB 159–61).

INDEX

A priori, 11, 82
Absence, 35–36, 60–61, 64, 66–67, 70, 75, 141
Absolute, xi, 53, 59, 61–62, 69–72, 74–75, 77, 123, 136, 155, 158
Absolution, 53, 62–63, 74–75
Accusation, 88–89, 102
Accusative, 87–88
Action, 50
Adequation, 13, 15, 152, 159
Administration, 12, 15–16
Affection, 159–60
Affectivity, 134–35, 139, 142, 152, 160
Alterity, 1, 11–12, 21, 48, 52, 65, 68, 72, 155, 167; and symmetry, 14
Altruism, 18
Anachorism, 75
Anachronism, 72, 77, 81, 106, 119, 146
Anarchy, 80–82, 87–89, 91–92, 103
Antihumanism, 94
Antiplatonism, 42–43
Apology, 93
Appearance, 65, 98, 153
Appresentation, 168
Arche, 80–81
Aristophanes, 139–40
Aristotle, 4, 47, 87, 97, 100
Art, 10, 41–42, 48, 50, 57, 97, 100
Assignation, 74, 76, 144, 169
Asymmetry, xi–xii, 11
Atheism, 44, 71, 74
Athens, 24
Atomism, 35
Auto-affection, 92–94
Autonomy, 11, 14, 92, 105, 109
Autre, xiv–xv, 12
Autrui, xiv–xv, 5, 7, 12
Awakening, 132–33, 136–39, 143–46

Being, 1, 5–6, 9, 11–13, 15–16, 30–31, 41–42, 46, 57, 62, 66, 73, 75, 77, 80, 84, 88, 97–100, 104, 109–10, 112–16, 122, 130–32, 147, 153–54, 170; access to, 101; act of, 15; alterity of, 64; analogy of, 110; as a whole, 42; assembling of, 41, 52; beyond, xi, 21, 31, 61, 67, 74, 76–77, 80, 100, 101, 107, 109, 113–15, 122, 124–25; comprehension of (Seinsverständnis), 1, 3–4; disclosure of, 74,

83, 97, 101, 143; essence of, 46; gathering of, 37, 39–41, 47; guardian of, 41; horizon of, 5, 8; idea of, 12, 15, 21, 48; -in-the-world, 4; logic of, 41; meaning of, 46, 91; of beings, 14, 62, 74, 83, 110; other than, 74, 115; otherwise than, 109–11, 113–16, 122, 125, 126, 143; outside of, 93; position of, 99; play of, 13; qua being, 3, 13; relation with, 6; sense of, 45, 57; shepherd of, 13; significa-tion of, 94; totality of, 42, 46; -toward-death, 86; truth of, 85, 97, 99–100; understanding of, 41, 67–68; unity of, 46; universal, 8
Beings, 5–9, 11, 30–31, 53, 109, 111–12, 114, 130, 154
Bergson, Henri, 13, 28, 38, 42–45, 68, 151, 156–57
Berkeley, George, 5
Beyond, 55–56, 59–61, 67, 80, 122, 141
Bible, xii, 130–31
Blum, Léon, 50–51
Body, 39–41
Brentano, Franz, 97, 99
Brunschvicg, Léon, 26, 58
Buber, Martin, 20, 26, 63, 119, 163

Care, 51
Certainty, 71
Civilization, 46, 58; Western, 58
Cogito, 153, 157–60. See also "I think"
Cognition, 75–77
Command, xi, 21, 54
Communication, 92
Compassion, 52, 91
Comprehension, 1–10, 17, 21
Conatus, 102, 111–12
Concealment, 59–60, 62
Concept, 154
Conscience, 11, 23–24, 68
Consciousness, 4, 6, 11, 15, 17–18, 20, 35, 54–56, 80–88, 92–93, 95, 98, 101, 119, 132–34, 136–38, 152, 155; freedom of, 89, 95; moral, 25; temporality of, 88. See also Unconscious
Consolation, 71
Contemplation, 101
Context, 36
Contraction, 87
Conversion, 54

Ontology, xi, 2–7, 11–12, 21, 33–34, 44, 65–66, 79, 83, 88–89, 99, 101, 109, 129, 131, 147, 156; fundamental, 1–2; transcendental, 15

Openness, 3–5, 53

Opinion, 131

Order, 61, 68–72, 77, 105–106; ancillary, 169; angelic, 171

Orientation, 46–52, 55–56

Other, ix–xi, xiv–xv, 1–2, 6, 8–9, 11–20, 23, 26–28, 34, 48–51, 52–54, 56–57, 60, 65, 68, 94–95, 109–10, 118, 122, 124, 151, 153, 155; absolutely, 49, 54, 61–62, 64, 77; affection by, 93; and the third, 170; as absolute, 167; as outside, 20; as you, 65, 76–77; being-for-the-, 97; desire for, 12; epiphany of, 53; -in-the-same, 106; not a phenomenon, 65; one-for-the-, 102; presence of, 52–53, 63; relation with, 7, 16, 27, 29; representation of, 7; understanding of, 52; wholly, 29. *See also Autre* and *Autrui*

Otherwise, 110

Ousia, 109

Pardon, 91

Parmenides, 59

Pascal, Blaise, 131, 134, 140

Passage, 72, 74, 81

Passion, 82, 91, 95

Passivity, xi, 82, 86, 87–93, 121, 136–37, 139–40, 142–45; absolute, 87, 95; anarchic, 89–90

Past, 61, 63, 69, 72, 76, 105, 116–19, 121; absolute, 61, 75; anarchical, 116; immemorial, xi, 60, 69, 75, 77; irrecuperable, 75; irreversible, 60–62, 69, 75; preoriginal, 116–17; trace as presence of, 63, 65; unrepresentable, 69

Patience, 50

Peace, 24, 111, 163–71

Penelope, 16

Perception, 35–36, 38–42, 44

Perhaps, 71, 75

Persecution, 71, 81, 87–91, 93–94, 121

Phenomenality, 33

Phenomenology, vii, x–xi, xiii, 33–34, 42–45, 61, 65–66, 85, 92, 95, 97, 151–52, 160, 168; and constitution, 58; and reduction, 56, 58; another, 151, 155

Phenomenon, xi, 52–53, 60, 66, 69–75, 85, 92, 103

Philosophia perennis, 3

Philosophy, xii–xiv, 4–5, 11, 13, 21, 25–27, 33, 42, 48, 66, 83, 95, 107, 113, 126, 129, 130, 147–50, 171; and life, 4; beyond, 129; distinguished from theology, 30, 130; failure of, 14; first, xii, 20, 163; transcendental, 39; Western, 87–88

Pity, 19

Plato, x–xi, 5, 11, 13, 21, 31, 34, 35–36, 42–45, 51, 55–56, 58–59, 66, 87, 111, 115, 119, 125, 129, 139–40, 147

Platonism, 58–59

Play, 50, 112

Pleasure: pure, 51

Plotinus, 13, 21, 31, 63

Pluralism, 46, 48

Poetry, 40–42

Politics, xiv, 163, 167, 170

Positivism, 34–36

Possession, 9, 18

Power, 8–9, 19

Prayer, 7, 106

Presence, 52–54, 61, 63, 65–67, 69, 71–72, 75–77, 81, 83, 91, 94, 97, 101, 103–105, 111, 116–19, 121, 131–35, 138, 142, 147, 151–54, 156, 170; divine, 66–67

Principle, 80–81, 89

Proper names, 36–37

Prophecy, 97, 105, 107, 146–47

Providence, 47

Proximity, xii, 65, 69, 74, 77, 80–82, 122

Psychism, 97, 101–102, 105

Psychoanalysis, 83

Putting into question, 12, 16–18, 20–21, 55, 57

Real, 44, 98

Realism, 11–12, 14–16, 21

Reality, 45

Reason, 5, 8, 23, 25, 30, 111, 130; beyond, 66

Receptivity, 36, 39, 41–42

Reciprocity, 49

Rectitude, 60. *See also* Straightforwardness

Recurrence, 82–87, 89–90, 93, 106

Reduction, 107; of ego to self, 88; phenomenological, 56, 58

Reflection, 10, 18, 20–21, 25, 29, 56–57, 84, 88; consciousness without, 56–57

Relation, 10–11; between the Same and the Other, 11–12, 20–21; ethical, 55; moral, 57; with the Other, 12, 52

Religion, xii–xiv, 2, 7–8, 28–29, 34, 48, 72, 143, 157–58, 161; positive, 50, 67

ADRIAAN T. PEPERZAK is the Arthur J. Schmitt Professor of Philosophy at Loyola University of Chicago. He has published *To the Other: An Introduction to the Philosophy of Emmanuel Levinas* and is preparing another book on Levinas entitled *Beyond.*

SIMON CRITCHLEY is Reader in Philosophy at the University of Essex. He is author of *The Ethics in Deconstruction and Very Little . . . Almost Nothing,* co-editor of *Deconstructive Subjectives, Blackwell's Companion to Continental Philosophy,* and (with Robert Bernasconi) *Re-Reading Levinas.*

ROBERT BERNASCONI is Moss Professor of Philosophy at the University of Memphis. He is author of *The Question of Language in Heidegger's History of Being* and co-editor (with Simon Critchley) of *Re-Reading Levinas.*